A VICTORIAN CURATE

A Victorian Curate

A Study of the Life and Career
of the Rev. Dr John Hunt

David Yeandle

https://www.openbookpublishers.com

© 2021 David Yeandle

This work is licensed under a Creative Commons Attribution 4.0 International license (CC BY 4.0). This license allows you to share, copy, distribute and transmit the text; to adapt the text and to make commercial use of the text providing attribution is made to the authors (but not in any way that suggests that they endorse you or your use of the work). Attribution should include the following information:

David Yeandle, *A Victorian Curate: A Study of the Life and Career of the Rev. Dr John Hunt*. Cambridge, UK: Open Book Publishers, 2021, https://doi.org/10.11647/OBP.0248

Copyright and permissions for the reuse of many of the images included in this publication differ from the above. This information is provided in the captions.

In order to access detailed and updated information on the license, please visit, https://doi.org/10.11647/OBP.0248#copyright

Further details about CC BY licenses are available at https://creativecommons.org/licenses/by/4.0/

All external links were active at the time of publication unless otherwise stated and have been archived via the Internet Archive Wayback Machine at https://archive.org/web

Updated digital material and resources associated with this volume are available at https://doi.org/10.11647/OBP.0248#resources

Every effort has been made to identify and contact copyright holders and any omission or error will be corrected if notification is made to the publisher.

ISBN Paperback: 9781800641525
ISBN Hardback: 9781800641532
ISBN Digital (PDF): 9781800641549
ISBN Digital ebook (epub): 9781800641556
ISBN Digital ebook (mobi): 9781800641563
ISBN XML: 9781800641570
DOI: 10.11647/OBP.0248

Cover image: St Ives Vicarage, c. 1880. Courtesy of the Norris Museum, St Ives, Cambridgeshire, UK.
Cover design: Anna Gatti.

Fig. 1 John Hunt in middle age, c. 1878, courtesy of Mr John Hunt.

Contents

Preface	xi
Introduction	1
1. John Hunt	5
1.1 Family and Upbringing	7
1.2 Education	9
1.3 Hunt's Scholarship	11
1.4 Hunt's Marriages	13
2. Clergymen Made Scarce	15
3. Town Life	19
3.1 Ordination and First Curacy	19
3.2 First Metropolitan Curacy	20
3.3 Search for a New Curacy	25
4. *Essays and Reviews* Controversy	35
5. Unemployment and Applications	41
5.1 Theological Differences and 'Evangelical' Credentials	41
5.2 The Curates' Registry	43
5.3 *The Guardian*	44
5.4 English Graduates Only	44
5.5 Privilege and Parsimony	45
6. Final Metropolitan Applications	47
6.1 Mistaken Identity	47
6.2 Hoxton	48

7. The Anatomist Curate	51
8. Country Life	57
8.1 Swallow, Lincolnshire	58
9. St Ives, Hunts.	61
9.1 Advowson for Sale	68
9.2 Ritualism	74
9.3 Beyond St Ives	86
10. Conclusions	87
11. Postscript: John Hunt in Otford	93
11.1 Transcription of Hunt's Epitaph in Otford Church	101
12. Chronological Table of John Hunt's Life	103
Appendix: Documents and Press Quotations	107
Text of Clergymen Made Scarce	108
[3] LETTER, &c.	110
P O S T S C R I P T.	141
Appendix II	181
The Anatomist Curate	181
An Inquest on an Inquest (*Punch*)	185
Clergymen Made Scarce (*Punch*)	186
Extraordinary Charge against a City Clergyman	188
Singular Freak of a Clergyman	192
Presentation of a Testimonial to the Rev. John Hunt	192
Lecture on St Augustine	196
Review of *Religious Thought in England* I	197
Review of *Religious Thought in England* II	198
Review of *Religious Thought in England in the Nineteenth Century*	202
Review of *Religious Thought in England in the Nineteenth Century*	203
Dr. Hunt's Travels.	204
John Hunt, the Poor Man's Friend	216

His Services to Literature	217
His Views on Sunday Observance	218
His Views on the Church	219
His View on Temperance	220
His Views on Politics	220
His Journeys Abroad	221
John Hunt's Obituary	228
Death of the Vicar of Otford	228
Dr. Hunt's Sudden Demise.	228
The Funeral.	230
Bibliography	233
Select Works by John Hunt	233
Other Works Cited	234
Index	249

Preface

My interest in John Hunt began during the time when I was Organist and Choirmaster of All Saints' Church, St Ives, Cambridgeshire (2001–2011). In the course of my enquiry into previous clergy at the church, my attention was drawn by Mr Bob Burn-Murdoch, former Curator of the Norris Museum, St Ives, to the rare copy in that museum's library of the booklet by the Rev. Dr John Hunt, entitled *Clergymen Made Scarce*, which contains manuscript annotations by Mrs Eliza Hunt. Mr Burn-Murdoch, who deserves my special thanks, kindly provided me with a copy of the text. I am further indebted to the staff of the Norris Museum for help with locating material and permission to reproduce images from the Museum.

My thanks are due to all those who have provided me with information and materials for this book: Mr John Hunt, the great-great-nephew of the Rev. Dr John Hunt, for answering my questions and for providing me with a photograph of his ancestor, as well as a family tree and other relevant documents and photographs; Mr Clive Southgate of St Bartholomew's Church, Otford, for providing me with information about John Hunt's time as Vicar of Otford; Mr Edwin Thompson of the Otford and District Historical Society, who has been very accommodating in supplying me with several items of importance from the Otford and District Historical Society archive, including the text of Harold Hart's pamphlet and several photographs of interest.

This book has been published with the generous support of the Goodliff Fund of the Huntingdonshire Local History Society, to which I am deeply indebted.

Finally, I should like to thank friends and others who have helped me with suggestions and information or read and commented on parts of the manuscript, in particular Dr Charles Beresford, Professor Nicholas Boyle, Mr Ian Dobson, Mrs Bridget Flanagan, Professor John Flood, Mr Peter Glazebrook, Mr Rolf Lunsmann, Dr Carol Regulski, and Mr James Warren.

Introduction

The present work is based on a little-known booklet, published by the Rev. Dr John Hunt (born Bridgend, Perth, 1827, died Otford, Kent, 1907).[1] The original copy that I have used is in the possession of the Norris Museum, St Ives, Cambridgeshire (formerly Huntingdonshire) and contains manuscript annotations by Mrs Eliza Hunt,[2] the first wife of the author. These provide a key to the many anonymous and pseudonymous references in the text.

The first edition of the booklet (1865) appears to be extremely rare. Reference is made to its availability by post from the freethinking publisher of liberal tracts, Thomas Scott, of Ramsgate.[3] The second edition (1867) is still to be encountered in a number of libraries, including the British Library, but it is nonetheless rare, although it is now available online. The author of *Clergymen Made Scarce* remained anonymous, referring to himself as 'A Presbyter'.[4] The booklet was issued ostensibly as an open letter to the Bishop of London. The second

---

1   *Clergymen Made Scarce. Five Years' Experience as a Curate in the Diocese of London: A Letter to the Right Hon. and Right Rev. the Lord Bishop of the Diocese by a Presbyter. Second Edition, with a Postscript, Containing Two Years' Further Experience in the Country* (London: Hall & Company, 1867). The first edition (1865) was identical, save for the absence of the Postscript.
2   Mrs Eliza Hunt was born Eliza Meadows Shepard Thorp in 1845, in St Ives, Huntingdonshire. See p. 13, below.
3   The only copy that I have traced is in the Lambeth Palace Library: *Clergymen Made Scarce: Five Years' Experience as a Curate in the Diocese of London: A Letter [...] by a Presbyter* (London: Hall, 1865); call number H5133 298.05.
4   A similar anonymous publication appeared in 1843, though it was written from a more critically analytical and less personal viewpoint: Anon., *The Whole Case of the Unbeneficed Clergy; Or, a Full, Candid, and Impartial Enquiry Into the Position of Those Clergy Commonly Called the Curates of the Established Church. By a Presbyter of the Church, Etc.* (Second Edition). (London: Hatchard & Son, 1843), https://books.google.co.uk/books?id=YeFhAAAAcAAJ. An earlier work along similar lines had appeared in 1837: John Jordan, *A Curate's Views of Church Reform, Temporal, Spiritual and Educational* (London: Longman, 1837), https://books.google.co.uk/

edition was augmented by a postscript, containing 'two years' further experience in the country'.

The booklet deals with John Hunt's experiences as a curate in the Church of England.[5] The first part, which appeared also in the first edition, concerns the numerous curacies that Hunt held in London; the postscript relates directly to his time at All Saints', St Ives, in Huntingdonshire (now Cambridgeshire), where he served as curate from 1865 to 1866, when he was aged 38–39. Both parts provide a significant insight at parish level into the corruption and turmoil in the Church of England in Victorian times.

Hunt is not unique in writing about the lot of the struggling curate who is trying to make his way in the Victorian Church of England, but he offers a unique personal perspective. In his person, we encounter, a singular conjunction of factors: he is a Scotsman of lowly birth, educated at a Scottish university. He thus brings a distinctive, atypical viewpoint from which to observe the largely middle- and upper-class Church of England in the nineteenth century. He has no social connections, no influential patronage. He is intelligent and witty. He has only his natural intelligence on which to rely for preferment. He does not suffer fools gladly and is not prepared to submit to those in higher authority who are intellectually his inferiors. He is not dogmatic but is flexible and rational in all that he does. His industry is phenomenal. His published output is immense. He is adaptable in his ability to minister alongside Low-Church and more catholically minded incumbents in both town and country.

In many of these facets, he reflects the state of typical aspects of the Victorian Church but from a distinctive personal point of view and often in sharper focus.

Hunt's book traces the insecurities of a curate's existence and also the difficulties he had in establishing himself and gaining a permanent living, including the obstacles of class, origins, and education. The

---

books?id=KeXd8fpWE24C. Cf. also A. Tindal Hart, *The Curate's Lot: The Story of the Unbeneficed English Clergy* (London: J. Baker, 1970), pp. 129, 134.

5   The term curate is used throughout this book, as in everyday usage, to mean an 'assistant curate' or unbeneficed clergyman. Cf. E. A. Livingstone, ed., *The Concise Oxford Dictionary of the Christian Church* (Oxford: Oxford University Press, 2014), https://www.oxfordreference.com/view/10.1093/acref/9780199659623.001.0001/acref-9780199659623, s.v. curate.

conflict between theologies in response to an age of scientific advances, the sale of ecclesiastical livings, and the introduction of ritualistic practices in rural parishes also feature prominently.

The wit, learning, and good humour of Hunt shine from the pages of his booklet. His magnanimity and Christian integrity come to the fore repeatedly in his dealings with opponents, towards whom he apparently bears no malice. He recognizes the need for Christians to accept that even those of a different persuasion have access to the truth. A committed Protestant, he is not antipathetic to traditional catholic teaching or indeed to many of the practices promoted by the Oxford Movement. A staunch Anglican minister, he is entirely orthodox in his teaching, in accordance with the Book of Common Prayer and the Thirty-Nine Articles. He is widely read in the classics and ancient fathers and seeks an opportunity to place his many talents at the service of others.

1. John Hunt

John Hunt was not a typical Anglican clergyman, and yet his life exemplifies starkly many aspects—both good and bad—of the career of an aspiring parson in the Church of England during the nineteenth century. He was an able, intellectual, liberal clergyman with moderate Evangelical views, but he tolerated other Christian traditions, both Anglican and beyond. He had rationalist sympathies—indeed reason was his guiding principle—and by his own admission he was 'a devout believer in Arminius and Wesley'.[1] He shares many similarities of character with one of his more famous near contemporaries, Archbishop Sumner (1780–1862), described by Chadwick in the following sympathetic terms: 'He was a temperate evangelical, and had none of that rigidity or aggression which cause unpopularity. He was moderate and gentle and amiable.'[2] Hunt's intellectualism and rationalism caused him increasingly to lean towards the Broad-Church party, the theology of F. D. Maurice and like-minded clergymen of high intellect.

His upbringing in Scotland was altogether different from that of a clergyman in England. Although Hunt is largely forgotten today, he was known—though not celebrated—in the Victorian Church and contemporary society for a variety of reasons, not all of them positive. He was a prolific author, with a fluent literary style, a skilled theologian, a controversialist, a competent linguist, with proficiency in both classical and modern languages, a man of letters, and an amateur natural scientist, with a particular interest in anatomy.

His epitaph, a memorial tablet in Otford Church, where he became vicar at the age of fifty-one, charitably sums up his life, drawing attention to his 'strong intellectual force' as 'one of the deepest philosophical

---

1 See *Clergymen Made Scarce*, p. 4.
2 Owen Chadwick, *The Victorian Church, Part I* (London: Adam & Charles Black, 1966), p. 452.

© 2021 David Yeandle, CC BY 4.0   https://doi.org/10.11647/OBP.0248.01

thinkers of the church', his 'faith based on the divinity of Jesus Christ', and his 'rare simplicity of nature'.[3] We are further told that 'he was humble, straight and honourable in all his dealings, and transparently truthful'.[4] These are attributes that can be observed repeatedly in his life, attributes that were rarely to be found in the clergy of his day but which, sadly, caused suffering and rejection for the gifted man who espoused them.

Such an aggregation of talents would perhaps, in a more enlightened society, have led to a senior post at a university or to high preferment in the Church, possibly even a bishopric; however, Hunt's background did not constitute a normal path to such advancement, and he struggled to find employment in the Church of England. He never rose to particular prominence nationally and, despite his many talents, was denied a position of seniority in the Church of England. He was not from the social classes that sent their sons into the Anglican Church,[5] nor was he rich, nor well connected, nor even an Englishman. He was, however, naturally intelligent and a perceptive thinker. As a liberal and a rationalist, he engaged with the theological controversies of the day, and in doing so, he often made more enemies than friends. His acerbic wit and keen intellect led to difficult encounters with men of lesser ability and inferior learning, who were, however, predominantly his ecclesiastical and social superiors. His bearing could at times appear supercilious and condescending, as, for example, when he called a churchwarden 'a fool, and a big fool'.[6] His demeanour on occasions betrayed some rough edges. All this diminished his chances, as a Scotsman of humble origins, without private means or the right social connections, of obtaining preferment in the nineteenth-century Church of England.

---

3   See John Hunt's epitaph in Otford Church, p. 101, below.
4   Harold W. Hart, 'John Hunt, the Poor Man's Friend' (unpublished typescript, Otford and District Historical Society Archive, 1958), reproduced in the Appendix, p. 216, below.
5   The Anglican Church was notorious for favouring upper-class clergy, especially those with an Oxford or Cambridge education. Cf. Paul Nicholls, 'The Social Expectations of Anglican Clergy in England and Australia, 1850–1910' (unpublished doctoral dissertation, University of Oxford, 1988), Abstract, pp. 1–2.
6   Cf. *Oxford Journal*, Saturday, 19 November 1864, p. 6.

1.1 Family and Upbringing

Not much is known of Hunt's family; he was born to parents Thomas and Agnes Hunt as the second of eight surviving siblings, all of whom were male.[7] The family, which was of English extraction,[8] lived in Bridgend, Kinnoull, a district of Perth, Scotland, on the east of the River Tay. His father, Thomas, was a shoemaker, as Thomas's father, James, had been. He was apprenticed in shoemaking by his uncle, his father having died when Thomas was only six years old. Despite this relatively lowly manual occupation,[9] he was an astute man, of whom it is reported: 'He was a man of considerable mental power, a philosophic workman, whose lifelong hobby was algebra, and who spent his leisure, and possibly many of the hours which should have been devoted to his business, in the solution of abstruse algebraic problems.'[10] We are not informed how successful the business was, but it must at least have been capable of supporting a wife and eight sons.[11]

---

7   The children of Thomas (b. 1789) and Agnes Hunt (née Malcom, b. 1799), who married on 12 January 1822, were: 1. Janet Hunt (1823–1824); 2. Colin Anderson Hunt (1825–1895); 3. John Hunt (1827–1907); 4. James Hunt (1829–1892); 5. Ninian Malcom Hunt (1831–1913); 6. Thomas Hunt (1833–1885); 7. William Hunt (1836–1876); 8. Alexander Allan Hunt (1838–1876) 9. Robert Hay Hunt (b. 1841). The family and its circumstances are discussed in: David Crawford Smith, *The Historians of Perth, and Other Local and Topographical Writers, up to the End of the Nineteenth Century* (Perth, J. Christie, 1906), pp. 195–202, http://archive.org/details/historiansperth01smitgoog

8   John Hunt's father, Thomas (1789–1867), was the son of James (1762–1795). His father, Thomas (1734–1802), was one of ten children of John Hunt (1685–1756). He was born at Braiseworth, Suffolk, and became a soldier in the 31st Regiment of Foot (Royal Surrey Regiment). His regiment was transferred to Edinburgh Castle, where his son James was born. After leaving the Army, Thomas moved to Perth in 1768 and became a hatter (personal communication from Mr John Hunt); cf. also Smith, *Historians of Perth*, pp. 199f.

9   Although shoemakers were not prosperous in the nineteenth century, with many living at or below subsistence levels in meagre lodgings, it would appear that Thomas Hunt had advanced in this trade. Especially telling in the context of John Hunt's later career as a clergyman is a comment in George Eliot's 'The Sad Fortunes of the Reverend Amos Barton' about the eponymous curate: '"Rather a low-bred fellow, I think, Barton," said Mr Pilgrim [...] "They say his father was a Dissenting shoemaker; and he's half a Dissenter himself"', George Eliot, *Scenes of Clerical Life* (Edinburgh and London: William Blackwood, 1858) , p. 16, https://books.google.co.uk/books?id=6zcJAAAAQAAJ Cf. also Hart, *The Curate's Lot*, p. 132.

10 Smith, *Historians of Perth*, p. 195.

11 It is difficult to estimate his income, but a point of comparison is a shoemaker's earnings in Forfar (some thirty miles away from Perth), c. 1840, which are reckoned

He appears to have remained active in the same business until his death in 1867. His address changes from 3 Gowrie Street in Bridgend (outside the burgh) to the west of the River Tay, first to Melville Street (1850), afterwards to North Port (1854), and finally to the most prestigious of the addresses,14 Watergate (1856), where he appears to have resided for the rest of his life.[12]

Smith writes, concerning Thomas and Agnes: 'to the upbringing and education of their large family, in a time of general poverty and distress, all their energies were devoted.' Thomas did not become a freeman of Perth, which was a prerequisite for carrying on his trade within the burgh, 'probably for want of funds',[13] and this is deemed the reason why he settled at Bridgend, as it was 'outwith the burgh'.[14] That he might, given better circumstances, have been in contention to become a freeman, the fee for which was an initial £25 plus the usual small dues,[15] suggests that he might have aspired to the wealthier mercantile class, but that his financial situation precluded this.[16] In short, he might be described, in today's idiom, as 'upwardly mobile'. Moving out of the manual, or working, class into the lower middle class of small shopkeepers and tradesfolk was a realistic possibility.

---

to be 'about 12 shillings a week' (approx. £62.50 in 2020), equivalent in 1840 to two days' wages as a skilled tradesman. Cf. John Marius Wilson, *The Imperial Gazetteer of Scotland or Dictionary of Scottish Topography* (Edinburgh & London: A. Fullarton & Co., 1854), I, p. 564, http://archive.org/details/imperialgazettee01wils. Thomas Hunt appears to have been a successful, but not wealthy, shoemaker, so his earnings were doubtless somewhat higher.

12 The dates and addresses are based on the details in the various Post Office directories, e.g., *Post Office Perth Directory for 1845–6* (Perth: Fisher, 1845), https://digital.nls.uk/directories/browse/archive/85660224. On the Watergate, see Short History of the Watergate, Made in Perth — Official Website, 2014, http://madeinperth.org/a-short-history-of-the-watergate/

13 Smith, *Historians of Perth*, p. 200.

14 Cf. Smith, *Historians of Perth*, pp. 198, 200. Bridgend was originally an insalubrious and undesirable place to live, but by this time it was an up-and-coming area. Cf. John Marius Wilson, *The Imperial Gazetteer of Scotland or Dictionary of Scottish Topography* (London & Edinburgh: A. Fullarton & Co., 1866), II, p. 237, https://digital.nls.uk/gazetteers-of-scotland-1803-1901/archive/97473786

15 Smith, *Historians of Perth*, p. 198. £25 would be worth approx. £2,600 in 2020. This and all subsequent currency conversions are calculated using 'Inflation Calculator', http://www.bankofengland.co.uk/monetary-policy/inflation/inflation-calculator. All values are approximate.

16 Cf. Smith, *Historians of Perth*, p. 198.

Thomas and some of his sons, especially Colin, were autodidacts,[17] by which they were able to better themselves, and which afforded them the opportunity to aspire to a higher social status. Indeed, Colin, who is described as 'a well-known, useful, and much-respected citizen of Perth', and other sons became successful businessmen and thus joined the middle classes.[18] As far as it is possible to tell, John was the only one of the eight sons to study at university; at least, there are no other Hunt sons recorded at St Andrews University, which is located thirty-five miles away from Bridgend.[19]

1.2 Education

John Hunt relates how he was 'educated in a Presbyterian sect',[20] although he does not elaborate further. In fact, his theological nurturing was in the Church of Scotland, at St Leonard's, Perth,[21] where the celebrated pastor and evangelist John Milne was minister (1839–1853).[22] It was a very distinctive kind of evangelicalism,[23] described affectionately by Hunt:

---

17 Colin, who received a primary and secondary education, taught himself Latin and French. Cf. Smith, *Historians of Perth*, p. 196.
18 Cf. Smith, *Historians of Perth*, pp. 195f.
19 See 'University of St Andrews Biographical Register 1747–1897', https://arts.st-andrews.ac.uk/biographical-register/data/documents/1387291364
20 Cf. *Clergymen Made Scarce*, p. 3.
21 Cf. Wilson, *The Imperial Gazetteer*, I, p. 584, http://archive.org/details/imperialgazettee01wils
22 See W. Robertson Nicoll, 'Ian Maclaren', *The Life of the Rev. John Watson, D. D.* (London: Hodder and Stoughton, 1908), p. 17, http://hdl.handle.net/2027/wu.89099242844. On Milne, see Horatius Bonar, *Life of the Rev. John Milne of Perth*, 5th edn (New York: Carter & Brothers, 1870), passim, https://www.electricscotland.com/webclans/m/lifeofrevjohnmil00bona.pdf; also John Hunt, 'Review of Horatius Bonar, The Life of the Rev. John Milne of Perth', *Contemporary Review* 10 (1869), 456–460, https://babel.hathitrust.org/cgi/pt?id=ucl.b2972914&view=1up&seq=466
23 Cf. 'It will be observed that [John] Watson was brought up under the ministry of the Rev. John Milne, of St. Leonard's, Perth. Mr. Milne belonged to what was known in Scotland as the M'Cheyne school. This was made up of men who were noted for their sanctity and their evangelistic zeal. Milne left his ministry in Perth to become a missionary in Calcutta, and after an interval returned to his old church. His life was written by Dr. Horatius Bonar, and he has been most felicitously described by the Rev. Dr. John Hunt, Vicar of Otford, Kent, and author of many important books on the history of theology. Dr. Hunt [...] in his early years attended Mr. Milne's church', Nicoll, p. 18.

We have said that Mr. Milne's ministry was successful. He had no great gifts of intellect; he had no eloquence; his learning was not extensive; in fact, his reading seems to have been unusually limited. What, then, was the secret of his power? We might say at once it was that he preached religion rather than theology; and he lived what he preached. If he did not know the difficulties that beset men who think, he yet knew the wants of men in general. He knew the power of sympathy, and he knew that the story of the life and the death of Jesus will reach men's hearts to the end of time. And then he had mastered the evil that was in himself.[24]

Clearly, Hunt owed much of his way of thinking and acting to this upbringing in Presbyterianism and the influence of the 'saintly John Milne',[25] as will become apparent.

His secondary education was at Perth Grammar School.[26] He mentions having 'matriculated at a Scotch University', without naming it.[27] St Andrews, where he studied from 1847–1848, whilst being the oldest university in Scotland (founded in 1413), was very different from the ancient English universities, with their distinctive collegiate system, arcane traditions, exclusion of Dissenters, and privileges for aristocrats and wealthy undergraduates, who were often more interested in gentlemen's pursuits than scholarship.[28] It is not known how it was possible for John, coming from originally humble circumstances and having little in the way of personal financial means, to attend St Andrews University, but it is to be noted that he did not matriculate at the university until 1847, aged nearly 21, whereas the usual matriculation age was around 17, and some matriculated as young as 15.[29] He may have had some form of employment before matriculation, possibly with his father. The *Biographical Register* of St Andrews lists Hunt as being a

---

24 Hunt, 'Review of Bonar', *The Life of the Rev. John Milne*, p. 459.
25 The term is Smith's, *Historians of Perth*, p. 35.
26 Cf. Herbert E. Norris, *History of Saint Ives. From 'The Hunts County Guardian'* (St. Ives: Hunts County Guardian, 1889), p. 77.
27 *Clergymen Made Scarce*, p. 3.
28 Cf. Michael Sanderson, *Education, Economic Change and Society in England 1780–1870*, 2nd edn (Cambridge: Cambridge University Press, 1995), passim.
29 Cf. Neil T. R. Dickson, 'A Scottish Fundamentalist? Thomas Whitelaw of Kilmarnock (1840–1917)', in *Evangelicalism and Fundamentalism in the United Kingdom during the Twentieth Century*, ed. David W. Bebbington and David Ceri Jones (Oxford: Oxford University Press, 2013), pp. 35–52, p. 38.

student at United College[30] and having studied only Latin 1 and Greek 1. Thus, he appears to have taken only first-year courses and may have left, possibly for lack of funds, without a degree, which required four years for the M.A.,[31] hence his use of 'matriculated', rather than 'graduated'.[32] His St Andrews D.D. was awarded much later, in 1878, apparently on the strength of his publications. In some of his later publications, e.g., *Religious Thought in England from the Reformation to the End of the last Century*, he is styled 'The Rev. John Hunt, M.A.'. After leaving St Andrews, he is to be found in 1851 in Preston in Lancashire, working as a private tutor. He spent two or three years here and during this time published *Select Poems: from the German* (1852) and a translation of *The Spiritual Songs of Martin Luther* (1853). He also served as the first editor of the *Preston Herald*.[33]

1.3 Hunt's Scholarship

This subject can be accorded only a brief mention in the context of the present work. Hunt was a prolific author. Throughout his long life, he published many hundreds of pages in books, pamphlets, journals, magazines, and ephemeral publications of varying types and quality on varying subjects, principally theology and religion.[34] He was also engaged in editorial activity, particularly while a member of staff (1867–1877) of *The Contemporary Review*,[35] for which he also wrote.[36]

---

30 On United College, see Charles Rogers, *History of St. Andrews* (Edinburgh: Adam & Charles Black, 1849), pp. 123–128, https://books.google.co.uk/books?id=f7MHAAAAQAAJ
31 Cf. Rogers, *History of St. Andrews*, p. 128.
32 The somewhat equivocal reference to Hunt's university career in Smith, *Historians of Perth*, pp. 195f., is possibly further evidence in support of this supposition: 'The second son, now the Rev. John Hunt, D.D., vicar of Otford, Kent, after passing through the University of St Andrews, joined the Church of England, and for nearly thirty years has held his present preferment.' See below, p. 44.
33 Norris, *History of Saint Ives*, p. 77.
34 His more important publications are listed in the Bibliography, p. 233, below.
35 Cf. Samuel Macauley Jackson, Philip Schaff, and J. J. Herzog, *Encyclopedia of Living Divines and Christian Workers of All Denominations in Europe and America; Being a Supplement to Schaff-Herzog Encyclopedia of Religious Knowledge* (New York: Funk & Wagnalls, 1887), p. 106, https://catalog.hathitrust.org/Record/005768313
36 E.g., 'Dr. John Henry Newman, A Psychological Study', *Contemporary Review* 27 (1876), 764–779. See also the letter by W.E. Gladstone, correcting an error, *Contemporary Review* xxviii (1876), 168.

This liberal periodical, which attracted progressive theologians, such as F. D. Maurice, and other figures of note, such as W. E. Gladstone, was published by Alexander Stuart Strahan, a moderate Scottish evangelical, with whom Hunt seems to have enjoyed a degree of friendship, since he was a witness at Hunt's first wedding.[37] Several of Hunt's major works were also published by Strahan and the related firm of W. Isbister.[38] His scholarship is rarely cited or consulted nowadays, and it called forth mixed reactions at the time of publication. It was noted for its almost excessive thoroughness and stylistic competence, but it was also criticized for assembling a collection of extracts from other writers and of being ponderous and dull.[39] Hunt's lack of lasting success as a theological writer was possibly in part due to his inability to express himself succinctly.

We can but marvel, however, at Hunt's monumental undertaking in producing his three-volume magnum opus of almost 1,400 pages: *Religious Thought in England*, together with his 384-page *Essay on Pantheism*, which, he explains, was intended as the first chapter in this enterprise. He writes about the task in the following revealing terms, showing not only that he enjoyed the mentorship of no less a theologian than F. D. Maurice,[40] but also that, during his many troubles as a curate, he was constantly engaged in writing this very substantial work of scholarship, as well as making many lesser contributions:

> In the preface to my essay on Pantheism I have recorded the circumstances which determined me to devote some years to the special study of theology. When I came to London, in 1859, I began a course of reading with the object of inquiring into the nature of revelation and the evidences by which it is supported. At the end of four years I had formed a plan of something like a complete history of theology, which

---

37 Parish Register: St Mary, Lambeth, England, 2 September 1873, p. 101.
38 *Poems by Robert Wilde D.D.* (London: Strahan, 1870); *Religious Thought in England, from the Reformation to the End of Last Century* (London: Strahan, 1870–1873), 3 vols; *Contemporary Essays in Theology* (London: Strahan, 1873) [reprinted from various sources]; *Pantheism and Christianity* (London: W. Isbister, 1884) [second edition of *An Essay on Pantheism* (London: Longmans, 1866)].
39 E.g., 'Mr. Hunt is painstaking and industrious indeed, but ponderous beyond belief or endurance', *Saturday Review of Politics, Literature, Science and Art* 83 (1897), 154. Cf. the reviews of *Religious Thought in England*, pp. 197–204, below.
40 See 'Maurice, (John) Frederick Denison (1805–1872), Church of England Clergyman and Theologian', in *Oxford Dictionary of National Biography*, https://doi.org/10.1093/ref:odnb/18384

would set forth the special character of Christianity and its relation to other religions. In the spring of 1863 I showed the outlines of my work to the late Professor Maurice, who had gone over large portions of the same field, and whose writings had been of great service to me. The Professor looked over the paper, and returning it, said with an incredulous smile 'you have twenty years' work before you'. He advised me to try one part first, and to go on with the rest if that succeeded.[41]

1.4 Hunt's Marriages

Hunt was not a family man. Although he married twice, both marriages—each time to women considerably his junior—were without known issue. It seems that he met his first wife, Eliza Meadows Shepard Thorp,[42] in St Ives, Huntingdonshire, while he was curate there from 1865–1866. Eliza's father, Frederick William Thorp, was an attorney in St Ives, having been articled there to George Game Day, a prominent, wealthy local figure.[43] In 1851, the family lived at 26 The Pavement, St Ives. Eliza was the eldest of four siblings, and her mother was Eliza Meadows Shepard. By 1861, they had moved to 33 Cromwell Place, on or near the site of Oliver Cromwell's probable former residence, old Slepe Hall.[44] There were seven children living at this address, but Eliza is no longer registered as living there. In the 1871 census, she is employed by Joseph Topham, a farmer and magistrate, as a governess, aged twenty-five, in the village of Great Staughton, Huntingdonshire.[45] She married Hunt in 1873 at St Mary's, Lambeth, where Hunt was curate, when she was twenty-eight and he was forty-six. Eliza was the author of several literary works, the most prominent being a three-volume novel, *The Wards of Plotinus*.[46] She died from diphtheria in 1890

---

41 *Religious Thought in England*, III, pp. vf.
42 Although variant spellings are found, this would appear to be the canonical form, as recorded in the *England & Wales Civil Registration Birth Index, 1837–1915*.
43 *The Legal Guide*, IV (1840), p. 56.
44 'Oliver Cromwell, the Farmer of St Ives', https://stives.cambs.info/citizens/cromwell.asp
45 1871 England Census, Folio: 78; Page: 11.
46 Hunt, Eliza [Mrs John Hunt], *The Wards of Plotinus*, 3 vols (London: Strahan, 1881), http://archive.org/details/wardsofplotinus01ward. The book contains a dedication 'To the Very Reverend Arthur Penrhyn Stanley, D.D., Dean of Westminster, These volumes are inscribed with mingled feelings of admiration and gratitude.' The Preface (pp. vii–xiii) is written from Otford Rectory by John Hunt, who had a hand

at the early age of forty-four,[47] leaving Hunt ten years a widower, until in 1899, aged seventy-two, he married Margaret Allen Foote, aged forty-one, from Cupar, Fife, at St Peter's, Clerkenwell, Islington. Interestingly, he gave 'Gentleman' as his deceased father's 'Rank or Profession' in both marriage registers. There was no hint of the latter's lowly origins as a shoemaker. Margaret outlived him, and in 1908, a year after Hunt's death, married the Rev. John Martin, from Carluke, Lanarkshire, Hunt's former curate. A strong Scottish connection is apparent.

---

in collecting the material. The online copy, from the Illinois University Library, contains a messy manuscript dedication, signed by 'Elise Hunt', for 'Theodore Watts, In memory of other days'. Theodore Watts-Dunton, who was from St Ives, where his father, like Eliza's father, was a solicitor, moved in the same literary and artistic circles as Tennyson, Swinburne, and Dante Gabriel Rossetti. The Hunts were on the periphery of these well-known figures' social group. The spelling Elise may be a deliberate affectation to hint at more exotic, possibly German, origins. The Hunts were certainly very fond of things German. Cf. 'Dunton, (Walter) Theodore Watts-(1832–1914), Writer and Poet', *Oxford Dictionary of National Biography*, https://doi.org/10.1093/ref:odnb/36785

47 Cf. 'Mrs. Hunt, wife of the Rev. Dr. Hunt, vicar Otford, died on Sunday last, after a few days illness, from diphtheria, and was buried this afternoon. The deceased lady, who was well-known as an author, was greatly respected', *Sevenoaks Chronicle and Kentish Advertiser*, 7 March 1890, p. 5.

2. Clergymen Made Scarce

Hunt's career as a curate was wearisome; indeed, it was not until 1878, some twenty-three years after his first curacy, at the age of fifty-one,[1] that he secured, through the good offices of Dean Stanley, a permanent living as Vicar of St Bartholomew's Church, Otford, near Sevenoaks, Kent, a village of approximately 1,200 inhabitants. Biographical details for this undervalued and largely forgotten clergyman would be almost non-existent if Hunt had not published a booklet in 1864/5, entitled *Clergymen Made Scarce*, a somewhat disgruntled and dejected account of his career to date, written at Swallow, near Caistor, in the Wolds of Lincolnshire.[2] The booklet, the second edition of which (1867) enjoyed some degree of circulation, purports to be an open letter to the Bishop of London, penned after an incident that led to Hunt's dismissal as curate from St Botolph's, Aldgate. The second edition includes a Postscript in smaller type (pp. 26–48), dealing with Hunt's experiences in St Ives, Huntingdonshire. The Postscript is nearly 4,000 words longer than the first (main) part of *Clergymen Made Scarce*.

The autobiographical account makes interesting reading. It contains allusions to personages and places that are referred to by pseudonyms or anonymously. Although some of these might be identifiable by a modern reader, others are obscure. Fortunately, there exists in the Norris Museum Library, St Ives, a rare copy of the booklet, with manuscript annotations by Mrs Eliza Hunt.[3] Although not all of the spellings are accurate, they provide a most useful key to the persons and places

---

1 On long probatory curacies, see Nicholls, 'Social Expectations', passim, esp. p. 147.
2 There are a few references to the work in the wider press, e.g., *Lloyd's Weekly Newspaper*, 16 April 1865, p. 27; *Cambridge Independent Press*, 30 March 1867, p. 6.
3 On the annotations, see fn. 1, p. 110, below

© 2021 David Yeandle, CC BY 4.0   https://doi.org/10.11647/OBP.0248.02

mentioned, sometimes disparagingly, in the text. The booklet caused a degree of controversy in St Ives.[4]

Hunt's booklet is not without humour, often of a down-to-earth nature. Even on the title page, he displays his scathing wit and keen intellect, with erudite epigraphs, which he modifies with mockingly ironic variations. His better-educated readers would have understood his ulterior motive, that of illuminating and criticizing privilege, preferment, prejudice, and folly in the Victorian Church.

The first epigraph, a modified popular saying, is a quotation from the satirical magazine *Punch*, which had published an article with the same title as Hunt's booklet viz. 'Clergymen Made Scarce'.[5] Which came first is unclear. The epigraph alludes satirically, and largely in Hunt's favour, to his predicament at losing the curacy at St Botolph's, Aldgate: 'Make the greatest fool in the family a parson, that is, if he will let you.' The circumstances of this loss will be examined in Chapter 7. The main thrust is that none but a fool would enter upon the career of a parson, if his family had 'not got a good fat living for him to step into as soon as he is ordained'.[6] As we have seen, this was very far from being the case with Hunt.

Continuing in similar vein, Hunt's second epigraph ironizes the motto of the City of Edinburgh *inter alia*. The motto, a shortened version of Psalm 127, v. 1 (*nisi Dominus frustra*) is deliberately misinterpreted by means of a 'Scotch translation', i.e. an ironically blunt and distorted rendering, to mean that a man without resources and social connections need not apply for a post in the Church of England: 'Unless ye be a lord's son, ye need'na come here.'[7]

The third and final epigraph is a modified quotation from Juvenal's First Satire (ll. 79f.), substituting *Ecclesia* for *natura*: 'si Ecclesia negat, facit indignatio versum Qualemcumque potest.' The likely sense is 'if the Church denies (or fails), indignation creates a verse as best it can.'[8]

---

4   Cf. Hunt's lecture on St Augustine, *Cambridge Independent Press*, 30 March 1867, p. 6, reprinted in the Appendix, p. 196.
5   '*Clergymen Made Scarce*', *Punch*, 17 December 1864, p. 251. A previous article about the inquest on the 'anatomy scandal' had already been published in *Punch* on 26 November 1865, p. 215.
6   *Punch*, 17 December 1864, p. 251 [cited in the Appendix, pp. 186f., below.].
7   Cf. Hart, *The Curate's Lot*, p. 130.
8   The original is translated 'If nature fails, then indignation generates verse, doing the best it can'. See *Juvenal: The Satires*, ed. William Barr, trans. Niall Rudd (Oxford; New York: Oxford University Press, 2008), p. 5.

Whether the addressee of this open letter, Archibald Campbell Tait, Bishop of London (1856–1868, Archbishop of Canterbury, 1868–1882)[9] ever read its contents we do not know, but he certainly encountered Hunt, including by negative report, in his large diocese. Some occasions are documented below. Indeed, Hunt may have had special reasons for choosing Tait as the addressee. Apart from his being Hunt's ordinary, with liberal sympathies and a penchant for evangelism and innovation, Tait was, like Hunt, a Scotsman, who, like Hunt, had grown up in the Presbyterian tradition. Like Hunt, he rejected Calvinism. Like Hunt, he was interested in education beyond the confines of the ancient English universities, with their arcane practices, which he had experienced firsthand while a tutor at Balliol. What more suitable recipient of this letter could there possibly have been? What better figure of authority was there to ensure that the wrongs done to an able, intellectual clergyman would not be repeated? Who better to bring reform to the corrupt nineteenth-century Church?

Hunt's booklet, then, provides a penetrating insight at parish level into the social foibles, corruption, and turmoil in the Church of England during Victorian times. It highlights curates' often poor employment prospects, their insecurity of tenure, their lowly status and poor remuneration, their subservience to incumbents, their struggles in gaining preferment on merit in the context of the sale of ecclesiastical livings. Clashes with incumbents on account of differences of theology and churchmanship abound. These details are seen in the context of social class, ethnic origins, and education.

Hunt begins by addressing his 'Letter' to the Bishop of London, setting out his learning initially by means of an allusion to the *Metamorphoses* or *Golden Ass* of Apuleius (born c. 125 AD).[10] He flatters the Bishop by referring to the Golden Ass and mentioning the name of its author, deferentially adding 'as your lordship knows'.[11] At first, there is no obvious connection with the Church when he states in the context of the *Golden Ass*: 'He [Apuleius] wished to show that wisdom might

---

9   Cf. 'Tait, Archibald Campbell (1811–1882), Archbishop of Canterbury', *Oxford Dictionary of National Biography*, https://doi.org/10.1093/ref:odnb/26917
10 See Stephen J. Harrison, 'Apuleius Writer and Orator, b. c. 125 CE', *Oxford Research Encyclopedia of Classics*, 2015, https://doi.org/10.1093/acrefore/9780199381135.013.628
11 *Clergymen Made Scarce*, p. 3.

sometimes exist even under an asinine exterior, and that there might be observing eyes where people did not expect to find them.'[12] The 'asinine exterior' soon reveals itself as belonging to the Church of England. The obscured wisdom would seem to be the preserve of figures like Hunt and Bishop Tait. The somewhat cryptic reference to himself as the 'Golden Curate',[13] which, he suggests, 'would seem self-laudatory if not egotistical', were he not to 'keep in check the spirit which has suggested the comparison', turns out to be far from self-laudatory at the end of the main part of the 'Letter':

> In the beginning I likened myself to the priest of Isis, but I checked the comparison. I again check it in the end. Apuleius wrote a fable, I have written the truth. Apuleius was at last delivered from his asshood; my curate-hood remains.[14]

Having displayed his classical erudition, Hunt next refers to theology and philosophy, with references to St Augustine and Rousseau. A quotation from Goethe's *Faust*, albeit in English translation, extolling the value of experience over theory,[15] provides the final literary allusion and display of learning before Hunt launches upon his real topic. And although he notes 'Curates are men who rarely speak for themselves', he feels under a 'divine impulse' to speak out.[16]

In this mood of emboldened militancy and divine justification for his cause, Hunt begins to recount to his bishop his life's story and philosophy.

---

12 *Ibid.*
13 *Ibid.*
14 *Clergymen Made Scarce*, p. 26.
15 'Grey, dear Friend, is all theory, | But green is the golden tree of life'; 'Grau, theurer Freund, ist alle Theorie | und grün des Lebens goldner Baum', Mephistopheles, *Faust* I, 2038f.
16 *Clergymen Made Scarce*, p. 3. For a general overview of a curate's position in society in the nineteenth century, see Hart, *The Curate's Lot*, pp. 127–173.

3. Town Life

3.1 Ordination and First Curacy

Hunt explains how, being out of sympathy with Calvinist theology,[1] he was ordained in the Church of England. The details of his ordination are not transparent. He states: 'The late Bishop Maltby admitted me to Holy Orders',[2] without distinguishing between deacon's and priest's orders. Whether 'admitted to Holy Orders' means 'ordained' is unclear. The chronology is puzzling, since Maltby retired in 1856, whereas, according to *Crockford's*, Hunt was priested in 1857.[3] Moreover, his diaconal ordination in 1855 is recorded as having been performed by the Bishop of Manchester (James Prince Lee) for the Bishop of Durham.

This provides Hunt with an opportunity to assert his academic prowess, by mentioning how well he performed in the examination: 'His [Maltby] examining Chaplain said that I had passed the best examination of all the Candidates, though there were present men who had stood well at Oxford and Cambridge.'[4] He is proud, it seems, to affirm his Scottish academic credentials over and against those of 'Oxbridge' men.

---

1 Cf. 'Difficulties as to some doctrines of the Westminster Confession, which always appeared to me without a foundation in the Holy Scriptures, presented a barrier to my admission to any of the orthodox communities in Scotland. I came to England full of one doctrine, compared with which every other seemed of small importance,— this doctrine was that "Christ had tasted death for every man." I found the Prayer Book full of this momentous truth, and waiving all other considerations I united myself to the Church of England', *Clergymen Made Scarce*, pp. 3f.
2 *Clergymen Made Scarce*, p. 4. Edward Maltby was Bishop of Durham, 1836–1856. See 'Maltby, Edward (1770–1859), Bishop of Durham', in *Oxford Dictionary of National Biography*, https://doi.org/10.1093/ref:odnb/17900
3 *Crockford's* 1885, p. 618, records 'd[eacon] 1855 by B[isho]p of Man[chester] for B[isho]p of Dur[ham] p[riest] 1857 by B[isho]p of Dur[ham]'.
4 *Clergymen Made Scarce*, p. 4.

Hunt obtained his first curacy at a 'Parish in the suburbs of a large town in the North of England' with 10,000 parishioners. Mrs Eliza Hunt identifies the place, naming its incumbent, as Deptford St Andrew's, Bishopwearmouth, Sunderland, some 180 miles south of Perth.[5]

Hunt remained from 1855–1859 in this parish, which he describes as 'entirely of the working class',[6] and which was usually regarded merely as a stepping-stone to an incumbency. Whether, because of his roots, he empathized with the working-class parishioners, we cannot tell, but he clearly enjoyed, and was fulfilled in, his first curacy, since, on account of the incumbent's ill health, he was practically in charge of the parish and set about assiduously visiting, organizing lectures and the like, and generally enjoying the freedom that this responsibility afforded him.[7] The parishioners responded accordingly and wept repeatedly during his farewell sermon. Despite their poverty, they presented him with a leaving present of £20.[8]

3.2 First Metropolitan Curacy

At this point in the narrative, Hunt praises the newly appointed (1856) Bishop of London for some of his innovations and declares how his earnest desire was to go to London and be under the Bishop's jurisdiction so that he could do a considerable 'amount of good'.[9] His dream was to 'have a Church and District' to himself in a short space of time. His age (thirty-two) would surely have warranted such enthusiasm, but as we have observed, he was to wait another nineteen years for such preferment.

---

5   *Ibid*. In her annotations, Mrs Eliza Hunt writes 'W H Bulmer. Bishops wearmouth Sunderland'. William Henry Philip Bulmer was appointed in 1843 as incumbent of Deptford St Andrew's, Bishopwearmouth, Sunderland (*Crockford's* 1865, p. 94). Cf. 'Saint Andrew's, Deptford. Was built in 1841, at a time when the Ayres Quay area was establishing itself as a centre of industry. Shipyards and glassmakers were thriving and new streets of housing were springing up on land reclaimed from the salt grasses bordering the river. The church cost £2000 [approx. £212,184 in 2020] and was built by subscription. The style and shape of St. Andrews was plain Gothic rectangular, very typical of Anglican architecture of that period. The building did not survive beyond 1980s slum clearance', Norman Kirtlan, *Places of Worship in Old Sunderland* (Washington: Stone Boy Studio), pp. 15–16, http://www.sunderland-antiquarians.org/assets/Uploads/OPGM/WAP/PlacesofWorshipinOldSunderland.pdf
6   *Clergymen Made Scarce*, p. 4.
7   *Ibid*.
8   *Clergymen Made Scarce*, p. 5. £20 was worth about £2,570 in 2020.
9   *Clergymen Made Scarce*, p. 4.

His desire to move to London soon found fulfilment in 1859, in what he calls his 'first Metropolitan Curacy [...] in the north of London',[10] which was funded by the Church Pastoral Aid Society.[11] Hunt's not-so-cryptic pseudonym names the incumbent of the parish as 'the Rev. Simon Arlington'. His real name was James Rose Sutherland.[12] The church was St Philip the Evangelist's, Arlington Square, Islington. It had only very recently been opened in 1858,[13] although Sutherland had been appointed Perpetual Curate[14] of St Philip's in 1856. Prior to coming to St Philip's, Sutherland had been senior curate of St Mary's, the parish church of Islington, and Lecturer[15] at St Botolph's, Aldersgate.[16]

There soon proved to be differences of opinion with the incumbent, whom Hunt calls 'a man advanced in life', and who 'had been a Curate until within a very few years of the time when [Hunt] first knew him'.[17] He refers to him later as having been a 'non-preaching Curate for nearly twenty years'.[18] This is clearly only approximate. His first curacy was in

---

10 *Clergymen Made Scarce*, p. 5.
11 Cf. *Clergymen Made Scarce*, pp. 6f. This evangelical society was founded in 1836. Cf. Chadwick, *Victorian Church* I, pp. 446, 449–450.
12 Mrs Eliza Hunt notes: 'James Sutherland Arlington Square Islington', *Clergymen Made Scarce*, p. 5. He was a BA of Queens' College, Cambridge, *Crockford's* 1865, p. 605.
13 It was closed and demolished in 1953. The parish was united with St. James the Apostle. Cf. GENUKI, 'Genuki: Anglican Churches in Islington, Middlesex in 1890, Middlesex' (GENUKI), https://www.genuki.org.uk/big/eng/MDX/Islington/churches
14 A perpetual curate was 'In the C of E the technical name given before 1969 to a clergyman who officiated in a parish or district to which he had been nominated by the impropriator and licensed by the bishop ...' See 'Perpetual Curate', in *Concise Oxford Dictionary of the Christian Church*.
15 'One of a class of preachers in the Church of England, usually chosen by the parish and supported by voluntary contributions, whose duty consists mainly in delivering afternoon or evening "lectures"' (OED).
16 Sutherland's biography is recorded in Venn and Venn, *Alumni Cantabrigienses 'S'*, pp. 1–103 (p. 85): 'SUTHERLAND, JAMES. Adm. pens, at QUEENS', Oct. 8, 1838. Matric. Lent, 1839; B.A. 1843. Ord. priest (Peterb.) 1843; C. of Fleckney, Leics., 1843-5. C. of Islington and Lecturer of St Botolph's, Aldersgate, London, 1846-56. V. of St Philip's, Islington, 1857-71. Died in 1871. (Clergy List; Crockford.)' The 1851 census records for 17 Park St., Islington: 'James Sutherland, born in Madras, India, Curate of St Mary's Islington, Lecturer of St Botolph's Aldersgate, aged 41'. Members of the household were: Catherine Sutherland (wife) 40, Emily Sutherland (daughter) 18, Sophia Sutherland (daughter) 10, Jane Bewley (mother-in-law) 70, Louisa Richardson (servant) 25.
17 *Clergymen Made Scarce*, p. 5.
18 *Clergymen Made Scarce*, p. 7. Preaching was regarded as their primary function and a privilege by many of the Victorian clergy, especially those of the Low Church. Cf. E. A. Livingstone, 'Preaching', in *Concise Oxford Dictionary of the Christian Church*,

1843, so he had been a curate for sixteen years in 1859. Hunt later states that Sutherland 'displayed the senile vanity of an old man just elevated into position'.[19] In the 1851 census, he is recorded as being forty-one years of age, which would equate to a birth date of 1810. However, the 1861 census records him as being fifty-six, indicating a birth date of 1805. This would appear to be the accurate date. If this is so, he did not matriculate at Cambridge until he was thirty-four, which is curiously late. He was thus about fifty-four in 1859, when Hunt first met him, hardly an age for senility but perhaps old enough to explain Hunt's reaction at the age of thirty-two. It can be assumed that Hunt's unsympathetic description referred to his bearing. His 'elevation' occurred three years previously, in 1856. He was reported, upon his death in 1871, to have been about twelve years a curate at St Mary's and about fifteen years at St Philip's.[20] Hunt declares Sutherland to be 'about the worst [incumbent] into whose hands [he] could have fallen'.[21] He does not spare his disdain for this 'man of meagre abilities, but of considerable craft'. Before we investigate the details of this fraught relationship, a word should be said about Sutherland's family circumstances. He was married to Catharine,[22] who, according to the census, was aged 50 in 1861. She is described as being 'of delicate health, and requiring constant medical advice'.[23] They had two surviving daughters, aged 28 and 20 in 1861. The younger, Sophia Jane, was in good health and capable of earning her own living, but the elder daughter, Amelia Elizabeth, was disabled. Her health is described as having 'always been most delicate', and she was 'in other respects [...] most grievously afflicted and utterly incapable of working for her living'.[24] Catharine died in 1864.[25] When Sutherland died in 1871, he left

---

s.v.; Chadwick, *Victorian Church* II, pp. 172f. The sermon provided an occasion for 'mass entertainment', in some cases rivalling the music hall. Cf. George P. Landow, 'Charles Haddon Spurgeon at Exeter Hall, London', http://www.victorianweb.org/religion/sermons/exeter.html

19 *Clergymen Made Scarce*, p. 5.
20 See *Islington Gazette*, 24 October 1871, p. 1.
21 *Clergymen Made Scarce*, p. 5.
22 Mrs Sutherland seems to have preferred the spelling Catharine, e.g., on her marriage register entry in Manchester Parish Church (28 July 1831), though the form Catherine is used elsewhere. Her maiden name was Bewley [details retrieved from Ancestry.com].
23 *Islington Gazette*, 24 October 1871, p. 1.
24 *Ibid.*
25 'April 28, at 34, Halliford-street, Downham-road, Islington, Catharine, the beloved wife of the Rev. James Sutherland, aged 57', *John Bull*, 30 April 1864, p. 16.

the two daughters 'totally unprovided for',[26] so the parishioners set up a fund to help especially the elder daughter. A substantial committee oversaw this, and it was advertised eleven times in the *Islington Gazette*, often on the front page.[27] It was stated that 'his income was always very limited, and precluded the possibility of his saving money'.[28] Maybe this was as a result of the long time he had spent as a curate, for whom the annual income was usually about £100.[29] The incumbent's income at St Philip's, however, was £355 per annum,[30] which, compared with Hunt's annual income at Otford of £210 in 1878,[31] was substantial. Looking after his ailing family, together with the cost of living in the metropolis, must also have made considerable demands on Sutherland's finances. His family circumstances may well have contributed to feelings of dejection and frustration, caused by his lacklustre career.

The first contretemps occurred very soon after Hunt's arrival in Islington. Sutherland, upon scrutinizing the books that Hunt had purchased with his leaving present from Deptford, works of progressive theologians and writers such as Frederick Denison Maurice, Charles Kingsley, and August Neander, labelled these disparagingly as 'neology'.[32] Hunt had truthfully to deny that he had read any of them in order to placate Sutherland and to be engaged as his curate.

Hunt's first metropolitan curacy was noteworthy for a variety of negative reasons. His initial enthusiasm was quickly extinguished; his self-esteem soon abased, firstly by an eagerly anticipated meeting with the Bishop. It will be remembered that Hunt had sought a placement in London in order to be under Bishop Tait's jurisdiction. His hopes of a personal discussion of his work with the Bishop were soon dashed—he was introduced along with six other curates and had no opportunity to impress upon the Bishop the importance of his coming to London. He

---

26 *Islington Gazette*, 24 October 1871, p. 1.
27 E.g., *ibid*.
28 *Ibid*.
29 Approx. £12,045 in 2020. Hunt mentions the figure of £100 as his salary, *Clergymen Made Scarce*, p. 27. Substantially lower figures were not uncommon. Cf. Hart, *The Curate's Lot*, p. 135 and passim. Cases of particular hardship are documented in William George Jervis, *Startling Facts Respecting the Poverty and Distress of Four Hundred Clergymen of the Church of England* (London: Thompson, 1860).
30 Approx. £42,760 in 2020.
31 Approx. £25,563 in 2020.
32 On the use of this term to disparage modern theology, mainly of German origin, see Chadwick, *Victorian Church* I, pp. 528–544.

was given a licence in exchange for a sovereign,[33] and the early adulation that he felt towards the Bishop quickly gave way to resentment—afterwards, he viewed him as the man, the sight of whom had cost him a sovereign out of his meagre resources.[34]

More disappointment was yet in store for him when it came to the apportioning of his duties. His positive experiences in Deptford had possibly led him to expect to be able to act in a similarly independent way in Islington. However, this was far from being the case. He was allowed to preach only occasionally, this being deemed by his incumbent a 'privilege'.[35] Likewise with pastoral visiting, he was severely restricted, being given only poor areas and no resources such as a meeting hall.[36] A revealing aspect of the Victorian Church emerges in this context. Hunt complains that he could not invite the poor people to church, 'for even if they had been willing to come, we had not pews for people who could not pay pew rents'.[37] The topic of pew rents was one that exercised the nineteenth-century Anglican Church, with many people regarding them as an ill that was unchristian and deterred the poor from attending, whereas many churches regarded them as an essential source of income.[38] A limited number of 'free' pews were provided in many churches. But, as Hunt observes, even if he had 'taken pews for them' and got them to come in their best clothes, the 'officers at the Church would have warned them off'.[39] Here, the arrogant and uncharitable attitude of many middle-class churchgoers especially of the Evangelical party in the nineteenth century manifests itself, whereas the ritualists frequently directed their work at the poor, encouraging them to come to church and receive the consolation of religion.[40] For many middle-class Victorians, church services, sermons, and lectures were a way of occupying their leisure time, amounting to a form of edifying entertainment.

---

33 Approx. £129 in 2020.
34 *Clergymen Made Scarce*, p. 6.
35 *Clergymen Made Scarce*, p. 6.
36 'A District was assigned to me, which consisted of Misery Lane, Poverty Corner, Starvation Street, and a few similar streets, terraces, and even parades, for so they called them', *Clergymen Made Scarce*, p. 6.
37 *Clergymen Made Scarce*, p. 6.
38 Cf. B. F. Austin, *The Gospel to the Poor versus Pew Rents*, CIHM/ICMH Microfiche Series = CIHM/ICMH Collection de Microfiches; No. 06703 (Toronto: Montreal: W. Briggs; C. W. Coates, 1884) https://catalog.hathitrust.org/Record/100250786
39 *Clergymen Made Scarce*, p. 6.
40 Cf. Chadwick, *Victorian Church* II, pp. 311f.

Hunt's ministrations in Arlington Square were soon to come to a premature end. It appears that he, as curate, was in the incumbent's way and that the latter devised ways of making him feel unwelcome, such as not allowing him to participate in services, instead leaving him to sit alone in a pew.[41] This culminated in what Sutherland described as a 'deputation' of congregants, who had allegedly complained about Hunt's 'Scotch accent' when he read the service. The situation caused some degree of unpleasantness, with people taking sides and Sutherland allowing Hunt to read only the Epistle at the Communion. Hunt, however, refused to sit 'enthroned' in church, doing hardly anything. The 'deputation' proved to have been highly exaggerated and was most likely little more than gossip.[42] Nevertheless, the ill-feeling caused Hunt to resolve to seek another curacy, so he went to see the Bishop. The following day, it transpired that Sutherland had, in an underhand way, persuaded Bishop Tait to countersign a legal notice, requiring Hunt to quit in six months' time. This was an unkind, unjust, and hurtful act by Sutherland, as Hunt noted: 'I was sorry the Bishop had been a party to this, for I had given notice to leave at the end of three months, so that this notice was a studied insult on the part of Mr. Arlington'.[43] Hunt's first metropolitan curacy had thus lasted but a few months, had included much unpleasantness, and had ended disastrously. He must have felt completely downcast and dejected.

3.3 Search for a New Curacy

Hunt set about searching independently for a curacy, having obtained no help or encouragement from Bishop Tait. As he put it, 'I had now my first experience in the way of looking out for a Curacy. I advertised in the *Record*, and had a multitude of answers.'[44] The *Record* was an evangelical paper that listed advertisements for curacies, many funded by the Pastoral Aid Society.[45] In response to one answer, he preached a

---

41 *Clergymen Made Scarce*, p. 7.
42 *Ibid.*
43 *Clergymen Made Scarce*, p. 8.
44 *Ibid.*
45 The newspaper was founded in 1828. See Doreen M. Rosman, *Evangelicals and Culture* (Cambridge: James Clarke, 2012), p. 23; Josef L. Altholz, 'Alexander Haldane, the "Record", and Religious Journalism, *Victorian Periodicals Review*, 20 (1987), 23–31:

well-received trial sermon on St Augustine at another fairly new church in the north-west of London (St Paul's, Lisson Grove, built in 1836), but, declaring himself in conversation to agree on a point of theology with 'Mr. [F. D.] Maurice', a clergyman noted for his liberal views and a strong influence on Hunt,[46] he incurred the incumbent's disapproval, so that his application came to nought.[47]

Further interest came from a 'Vicar in the South West' [of London][48] by whom Hunt was invited to luncheon, together with the vicar's 'bevy of daughters', who behaved vainly and impolitely. He was seeking a curate who would take 'Temporary Duty [...] in a School Room'. The chance to minister to an influx of working people in the parish greatly appealed to Hunt. The incumbent disparagingly labelled them all as 'infidels'.[49] Once again, Hunt's progressive thinking and his honesty in declaring his position openly were his undoing: he professed his admiration for the sermons of the social reformer Frederick Robertson,[50] which made it plain that there could be no engagement there.

Hunt remarks ironically: 'I thought a man who wished to convert working men from infidelity, should teach his family to bridge the distance between the grades of society, especially that between a Clergyman who has a benefice and one who has not'.[51] Yet again his ambitions had been thwarted, partly through his probity, partly through the prejudice of the senior clergyman.

His next application, the third in 1860, was to St John's, Melmoth Place, Walham Green, in Fulham, in the south west of London.[52] This

---

'The Record came to be known for its vitriolic partisanship as the organ of the Evangelical party in the Church of England; but it began mildly enough', p. 23. Hunt, who appears to have used it principally for its advertisements, comments passim on the paper, e.g., 'I again had recourse to that valuable periodical the Record, and I should say here that it is the best medium for Curates and Incumbents to make known their wants. It is cheaper than the Guardian and the people in the office are vastly more civil', *Clergymen Made Scarce*, p. 6.

46 *Clergymen Made Scarce*, pp. 8f.
47 Mrs Eliza Hunt notes 'Lissom [sic] Grove. Name forgotten'. The name of the incumbent of St Paul's, Lisson Grove, was James Keeling, *Crockford's* 1865, p. 363.
48 'Jenkins Battersea', Mrs Eliza Hunt. Probably this was John Simon Jenkinson, Vicar of St Mary's, Battersea (1847–1872), *Crockford's* 1865, p. 347.
49 *Clergymen Made Scarce*, p. 9.
50 Cf. 'Robertson, Frederick William (1816–1853), Church of England Clergyman', *Oxford Dictionary of National Biography*, https://doi.org/10.1093/ref:odnb/23792
51 *Clergymen Made Scarce*, p. 9.
52 Cf. *Clergymen Made Scarce*, pp. 9f. The church is situated in North End Road/ Vanston Place, Fulham, founded 1828, GENUKI, 'Genuki: St John, Walham Green,

resulted in an engagement. Hunt's pseudonym for the incumbent is the 'Rev. Peter Walham'. Mrs Eliza Hunt's annotation reads 'William Garrat Walham Green'. The surname is misspelled. The clergyman in question is William Garratt, who was Perpetual Curate of St John's, Fulham, a post he had held since 1845. Garratt was a well-educated man.[53] He was about forty-five in 1860. He was succeeded by William Edmund Batty in 1862, after which he appears no longer to have been in active ministry, and died in 1874. Hunt therefore first made his acquaintance almost at the end of his ministry. At first, the two clergymen got on very well with each other. Hunt declares that he 'greatly liked the man, perhaps because he was such a contrast from Mr. Arlington'.[54] Garratt showed friendliness and humour and even held out the prospect of some unmarried women from good families belonging to the parish. The incumbent and congregation were 'well pleased with [Hunt's] sermon',[55] and he was offered the curacy. It remained only to gain the approval of the Pastoral Aid Society, which paid the curate's salary. Notwithstanding this, Garratt was prepared to conclude a 'temporary engagement for four or five months', since he wished to 'leave Town immediately'.[56] Hunt anticipated no difficulties in gaining the approval of the Society, since he had been in its service since his ordination. Thus, he was left in charge of the parish during Garratt's absence, no references having been required of him.[57]

Matters, however, soon became complicated over the question of references. James Sutherland showed his disgruntlement over the way Hunt had left his parish, having found a substitute, albeit one who was not acceptable to him, thus obviating the need for Hunt to remain a further three months in the parish. Sutherland's displeasure had been incurred, in Hunt's opinion, both by Hunt's obtaining a new curacy so soon and because no reference had been made to him. Hunt was elated at

---

Church of England, Middlesex' (GENUKI), https://www.genuki.org.uk/big/eng/MDX/Fulham/StJohn. It subsequently espoused an Anglo-Catholic tradition.

53 See Venn and Venn, *Alumni Cantabrigienses*, II, pt 3, p. 18, https://books.google.co.uk/books?id=Abx6EqTRfqEC
54 *Clergymen Made Scarce*, p. 10.
55 *Ibid*.
56 *Ibid*. It later transpires that he went to fashionable Brighton, apparently for the summer season, since Hunt had begun his quest in July 1860. See *Clergymen Made Scarce*, pp. 8, 11.
57 *Ibid*.

the outcome and overjoyed at taking up residence in his new parish. His admiration for Garratt grew: God was in His heaven, and all *seemed* right with the world. However, his 'hopes were short lived';[58] the Pastoral Aid Society required a reference from his previous incumbent and would accept no other. His assertion that unpleasantness had existed between him and his last incumbent and that reference should rather be made to his curacy in the north of England fell on deaf ears. Thus it was that he was vulnerable to a spiteful reference by Sutherland. Under the guise of a generally positive assessment of Hunt's work, Sutherland was able to intimate Hunt's unsuitability by underhand means:

He gave me a testimonial which was on the whole satisfactory. He certified among other things that I was an 'able preacher and a diligent student;' but the cunning man knew the crotchets of this Society, and added not on his own authority, but that some one had said that my sermons were not thoroughly 'Evangelical'.[59]

Hunt's new incumbent came to his defence, and, after a succession of correspondence, was able to persuade the Society to appoint him as curate: 'He [Garratt] had taken the high ground, and fought [Hunt's] battle manfully'.[60] Hunt's work blossomed and flourished, and the congregation 'visibly increased'; his opinion of Garratt 'was now at its height'.[61] This happy state of affairs continued for about two months; then came the bombshell: a letter from Garratt informed Hunt that his appointment had been confirmed by the Pastoral Aid Society, but *'only for three months!* and that he would give [him] three months' notice from the date of his letter'.[62] Hunt's former champion now proved to be his humiliation. Quite why this volte-face occurred it is difficult to tell. Perhaps the incumbent had lost the will to do battle with the Society. Maybe the Society had had second thoughts about funding Hunt's curacy, particularly in view of the ambivalent reference from Sutherland. Perhaps the curate was beginning to outshine the incumbent; perhaps he had outlived his usefulness to Garratt. Maybe Garratt was not willing to contemplate paying a curate out of his own or the parish's resources. At any rate, Hunt notes that 'It was a manoeuvre of Mr. Walham's

---

58 Ibid.
59 Ibid.
60 *Clergymen Made Scarce*, p. 11.
61 Ibid.
62 Ibid.

never to have licensed Curates.'[63] Hence, Hunt had no recourse to the Bishop in the matter, since he had not been licensed. Anyway, the Bishop hardly knew him, once mistaking him on a visit to the parish for the previous curate. Hunt comments ruefully on this lamentable aspect of the Victorian Church: 'If with a licence in my former Curacy he [sc. the Bishop] could only help the Incumbent to insult me, what could I expect here without a licence?'[64] Again, we see how the curate's lot was far from being a happy one. Furthermore, a conflict between the parishioners' interests and wishes and those of the incumbent is next seen to develop. Hunt reports how 'Three different gentlemen called to ask if I would sanction a Petition being got up and presented to Mr. Walham for me to remain.' His probity and pragmatism came to the fore, however, and Hunt rejected the idea, especially in view of the role of the Society in paying the curate's salary. The parishioners nevertheless continued to show their support for Hunt by agreeing 'to raise the salary in the Parish, and dismiss the Society'. Hunt observes: 'that was an amount of lay interference not to be tolerated'.[65] By this comment, he lays bare an aspect of the Victorian Church that was pronounced at the time, but which had existed previously and would continue to exist subsequently. Although Garratt had for the most part behaved amicably and properly towards Hunt, it would appear that he felt threatened by these developments and that, like so many clergymen, he regarded his parish as his personal fiefdom, in which he brooked no interference. His reaction was typical in such a situation, as Hunt relates: 'He not only peremptorily refused [to accept the petition], but immediately accused me of raising a disturbance in his Parish.'[66] Here we might note the haughtiness of this 'peremptory' refusal and the possessive attitude expressed towards 'his' parish. The incumbent had been riled and felt the need to reassert his authority. Hunt, as an intellectually able clergyman and an uncompromising personality, must have found it difficult to show humility and charity, which was so often lacking in his superiors. Yet, he managed to emerge from the situation with dignity and even preserved a degree of friendship with Garratt:

---

63 *Ibid.*
64 *Ibid.*
65 *Ibid.*
66 *Ibid.*

'No charge could have been more unjust. I vindicated myself, and we remained apparently friends until the close of my time there'.[67]

Hunt's tally so far was three curacies, one of which had been good and long, one short and disastrous, and one short and unfortunate, but perhaps 'good in parts'. Added to that were two unsuccessful applications. Thus, he found himself seeking his fourth curacy in late 1860.

His previous incumbent, with whom, as we have seen, he remained on apparently friendly terms, offered to provide him with a reference in his quest for a new curacy. Hunt was grateful, since he had 'no other to whom [he] could refer'.[68] He 'happened to see' one of Garratt's letters, which confirmed that the latter wrote honestly and fairly. He agreed to omit a reference to 'Scotch predilections on the part of some' parishioners in any future references.[69]

Hunt's stay in Garratt's parish had been positive to a degree, partly because he 'had made some genuine[70] friends, whose friendship remains till this hour'.[71] Some parishioners tried to help him obtain a new position, suggesting an Indian chaplaincy or an appointment in the British Army. Both suggestions, however, came to nought: there was a very long waiting list for Army chaplaincies, and nothing was available in India.

Having moved away from traditional curacies, Hunt made further applications to overseas bodies, among which he 'wrote to the Secretary of the Colonial and Continental Society, asking employment on the Continent of Europe'.[72] This provided him with an opportunity to display the learning of which he was evidently proud:

> I mentioned, perhaps inadvisedly, that I had thoroughly studied the Roman Catholic Church, both on its good and its bad sides; that I was well acquainted with German Theology, from the Wolfenbüttel Fragments to

---

67 *Ibid.*
68 His first incumbent, William Bulmer, in Deptford, lived to be ninety-eight, hence he was still alive at the time. Hunt possibly did not wish to refer to him, owing to his poor state of health. Cf. 'On the 1st of March, the Rev. William Henry Philip Bulmer late rector of Boldon died at Doncaster in the 98th year of his age', *Monthly Chronicle of North Country Lore and Legend*, IV (1890), 188.
69 *Clergymen Made Scarce*, p. 12.
70 The word is underlined by Mrs Eliza Hunt, but without elucidation.
71 *Clergymen Made Scarce*, p. 12.
72 *Ibid.* The secretary since 1851 had been Mesac Thomas, who, in 1863, became Bishop of Goulburn, Australia. See 'Thomas, Mesac (1816–1892)', *Australian Dictionary of Biography*, https://adb.anu.edu.au/biography/thomas-mesac-4708/text7805

the latest development; that I knew Kant and all the ramifications from Kant. These I then thought, and still think, are the proper qualifications for an English Clergyman on the Continent...[73]

Sadly for Hunt, this cut no ice with the Society, and he remarked: 'I had an immediate answer as pompous (the writer is now an 'Evangelical' Bishop) as it was prompt, to the effect that there was no vacancy in their Society that would suit me.'[74]

The response appears to manifest an anti-intellectual, xenophobic arrogance that frequently affected British men in authority at the time, when the British Empire held sway over much of the world.[75] It simultaneously demonstrates how Hunt's credentials were little valued for their own sake, without wealth or family connections, and that his chances of employment were but slim.

Having been unsuccessful with foreign applications, Hunt next turned his attention to the countryside: 'About this time I had an unusual adventure in the country, in answer to an advertisement in the *Record*.'[76] The date would appear to have been late 1860 or early 1861.

Although the 'adventure' did not lead to an engagement, it is worthy of scrutiny for the light it sheds on the rural Church and its relationship to the 'squirearchy'. The parish of Burley was located in Rutland, as Mrs Eliza Hunt's annotation reveals.[77] The church's function was apparently to preserve the established order and especially to do the squire's

---

73 Ibid.
74 Ibid.
75 Cf. Hunt's observation: 'A well known Bishop has said in a book, called "Dangers, and Safeguards," &c., "A very general impression seems to prevail, that the very fact of a writer's showing any acquaintance with the Theology of Germany, may be taken as an *a priori* indication of unsoundness".' See A. C. Tait, *The Dangers and Safeguards of Modern Theology. Containing "Suggestions Offered to the Theological Student Under Present Difficulties"* (a Revised Edition), *and Other Discourses*, 1861, https://books.google.co.uk/books?id=T2BoAAAAcAAJ. The original publication, in which this quotation first appeared, is: *Suggestions offered to the Theological Student, under present difficulties. Five Discourses preached before the University of Oxford* (London: Murray, 1846), Preface, p. iv.
76 *Clergymen Made Scarce*, p. 12.
77 'Rutlandshire John Jones', Mrs Eliza Hunt. The Christian name would appear to be wrong. The Rev. Joseph Jones was Vicar of Burley-on-the-Hill, alternatively spelled Burleigh, Oakham, Rutland, from 1819 onwards. The living was in the gift of George Finch, Esq., *Crockford's* 1860, p. 346; 1865, p. 357. The church of the Holy Cross was adjacent to Finch's mansion. See 'Parishes: Burley | British History Online', https://www.british-history.ac.uk/vch/rutland/vol2/pp112-119

bidding. The squire, George Finch, 'combined evangelical Christianity with a love of hunting and cricket'.[78] His dominance over the church and village at large can be seen in the earnest advice given by the vicar's coachman on the ten-mile ride from the railway station to the village: 'Let me give you a bit of advice—Sir, tomorrow morning you must not begin the service until the squire comes in; some Clergymen as I bring this way go wrong there, and the squire does not like it.'[79]

By the time morning had come and Hunt and the vicar had repaired to church for morning service, the potential new curate had forgotten this piece of advice but by chance had begun to read the service just a few seconds after the entry of the squire. So far, so good. When it came to his sermon, however, he chose a text with a rural theme, which he thought would suit a 'congregation of simple farmers'.[80] He knew nothing of the squire's existence when preparing the sermon. His theme, the 'Rich man that pulled down his barns to build greater', proved to paint an unflattering, but accurate, picture of the squire, and the three-month engagement that was concluded with the vicar was later annulled by the arrival of the landowner, who did not find the sermon to his liking.[81] Hunt had stood up for his religious principles against prejudice and arrogance, albeit unwittingly, and had shown how, especially in rural parishes, the Church of England in the form of the country parson was willing to do obeisance to aristocratic wealth and status.

Hunt's narrative departs from the countryside as abruptly as he himself left the parson and squire to their own devices. His intellectual, forthright attitude was evidently not aligned with rural religion. He comments on the incomprehension that his career called forth: 'It seemed to my friends that I was doomed to misfortunes. They could not understand how a preacher who had pleased them so well, was not accepted wherever he offered himself.'[82] Who these friends were and where they were located is not revealed. It may have seemed logical to

---

78 'George Finch', Mrs Eliza Hunt. See Sue Howlett, 'Burley on the Hill' in Robert Ovens and Sheila Sleath, eds, *The Heritage of Rutland Water* (Oakham, Rutland: Rutland Local History & Record Society, 2008), pp. 55–92, p. 80, http://www.rutlandhistory.org/HRW/chapter-004
79 *Clergymen Made Scarce*, p. 13.
80 *Ibid*.
81 For details of this affair, see, for the light they cast on the rural Church's abject subservience to the gentry, *Clergymen Made Scarce*, pp. 13f.
82 *Clergymen Made Scarce*, p. 14.

blame the corrupt state of the Church, which is indeed what happened: 'They were sound Church of England people; but they began to think there must be something wrong in a Church, which made it difficult for such as me to get employment.'[83] Apparently, they had not perceived the discrepancies between Hunt's approach to religion (as manifested in his ministrations and applications) and that which was expected of him by his various potential employers. His friends proposed 'building a Dissenting Chapel', but Hunt's espousal of the Church of England caused him to reject this suggestion. Application was made to the Bishop of London to build a new church in 'the Parish'.[84] The location of this parish is typically not specified: Mrs Eliza Hunt has not supplied the details, nor does the use of the definite article unequivocally link to a previously mentioned location. Most logically, it would appear to be the parish in which Hunt had last been engaged (i.e. St John's, Melmoth Place, Walham Green). This is implied in the phrasing of his subsequent narrative: 'Before this scheme of a new Church was matured I had left Mr. Walham, to take charge of a Parish six miles north of London.'[85] Alternatively, it could mean All Saints', Fulham, the mother parish of the area.

---

83 *Ibid.*
84 *Ibid.*
85 *Ibid.*

4. *Essays and Reviews* Controversy

At the end of his stay in Walham Green and before the episode in Rutland, another misfortune befell the ill-fated curate: 'On the last day, he [Garratt] called with a petition for me to sign. It was the Clerical protest against the "Essays and Reviews." He asked me to sign it as a matter of course—all the Clergy were doing it.'[1] Whereas many clergymen signed the petition on the basis of hearsay and prejudice, like Garratt, not having read *Essays and Reviews*, which was first published in 1860,[2] John Hunt, always the scholar and progressive thinker, explained, to Garratt's surprise, how he had 'read it six months since'.[3] Whereas he was thus able to come to a sober appraisal of its contents and declined to sign the petition, Garratt's narrow-minded partiality in the matter caused him to suspect 'that [Hunt's] gospel was not the soundest in England'.[4]

After his lack of success in Rutland, Hunt moved to a new engagement, his fourth curacy, in 1860, a year that was very eventful for him and which saw storm clouds gathering in the debate between science and religion.[5] The parish is identified as 'Edmonton' by Mrs Eliza Hunt, without further elucidation.[6] At the time, Edmonton was a

---

1   *Clergymen Made Scarce*, p. 14.
2   A Broad-Church volume, which proffered an enlightened, scientific approach to religion and caused much controversy. See Victor Shea and William Whitla, eds, *Essays and Reviews: The 1860 Text and Its Reading*, Victorian Literature and Culture Series (Charlottesville and London: University of Virginia Press, 2000), https://books.google.co.uk/books?id=sJcf9rWn8nAC; Chadwick, *Victorian Church* II, pp. 75–97.
3   *Clergymen Made Scarce*, p. 14.
4   Ibid.
5   Darwin's *Origin of Species* was published in 1859. See Chadwick, *Victorian Church* II, pp. 1–35.
6   Anglican churches that were in existence at the time in Edmonton are: All Saints', Edmonton (founded in the twelfth century); Christ Church, until 1862 Weld Chapel, Southgate (founded 1615), St Michael's, Wood Green (founded 1844); St

separate town, not part of London. Since Mrs Eliza Hunt notes the name simply thus, without the name of the incumbent, we may reasonably assume that this was the ancient parish church of All Saints rather than one of the newer churches in the parish, as these would likely have had a more specific designation.[7] Hunt refers to the incumbent as the 'Vicar', whereas the other churches did not have a vicar, and the clergymen in charge are referred to as 'incumbent' in *Crockford's* (1860). In the absence of further information, it is impossible to be certain. The Vicar of All Saints' at the time was the Rev. Thomas Tate, MA,[8] who died on 21 January 1863. Thomas Tate's academic credentials were not the best; he was first of the 'Junior Optimes' (i.e. Third Class) in the Cambridge Mathematical Tripos in 1828. He had previously been curate at Edmonton, while his distinguished father, James Tate, was vicar. It is unclear whether Thomas Tate, who was aged fifty-six, was the incumbent with whom Hunt had to deal. Although Mrs Eliza Hunt does not identify this incumbent either, she names the other curate as 'John Goodwin', whom Hunt calls 'an ignorant man from St. Bees'.[9]

Initial encouragement from the congregation, who were very pleased with Hunt's sermons and packed the church, drew the admiration of the incumbent, and Hunt remarked: 'I seemed to be on my feet once more.'[10] Once again, however, his liberal, progressive opinions served to uphold his probity but not to further his temporal advancement. Once again, the argument was over *Essays and Reviews*, which he was able to appraise fairly and honestly, since he, unlike most, had actually read the volume, judging that 'There was truth in it that we needed—truth, some of it unpalatable indeed, but it was necessary for truth's own sake

---

Paul's, Winchmore Hill (founded 1828); St James's, Muswell Hill (founded 1850). See GENUKI, 'Genuki: Edmonton, Middlesex' (GENUKI), https://www.genuki.org.uk/big/eng/MDX/Edmonton

7   On the history of the various churches, see: 'Edmonton: Churches | British History Online', https://www.british-history.ac.uk/vch/middx/vol5/pp181-187
8   *Crockford's* 1860, p. 594.
9   St Bees Theological College in Cumberland was founded in 1816 as an alternative to Oxford and Cambridge, providing a route to ordination for 'literates', i.e., non-graduates. It was mostly looked down upon by graduate clergy. See Alan Graham Leigh Haig, 'The Church of England as a Profession in Victorian England' (unpublished doctoral dissertation, Australian National University, 1980), https://doi.org/10.25911/5d778863e864a; idem, *The Victorian Clergy* (London; Sydney: Croom Helm, 1984), p. 205 and passim.
10 *Clergymen Made Scarce* p. 15.

that it should come out.'[11] Predictably, the prejudice of those who had not read the text came again to the fore, this time more forcefully than before. Hunt's sober intellectual approach contrasts starkly with that of his congregation and fellow clergy. Once again, he receives notice to quit—this time immediately:

> My remarks brought me anonymous letters, expressing amazement and disappointment, that one whose ministrations they so much esteemed, should see any good in such a book. The Vicar too wrote that I must leave at once. The other Curate, an ignorant man from St. Bees, next Sunday denounced the 'Essays and Reviews' as the most atrociously infidel book that had ever been published. The Vicar came home, and he preached 'Essays and Reviews' till every servant girl in the Parish was reading 'Essays and Reviews.' The Curate of course had never read the book, and the Vicar made a vow he never would read it; but if his congregation wanted to go to hell, that, he said, was the book for them to read. It gave me great pain that I had been in any sense the cause of all this raving.[12]

Hunt's honesty and intellectual self-respect had once again been to his own detriment. This occurred more out of innocence, even naivety, than academic arrogance:

> I felt I had made a mistake, but it was done in innocence. I never could realize that religious people could be angry about a religious inquiry; least of all that Clergymen, the science of whose profession is theology, should be angry about theological Essays, displaying such ability and learning, as ought to make the Church glad that such gifts are still consecrated to her service.[13]

As before in Walham Green, Hunt did not have a licence in the parish, hence he had no possibility of appealing to the Bishop.[14] It appears that Hunt was not required literally to leave at once, since in the ensuing narrative he explains, with regard to a trial Sunday engagement in a new parish: 'As I had not left my other Parish I could not do this without giving up my emolument for the Parish I was now in.'[15]

Two metaphors enter the narrative at this point, the first, a rueful nautical one, 'I was again afloat in search of a Curacy', suggesting

---

11 *Ibid.*
12 *Ibid.*
13 *Ibid.*
14 *Ibid.*
15 *Clergymen Made Scarce*, p. 16.

drifting at sea, possibly after a shipwreck; the second, a witty literary allusion, 'Mounting my Rosinante (the *Record*), I set out in quest of new adventures.' The reference to 'Rosinante', Don Quixote's steed, well known for its former status as a workhorse or nag,[16] is on the surface a humorous quip, meaning 'mounting my trusty old workhorse'. But it implies greater subtlety, inasmuch as the *Record* had proved to be successful at finding Hunt new 'adventures' in the past, which, however, were mostly of a questionable nature. Moreover, Don Quixote, to whom Hunt implicitly compares himself, with its picaresque themes and problematic encounters, provides a fitting analogy to our clergyman himself, burlesque and tragic at the same time.

And so, Hunt applies for his fifth curacy, this time 'in the neighbourhood of Oxford Street West'.[17] This turns out to be All Saints' Church, Norfolk Square, Paddington, dating from 1847, closed in 1919. He had an earnest theological discussion with the incumbent, Edwin Henry Steventon, in which the latter showed a profound knowledge of theology, but Hunt's willingness to embrace, and engage with, complex contemporary theology, including aspects of *Essays and Reviews*, led to a situation where he judged 'it was evident from the beginning that we were not to make any engagement'.[18]

After this unsuccessful encounter, Hunt responded to 'another application from the South East'.[19] A missive from the Rev. Alfred William Snape, St Mary Magdalen, Old Kent Road, Bermondsey, distinguished itself from the rest by bearing a Latin motto, namely 'Timere vel mutare sperno'.[20] Hunt's testimonials proved not to satisfy the incumbent, and he was informed he 'would not be wanted on Sunday'.[21] He suspected

---

16   Cf. OED, s.v. 'Don Quixote gives this name to the horse on deciding to use him as his steed. It is formed as a deliberately noble-sounding name, punningly Spanish rocín horse, hack [...] + ante before [...], with allusion to the animal's former status as a workhorse or nag.'
17   *Clergymen Made Scarce*, p. 15.
18   *Clergymen Made Scarce*, p. 16.
19   'Snape, Old Kent Road', Mrs Eliza Hunt, viz. Alfred William Snape, St Mary Magdalen, Kent Road [Bermondsey]. Snape (b. 1825, MA Cantab., 1851) was the son of the Rev. Richard Snape, and the author of several short publications. Cf. *Crockford's* 1860, p. 571.
20   *Mutare Vel Timere Sperno* ('I scorn to change or fear') is the motto of the Dukes of Beaufort. The transposed order *Timere Vel Mutare Sperno* occurs also elsewhere, e.g., for the Deffray family. Whether any dynastic association was thereby implied by Snape is unclear. It might indicate a tenacious, pugnacious nature. Cf. Gustave de Rivoire de la Bâtie, *Armorial du Dauphiné* (Lyon: Perrin, 1867), p. 401.
21   *Clergymen Made Scarce*, p. 16.

Garratt of having referred to his refusal to sign the petition against *Essays and Reviews*. In his reply to Snape, in which he insisted on coming, as he had had to give up another engagement and would thus have been financially disadvantaged,[22] he wrote at the end of his reply 'in large letters *Timere vel mutare sperno*'. He thus showed fortitude and resilience, not without a hint of arrogance in displaying his classical education, by turning the motto against the originator. Presumably, the irony was not lost on his correspondent.

It is not clear whether Hunt actually 'read prayers', as he had initially been requested, but he was obliged to listen to a sermon that seemed 'specially written for [his] benefit', in which 'The preacher maintained that the Spirit never taught, except through the Bible.' Hunt was at odds with this theology and had in other ways made an unfavourable impression. Unfortunately, he had trusted that Garratt would write a favourable testimonial and 'reckoning that this engagement was certain', he had resigned his other parish. Thus, he 'was thrown out of employment altogether'.[23] In exasperation, Hunt explains:

> Three months were spent in advertising, corresponding, having interviews, and preaching trial sermons. I advertised in the *Record* twice a week, and had about a dozen answers to each advertisement. The working of the Curate system was revealed to me during these three months as I hope it never was to another before me, and I trust for the sake of the Church of England, it will never be so revealed in the experience of another after me.[24]

By this stage, he had reached a state of cynical disdain for the system of appointing curates. He relates a series of five luckless applications and the responses he received, ranging from one from Samuel Garratt, a relation of William Garratt's,[25] who was not on friendly terms with him,[26]

---

22 It had been agreed that Hunt would receive two guineas (approx. £261 in 2020) for his trial engagement.
23 *Clergymen Made Scarce*, p. 16.
24 *Clergymen Made Scarce*, p. 17.
25 'Garrat, Little Queen Street', Mrs Eliza Hunt, another misspelling. Little Queen Street ran between High Holborn and Great Queen Street, along what is now the northern end of Kingsway. See GENUKI, 'Genuki: Holborn Deanery Anglican Churches in 1890/1903, Middlesex' (GENUKI), https://www.genuki.org.uk/big/eng/MDX/HolbornStAndrew/churches. Samuel Garratt was incumbent of Trinity Church, St Giles-in-the-Fields, London (1856–1867), BA, Trinity Coll., Cantab., 1839; MA 1865, *Crockford's* 1860, p. 225.
26 Cf. *Clergymen Made Scarce*, p. 17.

to a feeble excuse from another incumbent[27] to the effect that he had changed his mind about having a curate, to the sanctimonious assertion that his trial sermon was 'lacking in the fulness of Evangelical truth',[28] to a position with no salary attached, to a bizarre interrogation on twelve numbered points by one who signed only with the initials H. L.,[29] to whom Hunt replied that he considered H. L. 'half-cracked', despite which he met him again later and was actually offered a position by him, which Hunt had to refuse because he had accepted another appointment. On this group of responses Hunt comments, with justification: 'Many of the letters were great curiosities.'[30] They exemplify the foibles and many of the idiosyncrasies of the contemporary clergy.

---

27 Not specified by Mrs Eliza Hunt.
28 'Krus, St. Judes, Lambeth or Southwark', Mrs Eliza Hunt, viz. St Jude's Church, Southwark, Saint George's Road, Southwark, closed 1976. See GENUKI, 'Genuki: St Jude, Southwark, Church of England, Surrey' (GENUKI), https://www.genuki.org.uk/big/eng/SRY/Southwark/StJude. Mrs Eliza Hunt's transcription of the name is incorrect. It should read 'Francis Cruse'. See *Crockford's* 1865, p. 156; Debbie Kennett, 'Cruwys News: Rev. Francis Cruse of Worthing, Sussex', *Cruwys News*, 2007, https://cruwys.blogspot.com/2007/02/rev-francis-cruse-of-worthing-sussex.html
29 'Robinson, Chelsea', Mrs Eliza Hunt. William Woolhouse Robinson, *Crockford's* 1865, p. 540, St John's Coll. Camb. B.A 1826, M.A. 1829; Deac. 1826, Pr. 1828 was incumbent of Christ Church, Chelsea. Amongst other things he wrote *A Clergyman's Reasons for Teetotalism* (1870), which would explain why one of his twelve questions concerned this subject. It is unclear what H. L. represented.
30 *Clergymen Made Scarce*, p. 17.

5. Unemployment and Applications

5.1 Theological Differences and 'Evangelical' Credentials

Our narrative now retreats a little to 'the first few weeks of [Hunt's] advertising',[1] but the chronology about this time is not altogether clear, and it is not possible to say whether 1860 or 1861 is meant. Sometime in 1860, during a three-month period of unemployment. Hunt refers to meeting the 'Rector of a large Parish, not far from London Bridge'.[2] Like Hunt, the rector, Hugh Allen, an extreme Protestant, was an educated man, with several degrees, including a Doctorate of Divinity from Trinity College Dublin (*ad eundem*, Cantab.). They enjoyed long theological discussions together, and Allen offered Hunt a curacy. At this point, the Pastoral Aid Society, which was to fund the curacy, again raised its head; it transpired in a reference that Hunt 'was reported to have said to some one in Mr. Walham's Parish, that the world was not made in six days out of nothing'.[3] Hunt's progressive theology again does him a disservice, but perhaps more importantly, his almost childlike trust in human nature[4] is of no benefit to him: he confided in the Curate of Edmonton, who promptly told the vicar, which led to them sending 'a

---

1   *Clergymen Made Scarce*, p. 18.
2   'Hugh Allen', Mrs Eliza Hunt; *Clergymen Made Scarce*, p. 18, i.e., Hugh Allen, Trinity College Dublin, B.A. 1835; M.A., B.D. and D.D. 1861, Rector of St George the Martyr, Southwark, 1859–1877, *Crockford's 1865*, p. 8. See also Chadwick: *Victorian Church* I, pp. 498f.
3   On the debate surrounding this, see Chadwick, *Victorian Church* I 'Genesis and Geology', pp. 558–572.
4   Cf. his epitaph in Otford Church, p. 101, below: 'He possessed a rare simplicity of nature'.

dispatch to the Society that [Hunt] was one of the rising infidels, who were to be crushed by every possible means'.[5] Naturally, this provoked a rejection by the Pastoral Aid Society. Hunt's tally of rejections had now reached well into double figures.

Continuing with the theme of the conflict between theologies, Hunt relates how about this time he 'chanced to call one day with a friend on the Principal of an important "Evangelical" Institution'.[6] Mrs Eliza Hunt duly provides details of the person.[7] A theological discussion ensued, in which the two disputants turned their attention to the philosophy of the Rev. Henry Longueville Mansel,[8] who at the time was Waynflete Professor in Moral and Metaphysical Philosophy at Oxford, later Dean of St Paul's. Here again, we observe a clash of the progressive, open-minded, more academically oriented rationalist churchman and the narrow-minded, more practically oriented Evangelical churchman. The latter, being the older man (Hunt was thirty-four, Green about forty-two), holding a position of seniority, treated Hunt arrogantly, maintaining that 'God has revealed Himself only in the book' (i.e., Bible). Hunt's considered reasoning carried no weight with Green, who declared him an atheist and ordered him to leave the premises.[9]

These two experiences caused Hunt 'great mental trouble' and led him to question his calling himself 'Evangelical'.[10] He realized that there were many of the beliefs and practices of the 'Evangelicals' that he did

---

5   *Clergymen Made Scarce*, p. 18.
6   Ibid.
7   'Thomas Green, Church Missionary College, Islington', Mrs Eliza Hunt. Green was the principal of the evangelical Church Missionary College in Islington, *Crockford's* 1865, p. 259. Cf. 'Church Missionary College, Islington, London, N.—Brasen. Coll. Ox. 2nd cl. Lit. Hum. and B.A. 1841, M.A. 1844; Deac. 1843 and Pr. 1844 ... Prin. of the Ch. Miss. Coll. Islington, 1858. Formerly P. C. of Friesland, near Manchester, 1849–1858', *ibid*. See also 'Church Missionary Society College, Islington', Wikipedia, https://en.wikipedia.org/w/index.php?title=Church_Missionary_Society_College,_Islington&oldid=995991744
8   See 'Mansel, Henry Longueville (1820–1871), Dean of St Paul's and Theologian', *Oxford Dictionary of National Biography*, https://doi.org/10.1093/ref:odnb/17988; Chadwick, *Victorian Church* I, pp. 556–558.
9   'At these words the Principal started from his seat, his form agitated with passion, he exclaimed, 'You are an Atheist! and I order you at once to leave these premises, that they be not polluted by your presence', *Clergymen Made Scarce*, p. 19.
10 On the Evangelicals, see Chadwick, *Victorian Church* I, pp. 440–455. An exaggerated, but telling, portrait of a hypocritical Evangelical clergyman is given by Anthony Trollope in *Barchester Towers* (Chapter 4 and passim) in the person of the bishop's chaplain, Obadiah Slope.

not share and concluded 'that the word "Evangelical" had come to be used conventionally in an improper sense'.[11] He was advised to move away from advertising in the 'evangelical' *Record*, especially since most of the curacies advertised there were funded by the Pastoral Aid Society. He was directed instead towards the Tractarian *Guardian*[12] and also the Curates' Registry at Whitehall.[13]

5.2 The Curates' Registry

Hunt comments on his experiences with the Curates' Registry with deep resentment: 'I never forget the feeling of degradation that came over me when I was first reduced to these expedients.'[14] His fraught quest for ecclesiastical employment had reached a low ebb when he sent in applications through the Registry. He tells how some incumbents continually advertised for curates because they 'do not know how to use them' and remarks further on the insensitive and high-handed way in which applicants were often treated. He relates how this fate befell him: 'One Incumbent,[15] whose name I took from this Registry, refused to see me, and sent an angry message that he had ordered the Secretary to take his name off these books two months ago.'[16] More than just suffering from dejection and low self-esteem, the rejected curates 'get the reputation of dangerous men'.[17] Their reputation thus makes it all the more difficult for them to break out of this vicious circle, and they find, in Hunt's words, that they 'lose caste with the Bishop and the beneficed Clergy'.[18]

---

11   *Clergymen Made Scarce*, p. 19.
12   Cf. 'The Guardian was a weekly Anglican newspaper published from 1846 to 1951. It was founded by Richard William Church, Thomas Henry Haddan, and other supporters of the Tractarian movement and was for many years the leading newspaper of the Church of England', 'The Guardian (Anglican Newspaper)', Wikipedia, https://en.wikipedia.org/w/index.php?title=The_Guardian_(Anglican_newspaper)&oldid=959850312; Chadwick: *Victorian Church* I, p. 238.
13   An office at 7 Whitehall, entitled 'Registry for Curates, Curacies, Temporary Duty and Titles for Holy Orders', it was 'under the sanction of the archbishops of both provinces'. See, for example, the advertisement in the *Clergy List*, 1866, p. 12.
14   *Clergymen Made Scarce*, p. 19.
15   'Courtney, St. James, Pentonville, an Irishman', Mrs Eliza Hunt. Another misspelling. This is the Rev. Anthony Lefroy Courtenay, D. D., incumbent of St James's, Pentonville, a Low Churchman and litigant. See Philip Temple, *Northern Clerkenwell and Pentonville* (New Haven, CT: Yale University Press, 2008), p. 379.
16   *Clergymen Made Scarce*, p. 20.
17   *Clergymen Made Scarce*, p. 19.
18   Ibid.

We can only applaud Hunt that he did not, under these circumstances, throw in the towel or change his principled approach.

5.3 *The Guardian*

The first advertisement in the High-Church *Guardian*, which Hunt had never used before,[19] provided an impressive total of thirty-six responses. Hunt 'was introduced to an entirely new class of men'.[20] The responses were from diverse clergymen, often with idiosyncratic wishes, habits, and sometimes devious motives.[21] The main drawback was their inability to offer adequate remuneration, since there was no High-Church equivalent of the Pastoral Aid Society.

5.4 English Graduates Only

Among the more eccentric responses from the *Guardian* was a disapproving observation from one incumbent that Hunt had not 'graduated at an English University'.[22] As we have already seen, there is no record in the St Andrews *Biographical Register* that Hunt graduated at all; his only recorded degree listed there being 'D.D. 9.2.1878'.[23] He is, however, presented as 'The Rev. John Hunt, M.A.' on the title pages of his comprehensive three-volume *Religious Thought in England from the Reformation to the End of the Last Century* and frequently in the press.[24] Earlier publications, such as the *Essay on Pantheism*, for which he attained a certain notoriety, and which was placed on the *Index*,[25] did not list a

---

19 'I had hitherto conscientiously avoided this class, as I had always looked on High Churchmen as a generation of simpletons. They had built Churches and kept them clean. They had abolished square pews in prominent places for the rich, and free benches in obscure corners for the poor. This exhausted the catalogue of their merits', *Clergymen Made Scarce*, p. 20.
20 *Ibid*.
21 The details are too many and varied to be discussed here in detail. See *ibid*.
22 *Ibid*.
23 See above, p. 10.
24 E.g., 'Rev. John Hunt, M.A., Christ's Church, Hoxton', *London Evening Standard*, 18 November 1861, p. 2.
25 See the review in the *Spectator*, 24 November 1866, p. 20: 'The curate of St. Ives has redeemed the credit of his order. The Church of Rome has awarded him its most distinguished honour of the *Index* in company with Dr. Pusey and the author of *Ecce Homo*...', 'Review of: *An Essay on Pantheism* by the Rev. John Hunt', *Spectator*,

degree, the author being given only as the 'Rev. John Hunt, Curate of St. Ives, Hunts.'[26] Non-Oxbridge graduates were evidently seen as inferior, while those from the theological colleges such as St Bees were looked down upon by all, as is apparent even from Hunt's acerbic remarks about 'clerical colleges':

> With one [incumbent] I entered into correspondence, and was finally refused, because I had not graduated at an English University. This indeed was the case with some of the most desirable Curacies that turned up. I felt this too as a hardship. It was not fair that I should be classed either with the 'literates,'[27] or the 'illiterates,' of the Church. I was not an ignorant man, and I knew I was not. I had sat at the feet of Sir David Brewster,[28] I had learned Metaphysics from Ferrier,[29] and other sciences from other great doctors eminent in their day. It was too bad that I should be classed with men from the Clerical Colleges—institutions whose very existence is one of the greatest scandals of the Church.[30]

This blatant discrimination evidently rankled with Hunt: he defends his alma mater and, it seems, the honour of his country of birth.

5.5 Privilege and Parsimony

One more fruitless application concludes this stage of Hunt's 'curacy hunting'.[31] It is a tale of privilege, wealth, and parsimony: 'One *Guardian* application was from a High-church Rector[32] in a fashionable part of

---

24 November 1866, p. 20. The *Index Expurgatorius* was 'strictly, an authoritative specification of the passages to be expunged or altered in works otherwise permitted to be read by Roman Catholics. The term is frequently used [as here] in England to cover the "Index Librorum Prohibitorum", or list of forbidden books (not authors, as sometimes thought)', Margaret Drabble, Jenny Stringer, and Daniel Hahn, *Index Expurgatorius* (Oxford: Oxford University Press, 2007), https://doi.org/10.1093/acref/9780199214921.013.3126

26 John Hunt, *An Essay on Pantheism* (London: Longmans, Green, Reader and Dyer, 1866).

27 'In the Church of England: a person who is admitted to holy orders without having obtained a university degree. Now hist.', OED.

28 Cf. 'Brewster, Sir David (1781–1868), Natural Philosopher and Academic Administrator', *Oxford Dictionary of National Biography*, https://doi.org/10.1093/ref:odnb/3371

29 Cf. 'Ferrier, James Frederick (1808–1864), Philosopher', *Oxford Dictionary of National Biography*, https://doi.org/10.1093/ref:odnb/9369

30 *Clergymen Made Scarce*, p. 20.

31 This is Hunt's term, *Clergymen Made Scarce*, p. 20 and passim.

32 'Thomas Jackson', Mrs Eliza Hunt.

London. He asked that I might preach on trial, as the congregation paid and selected the curate, "High Churchism for ever," I said, "if this is to be the practice."'[33] While the individual details will not be pursued here, the episode may serve to show Hunt's desperation to gain remunerative employment and his willingness, if only temporarily, to set aside his principles in a way reminiscent of the Vicar of Bray.

Of course, things did not turn out as he had hoped, but 'the whole affair was a swindle, no Curate was wanted. The Rector for certain reasons had to be out of the way, and by this device he got his duty taken without expense, for two months.'[34] A sharp contrast is painted between the beau monde, attending church in their fashionable carriages to hear the obese and dishonest rector preach and the poor folk in an impoverished part of town, to whom the same man had preached as a visitor on another occasion and from whom 10s. 6d. had been demanded for a carriage to convey the clergyman to and from church. Another ugly facet of the moral double standards that the Victorian Church tolerated is thus revealed.

---

33 *Clergymen Made Scarce*, p. 20.
34 *Clergymen Made Scarce*, p. 21.

6. Final Metropolitan Applications

Before our hapless clergyman introduces his 'grand finale', the episode he chose to conclude the first part of his open letter, which concerned mainly his experiences in the metropolis (i.e. the part which formed the first edition of the work), Hunt deals with his penultimate applications, one of which was successful and led to a longer engagement.

6.1 Mistaken Identity

The first application resulted in an amusing incident. In response to an advertisement by Hunt in the *Record*, an unnamed potential employer had contacted him under the misapprehension that he sought employment as a footman. The potential employer and his wife interviewed him, thinking he was a servant. Presumably, Hunt was not wearing clerical dress, as he had had to leave his lodgings in a great hurry, in order to keep the appointment, otherwise it is puzzling that his calling was not recognized. Of interest for our purposes is Hunt's reaction to his treatment. He feels that the haughty conduct of his potential master and especially mistress is a further and pronounced example of the condescension with which he had frequently been greeted during his curacy-hunting: 'During the two months I had been in search of a Curacy I had got a good many knocks on the head from unfeeling and fickle Incumbents that wanted Curates, but now I thought surely I have come to the last step of degradation, anything after this.'[1] Even more harsh words are devoted to the gentleman's wife, whom Hunt mistakes for a rector's spouse: 'And then these Incumbents' wives! What

---

1   *Clergymen Made Scarce*, p. 22.

mischief do they not make! If this gentleman is the Rector of a parish, evidently his wife is the Di-Rector. Shall not I as a Curate protest against this monstrous government of women? Shall I not assert the equality of all members of the priesthood?'[2] Such male chauvinistic language may strike a dissonant chord with a modern reader, but these attitudes were evidently acceptable in Victorian society. Just as Hunt, the presumed servant, is castigated by the lady of the house for sitting down in her presence without permission, so he in turn feels justified in chiding her for interfering in the all-male preserve of the Church. Nevertheless, the situation is resolved, and the humour thereof is perceived by all.

6.2 Hoxton

The successful application came at Christ Church, Hoxton, just to the east of St Philip's, Arlington Square, where Hunt had held his first metropolitan curacy. It is referred to first in a somewhat curious way in the context of university graduates:

> I had an interview with one Incumbent[3] who would have nothing but a University man for his Curate. He was an M.A. of Cambridge. It was about the time of the Prince of Wales' marriage. He was very wroth that it should be permitted in Lent. I asked if he knew the custom of the Catholic Church before the Reformation as to marriages in Lent. 'Reformation,' he said, 'was there *any Lent before the Reformation?*' I was thankful for once that I was not an M.A. of Cambridge.[4]

Hunt clearly cannot resist disparaging the inferior knowledge of this MA of Cambridge. Nonetheless, it appears that he felt a degree of inferiority himself with regard to his university education, as with his social status and upbringing: the phrase 'for once' appears to indicate that normally he would have been happy to be classed with the graduates of one of the

---

2   *Ibid.*
3   'Henry Kelly Christs [sic] Church Hoxton', Mrs Eliza Hunt, viz. the Rev. Henry Plimley Kelly, Incumbent of Christ Church, Hoxton, London: 'Kelly, Henry Plimley. Adm. pens. at Caius, May 8, 1851. [2nd] s. of the Rev. Anthony Plimley (1816), of Hoxton, Middlesex. B. there May 23, 1832. School, Charterhouse. Matric. Michs. 1851; B.A. 1855; M.A. 1858. Ord. deacon (Colombo, for London) 1855; priest (London) 1856; C. of Uxbridge, 1855–1857. C. of St John-the-Baptist, Hoxton, 1858–1860. V. of Christ Church, Hoxton, 1860–1902. Resided subsequently at Cheltenham, where he died Dec. 6, 1927', Venn and Venn, *Alumni Cantabrigienses* 'K', pp. 1–73.
4   *Clergymen Made Scarce,* p. 20.

ancient English universities and thus to belong to the privileged class of clergymen for whom it was scarcely necessary to exert themselves, in order to gain preferment.

Mrs Eliza Hunt identifies the incumbent and parish as 'Henry Kelly Christs [sic] Church Hoxton'. The reference to the 'Prince of Wales' marriage'[5] is puzzling, since Hunt had joined this parish much earlier, certainly by November 1861, when there is a reference to him in the press.[6] Maybe the 'interview' was not related to Hunt's application or the conversation about the Prince of Wales's marriage was not in any way related to Hunt's initial application. An alternative explanation would be that Mrs Eliza Hunt had misidentified the incumbent here (e.g. in the transcription of the names from another source), but this would not explain the dating unless this 'interview' came after Hunt left Hoxton and before he went to St Botolph's, Aldgate.

Instead of continuing with the narrative concerning this parish (assuming Hoxton is meant), which is not at this point accorded any kind of detail with which later to identify it, Hunt interposes two other episodes, with which we have already dealt above, viz. 'Privilege and Parsimony' and 'Mistaken Identity'. The church is henceforth referred to as 'the Parish adjoining Mr. Arlington's',[7] and it is not identified as being the same place that had been mentioned in the context of the 'Incumbent who would have nothing but a University man for his Curate'. Mrs Eliza Hunt does not identify it in this context, but, from press reports, we can establish that it was Christ Church, Hoxton.[8] Hunt reports how obtaining employment here caused him 'long toil and great waste of money'.[9]

Initial problems in gaining a licence here were exacerbated by an over-cautious attitude on the part of Garratt in providing a testimonial.

---

5   Albert Edward, Prince of Wales, later King Edward VII, married Alexandra of Denmark in St George's Chapel, Windsor, on 10 March 1863.
6   *Evening Standard*, 18 November 1861, p. 2.
7   'Parish adjoining Mr Arlington's', i.e., next to St Philip's, Arlington Sq., viz. Christ Church, Hoxton. It was founded in 1840, closed after 1953, GENUKI, 'Genuki: Christ Church, Hoxton, Church of England, Middlesex' (GENUKI), https://www.genuki.org.uk/big/eng/MDX/Shoreditch/ChristChurch
8   'The Rev. John Hunt, of Christ Church, Hoxton, spoke from I Numbers, 22nd chapter and 30th verse — Am I not thine ass? The sermon was eloquent ...', *Morning Post*, 22 November 1861, p. 2.
9   *Clergymen Made Scarce*, p. 22.

A further testimonial was given by 'the Vicar of the old Parish out of which Mr. Walham's [i.e. Garratt's] was originally formed', whom Hunt describes as 'a sensible man [who] had always been friendly to me'.[10] The problems were set aside when the Bishop gave him a licence 'without troubling any of them'.

The previous incumbent had been 'an extreme High Churchman', and when he left, the congregation left with him.[11] Hunt therefore had the opportunity to build up the congregation. A series of minor problems and disagreements slightly marred his stay, but he gradually increased the congregation and remained in the parish for two years.[12] Unusually, he left of his own accord to go to another parish.

---

10   'Baker Fulham', Mrs Eliza Hunt. Probably 'BAKER, Robert George, Fulham, London, S. W.—Trin. Coll. Cam. B.A. 1810, M.A. 1813; Deac, 1812 and Pr. 1813 by Bp of Lin. V. of All Saints, Fulham, Dio. Lon. 1834', *Crockford's* 1865, p. 26.

11   *Clergymen Made Scarce*, p. 23: 'At one time the Church had been in the hands of an extreme High Churchman, and was made a kind of rendezvous for the High Church people, in the surrounding Parishes. The ceremonies which attracted these people, drove away all the parishioners, who took their revenge by building a Wesleyan, and an Independent Chapel in the vicinity of the Church. That Incumbent was removed, and all the fantastical High Church people left with him, so that the new Incumbent had no congregation.' The previous incumbent was William Scott (1813–1872) who was a leading High Churchman and perpetual curate of Christ Church, Hoxton from 1839 to 1860.

12   *Clergymen Made Scarce*, p. 23.

7. The Anatomist Curate

Brief mention has already been made of Hunt's unfortunate experiences at St Botolph's, Aldgate. This episode brought him to national attention in the press. The more scurrilous reports criticized or ridiculed him, whereas a few publications came to his defence. We have fairly precise dating in Hunt's account: 'It was some time in September 1863, when I entered on my duties as Curate of one of the City churches.'[1] He continues by setting the scene:

The parishioners were 'Jews, Infidels, Turks, Heretics,' and other Dissenters. Those who attended the Church were a few shopkeepers and their families. Those who were of the Church, but did not attend it, were a multitude of paupers. As an old City parish it had immense charities, and as it consisted of many small tradesmen, it abounded in men eager for public offices.[2]

Hunt realizes that the kind of work that he wished to do with the 'working men' was unfeasible, and having tried unsuccessfully to find some suitable ecclesiastical occupation where he could work 'without the interference of any paltry Incumbent',[3] he took advantage of living in the capital city and pursued anatomical studies at St Bartholomew's Hospital. He writes: 'as a student of theology, seeing that nearly all theological questions impinged on the question of nature, I felt it my duty to include among my studies, anatomy and physiology.'[4] A reduction in the size of the parish by the Ecclesiastical Commissioners, who cut off half to form a new district, meant that Hunt's remaining time in the parish was reduced to three months.

---

1 'St Botolphs, Aldgate', Mrs Eliza Hunt; cf. L. Hatts and P. Middleton, *London City Churches* (Bankside Press, 2003), pp. 30f., https://books.google.co.uk/books?id=JezJorTtQnUC.
2 *Clergymen Made Scarce*, p. 23.
3 Ibid.
4 *Clergymen Made Scarce*, p. 24.

In the meantime, however, a scandal occurred that caused the incumbent to inhibit Hunt from acting as curate of the parish. The basic facts are simple, but the ramifications became complex. Hunt gives only a sketchy overview in *Clergymen Made Scarce* of what happened, not even mentioning the fact that at issue was a dead unborn child, a foetus, which Hunt had stored in the vaults of St Botolph's Church for the purposes of dissection.

Hunt's behaviour in this episode is telling. The information gleaned from articles in the press is more ample than that which Hunt divulges in *Clergymen Made Scarce*. The large number of identical or very similar articles and their content attest to the singularity of Hunt's conduct.[5] These are entitled 'Singular Freak[6] of a Clergyman' and similar. Some are longer and go into more ample detail, such as the article in *Reynolds's Newspaper*, entitled 'Extraordinary Charge against a City Clergyman', which gives us most factual information.[7] The proceedings are described as being of a 'very extraordinary character' and provoking both 'remarkable interest' and 'revolting rumours'.[8] The articles, without exception, are condescending to the church officials and often supercilious in tone. Those in *Punch* attempt to be humorous, while that in the *Spectator* provides a more intellectual and balanced assessment.[9] It treats the situation soberly from various different angles, including whether Hunt acted with common sense. As with the *Punch* articles, discussed below, condescension is shown towards the jurymen. Common to all the articles is the overt expression of opinions.

---

5 *Newcastle Journal*, 17 November 1864, p. 3; *Bedfordshire Times and Independent*, 19 November 1864, p. 7; *Berkshire Chronicle*, 19 November 1864, p. 6; *Beverley and East Riding Recorder*, 19 November 1864, p. 6; *Oxford Times*, 19 November 1864, p. 8; *Preston Herald*, 19 November 1864, p. 3; *Reading Mercury*, 19 November 1864, p. 8; *Maidstone Journal and Kentish Advertiser*, 21 November 1864, p. 7; *Bedfordshire Times and Independent*, 22 November 1864, p. 8.

6 Here used in the now less common sense of 'A sudden causeless change or turn of the mind; a capricious humour, notion, whim, or vagary', OED, s.v.

7 *Sheffield Daily Telegraph*, 16 November 1864, p. 4; *Sheffield Independent*, 16 November 1864, p. 4; *Southern Reporter and Cork Commercial Courier*, 17 November 1864, p.3; *Bedfordshire Mercury*, 19 November 1864, p. 7; *Sussex Advertiser*, 19 November 1864, p. 2; *Thanet Advertiser*, 19 November 1864, p. 3; *Lloyd's Weekly Newspaper*, 20 November 1864, p. 2; *Reynolds's Newspaper*, 20 November 1864, p. 3; *Sussex Advertiser*, 22 November 1864, p. 8; *Sussex Advertiser*, 23 November 1864, p. 4.

8 *Ibid.*

9 Reprinted below in the Appendix, pp. 181–185.

The dramatis personae are: 1. the enlightened intellectuals (Hunt, Drs Thynne, Holman, Barnes), 2. the unenlightened clergy (Roberton), 3. the petty bourgeoisie (Churchwarden King, William Bigg, Vestry Clerk Clines and the coroner's jury), 4. the proletarians (Gaslighter/Steeple Keeper Parkhole and Sextoness Hammond), 5. Coroner Payne.

The basic facts are these: Hunt obtained a male, seven-month-old foetus from a medical friend, Dr Thomas Thynne, for the purposes of dissection. The foetus was stored in the vault of St Botolph's Church.[10] Hunt sent a message via the Sextoness, Mary Hammond, to a church functionary, Walter Parkhole, the Gaslighter and Steeple Keeper, to buy a pot to boil water, for which he gave him a shilling. Parkhole, having seen the foetus, wrapped in newspaper, refused, thinking the pot was intended for boiling the foetus. Parkhole informed Hammond and one William Bigg, presumably another church official, possibly a churchwarden.

The mix of class and education is interesting. Hunt is high-handed in his instructions to the church functionaries and in refusing to divulge where he obtained the foetus. He clearly regarded it as a matter that did not concern the lower orders. It is not until the court proceedings that he gives full information and explains the circumstances, including his motives for dissection, namely, to increase his anatomical knowledge, which would in turn help his theological enquiry and his pastoral ministrations. His contempt, especially for Churchwarden King, who initiated the legal inquiry, and the coroner's jury is clear.

Hunt's comments about the people concerned in the incident show condescension towards those whom he considers to be of lower status and intellect:

> I kept these studies as secret as I could, till a Churchwarden,[11] one of the officious small tradesmen of the parish dragged them to light. A coroner's jury, consisting of sixteen of these small shopkeepers, condemned my studies, and brought down on themselves and the whole of the Parish

---

10 The vault is of brick. There are photographs of it in modern times when it was used as a shelter for homeless people. See 'Malcolm Johnson At St Botolph's | Spitalfields Life' https://spitalfieldslife.com/2014/03/11/malcolm-johnson-at-st-botolphs/. See also Malcolm Johnson and R. Londin, *Crypts of London: Past and Present* (History Press, 2013) https://books.google.co.uk/books?id=ksMSDQAAQBAJ.

11 'David King', Mrs Eliza Hunt. Hunt arrogantly refers to King as 'a fool, and a big fool' (cf. fn. 6, p. 6).

authorities, the ridicule of the public press, including the sarcasms of *Punch*.[12]

In fact, *Punch* published two articles that referred to the incident. The earlier article was published in November 1864 and pours scorn on the tradesmen who constituted the coroner's jury, especially for their temerity in suggesting 'it would be better if [Hunt] confined his studies to matters of a clerical nature to the exclusion of the study of anatomy'.[13] The style and approach of *Punch* in the nineteenth century were condescending in the extreme, and the 'humour' that was aimed for, using irony and sarcasm, finds little resonance with a twenty-first-century audience. To refer to members of a coroner's jury, however inadequate their education, as 'vulgar blockheads' is unthinkable to a modern reader. The second article, from December 1864, to which we had occasion to refer briefly above, once again takes up the cudgels against the jurymen and also this time ironizes the behaviour of the incumbent in sacking Hunt. This time the humour is perhaps better conceived: 'The rumour that the rector[14] of St Botolph's, Aldgate, has, under circumstances such as these above stated, discharged his curate, the Rev. Mr. Hunt, is evidently an invention of the Jesuits, designed to damage the Church of England.'[15]

As we have seen from the press articles, Hunt's misfortunes were still plaguing him—the incumbent dismissed him as curate, and the curate had no success in appealing to the Bishop.[16] St Botolph's had been Hunt's sixth curacy, which he left at the age of thirty-seven. His hopes of finding subsequent employment were now at a low ebb, as he was in need of suitable references. Despite the Bishop's exacting 'from the Incumbent a promise that he would be [Hunt's] referee', Roberton[17] 'took the first opportunity of breaking the promise'. Criticism of the Bishop is implied through Hunt's damning with faint praise: 'I had

---

12 *Clergymen Made Scarce*, p. 24.
13 See Appendix, below, p. 186.
14 The incumbent was a perpetual curate, not named by Mrs Eliza Hunt. His details are: 'ROBERTON, James Matthew, 16, Devonshire-square, London, N.E.—Magd. Hall, Ox. B.A. 1851, M.A. 1853; Deac. 1850 and Pr. 1851 by Bp of Win. P. C. of St. Botolph's, without Aldgate, City and Dio. Lon. 1860', *Crockford's* 1865, p. 535.
15 *Punch*, 17 December 1864, p. 251.
16 See *Clergymen Made Scarce*, p. 24.
17 Mrs Eliza Hunt's writing is only semi-legible here. The letters following 'Rober' are not easy to decipher.

heard it mentioned as one of the Bishop of London's failings, that he never took the side of a Curate, but I did not believe it. His lordship judged the matter with considerable impartiality.'[18] Hunt then explains how, 'but for the voluntary service of a neighbouring Rector, [he] would have had difficulty in getting a Curacy either in London or any other place'. At this point, he refers to the infamous case of Bishop Colenso.[19] It is noteworthy that Colenso's trial and appeal took place at the same time as Hunt's troubles at St Botolph's (1863–1865). The happenings are an occasion for criticism of Church government and the Church's lamentable treatment of curates:

> The decision in Bishop Colenso's case has demonstrated to the world that the Church of England is an ecclesiastical body without Church Government. The case of every Curate in the kingdom would prove the same thing. Every rightminded man will rejoice that the state has protected Bishop Colenso from the arbitrary persecution of the Metropolitan of the Cape; but that state which shields Bishops and Incumbents, leaves Curates unprotected. The law only enables the Incumbent to kick the Curate, and gives the Bishop the power to help the Incumbent to do it more effectually.[20]

One final application was made in the metropolis before Hunt left for the country—it was with 'an "Evangelical" Rector of the purest species', but the whereabouts of the parish is not specified.[21] It did not lead to an engagement but to some theological discussions with the incumbent. This first part of Hunt's 'letter' concludes with some telling words:

> After this eventful experience—this battling simply to be allowed 'to spend and be spent for Christ,' I speak seriously, many will ask if I am not sick of the Church, and of religion, too? Most men would have renounced both, I have renounced neither. My words, like those of the Abbé Lamennais are still *Les paroles d'un Croyant*. Frederick Robertson marks it as one of the characteristics of Jesus that He never despaired of humanity, though no man suffered more than He from the baseness and the hypocrisy of men. And Mr. Renan has a grand thought. He supposes that when Jesus came to Calvary, and His great soul was clouded with sorrow, a half repentant feeling may have crossed His mind that He was

---

18   *Clergymen Made Scarce*, p. 24.
19   See Chadwick, *Victorian Church* II, pp. 90–97.
20   *Clergymen Made Scarce*, p. 25.
21   *Ibid*.

suffering too much for such a worthless race. Such a feeling may indeed have crossed the mind of Jesus, but it could only have been a momentary temptation. The true spirit has within it a perennial spring of faith. We that do live, live by faith.

We walk by faith. In faith we follow the *'Noble Initiateur.'* In the beginning I likened myself to the priest of Isis, but I checked the comparison. I again check it in the end. Apuleius wrote a fable, I have written the truth. Apuleius was at last delivered from his asshood; my curate-hood remains.

I am, my Lord,
Your Lordship's obedient Servant,

A PRESBYTER. [22]

Within these words lie sentiments of dejection and resignation, but also an assertion of faith to persevere, despite the unfortunate hand that Hunt had been dealt.

---

22 *Ibid.*

8. Country Life

The second part of our investigation deals with the 'postscript' to Hunt's booklet. While the themes remain roughly the same, the scene changes to the country, to different mentalities and a different type of churchmanship. A not altogether convincing justification is given at the beginning for this part of Hunt's 'letter' being addressed to the Bishop of London:

> There is no special reason why this Postscript should be addressed to the Bishop of London. The events it records took place in another diocese.[1] The facts, however, concern the whole Church and therefore every Bishop in the Church. What concerns all Bishops must be of special interest to the Bishop of the Metropolis.[2]

Hunt begins the introduction to the Postscript by offering some reflections on the state of his career and fortunes after leaving St Botolph's, Aldgate, following the anatomy scandal. He includes some perceptive observations in expressive language:

> Notwithstanding the apparent egotism of this letter, nothing but a deep sense of duty would ever have allowed the writer to publish it, and nothing but the same sense impels him to write again. We do not make all the circumstances of our lives; most of them are made for us. It is our business to use them as best we can, so to serve our day and generation, that when the night cometh, wherein no man can work, we may lay our heads down to sleep with the peaceful assurance that we have not lived in vain.
>
> It is difficult, indeed, to determine how far we are the children of destiny, and how far our own character and acts create the circumstances of our lives. We seem carried on to do certain things by an impulse

---

1 Huntingdon Archdeaconry was transferred to Ely in 1837, before which it had been in Lincoln Diocese.
2 *Clergymen Made Scarce*, p. 26.

apparently irresistible, and when they are done we wonder what end they can serve. And yet how often after years have passed away do we see the necessity that these things should have been done, yea that they *should have been done by us*, and that they were worth our doing even if we had spent ourselves in the performance of them. There is a Wisdom teaching and guiding us all, shaping our ends, and making us the servants of a Divine Will in adversity as well as in prosperity.[3]

Whether we choose to interpret the sentiments in the same way as the author, they are certainly worthy of scrutiny. Hunt's reference to his 'apparent egotism'[4] is a clue to understanding his psychology, which may have been instrumental in some of his misfortunes. The observation that 'There is a Wisdom teaching and guiding us all, shaping our ends, and making us the servants of a Divine Will in adversity as well as in prosperity'[5] is a touching response of faith in the light of his difficulties. Particularly interesting are Hunt's ironically critical observations on the role of the curate: 'It is necessary always that a Curate be a man *of whom not much can be said*. It is with Curates as it is with young ladies, the more unknowing they are the more likely it is that some Rector will give them employment.'[6]

8.1 Swallow, Lincolnshire

In response to his advertisement in the *Record*, Hunt received two positive replies. He chose the one with which he had first corresponded, viz. Swallow[7] 'in the wolds of Lincolnshire', commenting: 'How different the course of events had I decided on the other.'[8] The date is December 1864, the time when the two *Punch* articles about the anatomy scandal appeared (November and December), both of which mentioned Hunt by name. He clearly did not wish to be identified with the scandal in the eyes of the new parishioners, so his solution was to borrow 'all the papers with the intention of never returning them'.[9] This strategy was evidently successful, as we hear no more about his temporary stay here,

---

3 *Clergymen Made Scarce*, pp. 26f.
4 Ibid., p. 26.
5 Ibid., p. 27.
6 Ibid., p. 26.
7 Mrs Eliza Hunt's annotation: 'Swallow near Caster' [viz. Caistor].
8 We do not learn which was the other parish or why things might have been different.
9 *Clergymen Made Scarce*, p. 27.

save for the deficiencies of the church, congregation, and sacred vessels. Swallow was his seventh curacy, which proved to be something of a rural haven, affording him time to pen the first edition of *Clergymen Made Scarce*: 'Here I meditated on the past, and formed plans for the future.'[10]

Owing to the temporary nature of the engagement in Lincolnshire, Hunt finds himself having to advertise again. He explains how he 'again came in contact with two Incumbents, not knowing which of the two to choose.' The 'Evangelical' incumbent wished to meet him in London, but Hunt was well aware that the journey from Lincolnshire would cost him time and 'about £2 10s. in money'. He compares this sum with his curate's salary of £100 per annum,[11] commenting, somewhat tongue-in-cheek, that 'the most "Evangelical" being in [the] world must know that £2 10s. is a very large sum for a man who lives on £100 a year' and asks the incumbent 'who was to bear the expense of [his] coming to London'. Hunt relates with cynicism: 'The Incumbent had recourse to the usual excuse—the very night he arrived in London, he had met an old friend who was willing to take his curacy.'[12] Another clerical foible is thus laid bare.

---

10 *Ibid.*
11 £2 10s. was worth approx. £325 in 2020, £100 approx. £12,993.
12 *Ibid.*

9. St Ives, Hunts.

The next answer came via an advertisement in the High-Church *Guardian*. It was from the curate of 'Ousebank', who would shortly be leaving for another parish and required a replacement for six weeks. 'Ousebank' is Hunt's pseudonym for St Ives in Huntingdonshire. His time there was clearly an important and largely happy episode in Hunt's life, not least because he met his first wife there and, after a successful curacy, nearly succeeded in gaining the incumbency. He devotes more words to his time at St Ives than in the whole of Part I, where he had described his previous curacies. Moreover, he writes in a more lyrical way about St Ives, both in *Clergymen Made Scarce* and in the Preface to the *Poems by Robert Wilde*.[1] For these reasons, we devote special attention to this section.

The new curate was to receive the salary of £1 1s. a week and to live in the capacious vicarage with the incumbent and his wife,[2] where the couple enjoyed a gentrified existence.[3] Hunt was allowed to 'enter at once on the duty',[4] thus travelling over 100 miles south to St Ives, on the north

---

1. John Hunt, ed., *Poems by Robert Wilde* [sic] *D.D., One of the Ejected Ministers of 1662, with a Historical and Biographical Preface and Notes by the Rev. John Hunt* (London: Strahan, 1870).
2. *Clergymen Made Scarce*, p. 27, esp. pp. 32f. 'The large salary was nominally £120 a year—actually £1 1s. a week, and live in the Vicarage.' The sum actually received was equivalent to £135 in 2020. Presumably Hunt's board and lodging were provided free of charge under this arrangement.
3. There are no detailed descriptions of everyday life in the vicarage under this incumbent, but the reminiscences of a domestic servant at the beginning of the twentieth century (c. 1907) during Oscar Wade Wilde's incumbency (1899–1931) give an impression of its size, grandeur, and gentrified living conditions: 'it was a beautiful vicarage [...] a huge vicarage, the staircase was [...] one of those lovely round staircases [...] a big square hall. We weren't allowed to use those stairs, we had the servants' stairs to go up. Same as we had the servants' hall where we had our meals, and never the same food as they had in the dining rooms, quite different food', Memories of St Ives, Cambridgeshire, http://saintives.org.uk/memories.html
4. *Clergymen Made Scarce*, p. 27.

© 2021 David Yeandle, CC BY 4.0   https://doi.org/10.11647/OBP.0248.09

Fig. 2 St Ives Vicarage, c. 1883, courtesy of Mr Rolf Lunsmann.

bank of the River Ouse, in Cambridgeshire (then Huntingdonshire),[5] a journey that took him roughly thirteen hours. St Ives was a thriving small town, with 3,500 inhabitants, an important market, and yearly fair.[6] In 1864, it had a quaint, old-world feel to it. Hunt records this, together with other features:

---

5   Mrs Eliza Hunt's annotation: 'St. Ives Hunts.' The town, anciently called Slepe, was renamed St Ives after Ivo, a Persian bishop, whose supposed bones were found in a field near Slepe by a ploughman (c. 1000) and claimed by nearby Ramsey Abbey (cf. 'Houses of Benedictine Monks: The Priory of St Ives | British History Online', https://www.british-history.ac.uk/vch/hunts/vol1/pp388-389. It was situated in the old county of Huntingdonshire. Huntingdon Archdeaconry belonged to the Diocese of Lincoln until 1837, when it was transferred, along with most of Bedford Archdeaconry, to the Diocese of Ely.
6   See *History, Gazetteer & Directory of Huntingdonshire, 1854* (Huntingdon: James Hatfield, 1854), https://specialcollections.le.ac.uk/digital/collection/p16445coll4/id/278541; 'Parishes: St Ives | British History Online', https://www.british-history.ac.uk/vch/hunts/vol2/pp210-223. In the 1851 census, its population was recorded as 3,572 inhabitants.

> The Parish of Ousebank had many attractions, but it had also some disadvantages. It was a quiet old-fashioned country town. It had no gentry, but the tradespeople were well-disposed, simple, industrious, and, perhaps I may say, with some qualifications, intelligent. There was an honest independence about them, —I might call it pride, but that word would express more than I mean. There were many efforts after caste—everybody tried to be above everybody, and nobody seemed good enough for nobody. Excepting the representatives of the professions, they were all people in business, so that one or two trying to form a class above the others, could not succeed. 'We are all tinkers and tailors,' said the richest man in Ousebank, to me, one day, 'and there is no use of any one trying to set himself above another.'[7]

The townsfolk could be divided into 'church' people and 'chapel' people. The former were mainly professional and some working people, the latter mainly tradesfolk. Hunt observes, not without irony:

> Ousebank had another disadvantage. It was emphatically a Dissenting town. There was but one Church, while there were seven or eight meeting houses, and the meeting houses were not small places which held only a few people, but large buildings, with congregations numbering three, four, and five hundred. One of them, indeed, was called the Free Church, a fine Gothic building, with a tall spire, and stained-glass windows, erected at an expense of £5000,[8] and dedicated by local wit to the gentleman who was the chief contributor, whom they canonised on the occasion of the dedication.[9]

Potto Brown, the principal benefactor, who was raised a Quaker, but ejected later, did not approve of a steeple being added to the Free Church and restricted his contribution to £3,000, leaving others to pay £2,000 for the spire.[10] The church, which was opened in 1864, replacing the former

---

7   *Clergymen Made Scarce*, pp. 28f. The 'richest man' refers to Frederick Mutton. See fn. 43, p. 145.
8   Approx. £649,663 in 2020.
9   *Clergymen Made Scarce*, p. 29. This humorous remark refers principally to Potto Brown, a wealthy miller and philanthropist, who ran Houghton Mill and the steam mill in St Ives. See 'Potto Brown', Wikipedia, https://en.wikipedia.org/w/index.php?title=Potto_Brown&oldid=994016050. He lived in a substantial mansion in Houghton called 'The Elms' (built in 1854). Cf. Bridget Flanagan, *A Commanding View: The Houses and Gardens of Houghton Hill* (Godmanchester: Great Ouse Valley Trust, 2019), p. 21.
10 £3,000 was worth approx. £389,800 in 2020, £2,000 approx. £259,865. See Oddities of St Ives, http://saintives.org.uk/oddities1.html.

Independent Chapel, stands impressively on the Market Hill,[11] beside the statue of Oliver Cromwell, who had been an inhabitant of St Ives; the statue was not unveiled until 1901. The untrained eye might, and often does, easily mistake the building for an Anglican Parish Church, despite its south-facing orientation. The spire was supposedly intended to rival that of the Parish Church. The interior of the original church, which has subsequently been re-modelled, gave the pulpit pride of place in the apsidal focal point at the south end.[12]

The other Dissenting meeting houses of St Ives are by no means as architecturally impressive. The following are listed for 1854: Independent (superseded by the Free Church), Wesleyan, Baptist, Particular Baptist, Primitive Methodist, Friends. Most had seating for several hundred people. Clearly, then, the Parish Church of All Saints was faced with considerable competition amongst the worshippers in the town, with its 680 sittings, as against a capacity of well over 1,500 in the various chapels.[13]

Hunt was evidently impressed by his newly found country parish. Church, town, and incumbent, whom he named 'Mr. Coldstream',[14] were all to his liking, and he was given a warm, enthusiastic welcome:

---

11 See 'Here's One I Made Earlier', in *Inspire: The Newsletter of the Free Church* (United Reformed) Saint Ives, December 2017, pp. 6–7, https://d3hgrlq6yacptf.cloudfront.net/5f41930a02cae/content/pages/documents/1511978737.pdf. Bateman Brown notes: '…the church standing on the Market Hill, St. Ives, was built in as commanding a position in the town as possible, and, instead of being called a Meeting House, was named "The Free Church, St. Ives," to denote it was supported by the free gifts of its worshippers, and not by aid derived from the State.' (Bateman Brown, *Reminiscences*, p. 68).

12 As a non-conformist church, this is oriented to fit in with the street layout. The south apse, furthest away from the street, would correspond to the east end in an Anglican church.

13 Cf. 'Kelly's Directory of Beds, Hunts & Northants, 1898', p. 51, https://specialcollections.le.ac.uk/digital/collection/p16445coll4/id/167113; *Clergymen Made Scarce*, p. 29.

14 Mrs Eliza Hunt: 'Yate Fosbroke'. Cf. 'JAN. 1. [1840] —Rev. Yate Fosbrooke [sic], M.A., formerly of Clare Hall [B.A. 1823, MA 1842], curate and lecturer of Enfield, Middlesex, has been instituted to the vicarage of St. Ives, Huntingdonshire' ('University Intelligence', in *The Cambridge University Magazine* I.1, 1840, p. 279). He died, aged sixty-five, on 6 July 1866. Cf. 'Deaths. August 1866', in *The Gentleman's Magazine and Historical Review* (J. H. and J. Parker, 1866), p. 278, https://books.google.co.uk/books?id=ZlNFAAAAYAAJ. Yate Fosbroke was the son of the Rev. Thomas Dudley Fosbroke, the antiquary (1770–1842). Cf. 'Fosbroke [Fosbrooke], Thomas Dudley (1770–1842), Antiquary', *Oxford Dictionary of National Biography*, https://doi.org/10.1093/ref:odnb/9954. The name is variously spelled Fosbrooke or Fosbroke. The family had aristocratic roots as the Fosbrookes of Shardlow and

> The Vicar and his lady gave me a hearty welcome. Before many minutes I was quite at home with them [...] The Church was a beautiful building and had been recently restored. It had eight or nine richly stained windows. The spire was the very perfection of symmetry. Mr. Coldstream was proud of his Church, and proud that it had been restored during his Incumbency.[15]

Hunt was allowed to preach *extempore* and did so to the great satisfaction of incumbent and congregation, so that he was asked to be entirely responsible for preaching and was offered a permanent position as curate; moreover, the prospect of additional funding by the congregation was held out to him.

He was overjoyed at this successful start:

> Did I not think myself a happy man? The lines had fallen unto me in pleasant places. I praised that wonderful Providence which by so many apparent accidents had brought me to such a Goshen as this.[16]

The situation in St Ives presents an interesting picture, not of the village parson and squire, such as we had encountered in Burley, but of a gentleman parson, who lived with his wife in a large vicarage and kept up customs of the gentry in a rural town environment comprising largely nonconformist shopkeepers and tradespeople:

> The new aristocracy was stronger than the old, or, to speak more correctly, the *meal*ocracy—for the richest men were millers—was too powerful a rival for the landocracy. The schism between them was wide and deep. There were but few Church people in the town—that is, people who went to Church from principle. The intelligence and wealth of the town, such as they were, were nearly all on the side of the Dissenters.[17]

Ravenstone. Cf. *Burke's Genealogical and Heraldic History of the Landed Gentry* (London: Harrison, 1875), p. 458, https://books.google.co.uk/books?id=ZNEKAAAAYAAJ. Yate Fosbroke's branch of the family preferred the spelling with one o.

15 During Fosbroke's incumbency, the church was equipped with attractive oak pews amongst other things and made a dignified impression. On the financing, including an attempt to levy a church rate, see Mary Carter, *19th Century St Ives* (St Ives: Friends of the Norris Museum, 2010), p. 50.

16 *Clergymen Made Scarce*, p. 28. The allusion is to Psalm 16:6 'The lines are fallen to me in pleasant places; yes, I have a goodly heritage.' On the Land of Goshen, see Thomas Römer, 'Goshen', in *Encyclopedia of the Bible and its Reception*, edited by Constance M. Furey, Joel Marcus LeMon, Brian Matz, Thomas Chr. Römer, Jens Schröter, Barry Dov Walfish and Eric Ziolkowski (Berlin, Boston: De Gruyter, 2010), https://www-degruyter-com.ezp.lib.cam.ac.uk/document/database/EBR/entry/MainLemma_8117/html.

17 *Clergymen Made Scarce*, p. 29.

Fig. 3 Interior of All Saints', St Ives, c. 1860, courtesy of the Norris Museum, St Ives.

Hunt, perhaps mindful of his own origins as the son of a cobbler, comments on the need for the Church to exist harmoniously alongside the tradesfolk: 'When the Church resolves to be independent of the trading community, it resolves to be independent of the nation.'[18]

Yate Fosbroke,[19] who was not kindly disposed towards the tradesfolk, is nevertheless described benevolently by his curate:

> Mr. Coldstream had been Vicar of Ousebank for nearly thirty years. He was an old-fashioned clergyman, and was proud of his office, not so much for the office itself, but because an English clergyman was equivalent to an English gentleman. A clergyman of the Church of England and an old English gentleman were to him nearly the same, and each was the ideal pre-eminently of all that was great, good, and desirable in this mortal life. His ancestors had been clergymen since the days of Charles I.[20]

Hunt and Fosbroke worked amicably together for the most part, though they differed occasionally on points of theology, a subject on which Fosbroke had rigid views but which did not otherwise greatly occupy him. His principal objective was to live the life of a gentleman. This involved at times an air of haughty superiority. He looked down on the lower classes, whom he called 'snobs' in the old sense of the word that had been used disparagingly with reference to the jurymen by *Punch* in the article about the anatomy scandal.[21] He was generally disparaging about Dissenters. He suspected Hunt of heterodoxy, especially with regard to the *Essay on Pantheism* that Hunt wished to publish at St Ives, for which he achieved a certain notoriety.[22] Hunt's prosecution of

---

18 *Clergymen Made Scarce*, p. 38.
19 See *Crockford's* 1865, p. 225: 'FOSBROKE, Yate, St. Ives, Hunts.—V. of St. Ives with Chapelries of Oldhurst and Woodhurst annexed, Dio. Ely. (Patrons, J. Ansley, Esq. and other Trustees; V.'s Inc. 500*l* and Ho; Pop. St. Ives 3395, Oldhurst 174, Woodhurst 554.) Surrogate'.
20 *Clergymen Made Scarce*, p. 29.
21 Cf. *Clergymen Made Scarce*, p. 30. *Snob* was originally a dialect or colloquial term for 'a shoemaker or cobbler; a cobbler's apprentice'. By the 1830s, it had developed to mean 'A person belonging to the ordinary or lower social class; one having no pretensions to rank or gentility', OED. A modern equivalent might be 'pleb' or 'prole'. It was particularly popular amongst Cambridge students in the sense of a non-university 'townsman'.
22 Although this substantial book (384 pp.) was published under the imprint of Longmans, Green, Reader and Dyer in London, it was printed at the St Ives Press, Crown Street, by the Rev. William Lang. Cf. 'Mr. Watts sold the press to the Rev. William Lang, who published there in 1866 an important book by the Rev. John Hunt, 'An Essay on Pantheism,' which attracted great attention at that time. The

progressive theology may have secured his book's inclusion on the *Index* of the Roman Catholic Church, but it did not cause him to be numbered among the celebrated proponents of liberal theology such as Stanley, Maurice, Kingsley, and Neander.

9.1 Advowson for Sale

As the Incumbent's final days on earth approach, Hunt's account assumes a somewhat novelistic tone, often with a melancholy or sentimental tinge. The narrative becomes much longer and at times more florid than in the case of the accounts of his previous curacies. Apart from tracing Fosbroke's declining health, Hunt concentrates on the succession and the sale of the living. Here we have a first-hand account of the scramble to acquire a living and to make money out of the process. Fosbroke was forbidden by his doctors to preach, owing to heart disease, but he would not accept this and said that he 'intended to live some time yet'.[23] In this context, he referred to the sale of the living: 'I'll make the value of the next presentation to this living fall in the market.' Hunt comments: 'This was in allusion to something which had greatly annoyed him ever since his last illness. The patrons had been advertising the sale of the living.'[24] Ironically, Fosbroke had himself purchased the living through an intermediary—in fact, his father-in-law.[25] Advertisements were usually placed through an agency or in the press.[26] Livings were frequently auctioned, as Hunt recounts:

---

press was closed in 1867', 'Parishes: St Ives | British History Online', https://www.british-history.ac.uk/vch/hunts/vol2/pp210-223

23 *Clergymen Made Scarce*, p. 35.
24 *Ibid*.
25 Mrs Eliza Hunt's annotation. His name was Joseph Pain. On the sale of benefices and the legal restrictions, see Chadwick, *Victorian Church* II, pp. 207–213.
26 As an example, cf. *The Ecclesiastical Gazette*, 14 May 1867, p. 293
'CHURCH PREFERMENT FOR SALE.
MR. BAGSTER's List of nearly 100 Livings for sale may be had on the confidential application of Principals or their Solicitors only free of charge.
The Advowsons Nos. 1117, 954, and 1125, and the Next Presentations Nos. 1029, 1137, 1142, and 1143 have been disposed of.
ADVOWSON.–EASTERN COUNTY.
MR. BAGSTER is instructed to DISPOSE OF the ADVOWSON of a LIVING one mile from the Sea, and near a Town and Railway Station. There is a capital house filled up with every convenience, and standing in its own grounds. The net income from rent-charge and glebe is 760 l. a year. The population is purely Rural. Church is very

> One day he [Fosbroke] stepped into the office of a London trader in Church benefices. The next presentation to the Vicarage of Ousebank was put up to auction. It was knocked down for £600.[27] He was the bidder, a friend [his father-in-law] was the buyer. Thirteen months after the purchase the living was vacant. Mr. Coldstream was little fitted to be Vicar in a Dissenting town as a man could well be. He had bought the temporalities and the spiritualities of Ousebank.[28]

This reveals the practice of buying the advowson of a living, often with an elderly or ailing clergyman still in post, of whom it could be expected that he would die soon, thus enabling the patron to present to the living his own choice of successor, frequently a son or other relative, in this case, his son-in-law. The law forbade the sale of a vacant living.[29] In this case, the incumbent, Cuthbert Johnson Baines, was not especially advanced in years, but he was an invalid, though not considered to be in imminent danger of dying. Nevertheless, he died suddenly, aged sixty-three, on 13 October 1839.[30] Hence, the advowson was a good speculative purchase, since the purchaser had had to wait only thirteen months before a presentation was possible.

When Fosbroke was presented, the patron was Gilbert Ansley Esq. (d. 1860), a wealthy landowner, who lived in a grand house in neighbouring Houghton.[31] Pain evidently purchased only the next presentation, rather than the advowson. By 1866, the advowson had passed to three heirs of the Ansley family: Gilbert Ansley's widow and two sons.[32] Hunt comments:

---

handsome and in good repair, and there are new and Endowed Schools. The whole circumstances of the parish are most unexceptionable. Very early possession. Price 8500*l*.' This was an expensive living, equivalent to £562,569 in 2020.

27 Approx. £62,500 in 2020.
28 *Clergymen Made Scarce*, p. 30.
29 Cf. Chadwick: *Victorian Church* II, p. 210.
30 Cf. *Cambridge Chronicle and Journal*, Saturday, 19 October 1839, p. 2; J. Nichols, *The Gentleman's Magazine* (E. Cave, 1840), p. 102, https://books.google.co.uk/books?id=TCVIAQAAMAAJ
31 Cf. *History, Gazetteer & Directory of Huntingdonshire*, 1854, p. 411. Ansley lived at Houghton Hill House, built in 1840 in eighty-nine acres of grounds. Cf. *Civic Society of St Ives: Annual Report 2013*, St Ives, 2013, pp. 17f.; Flanagan, *A Commanding View*, pp. 16f.). The Ansley family's rise to prominence begins with Gilbert's father, John Ansley, who was Lord Mayor of London in 1807–1808. Cf. Obituary 1845, in *The Gentleman's Magazine* 24, 1845, p. 546.
32 See David Yeandle, *The Clash of Churchmanship in Nineteenth-Century St Ives: The Coming of Anglo-Catholicism* (London: Anglo-Catholic History Society, 2021), p. 6.

A century ago, perhaps, the living of Ousebank was in the gift of the owner of the estates. As the estates came to be subdivided among the different branches of the family, the living had to be sold that the claims of each might be satisfied. The patrons at the present time were three in number. The first [Gilbert John Ansley] was our squire, a man of great integrity—a man who would not have sinned one jot against his conscience for all the wealth in the world. He wished heartily that a law were passed to prevent the sale of livings under any circumstances. The second patron [Benjamin Frederick Ansley] was a wine merchant in London. He declared without any reserve that his sole wish was to turn his right into money. His share in the living of Ousebank was a part of his ancestral inheritance. That inheritance was now but small, and he could not afford to lose any of it. The third patron [Mary Anne Ansley] was of the 'female persuasion.' She was the acting partner in the firm.[33]

The use of the terminology *female persuasion*,[34] *acting partner*, and *firm* is no doubt intended to indicate a certain ironic distance—possibly with

---

On the history of the advowson, see 'Parishes: St Ives', in British History Online: '"Mr. Pigot" was returned as patron in 1817. Shortly after this date the advowson passed to the Ansley family, probably to John Ansley of London. Joseph Pain [Fosbroke's father-in-law] presented for one turn in 1839, but Gilbert Ansley of Houghton Hill House had the advowson in 1855 and died in 1860. His widow, Mary Anne, daughter of Horatio Martelli, died in 1896. The advowson seems to have been held by trustees under the marriage settlement of Gilbert Ansley, who shortly after 1899 conveyed it to the Rev. S. J. M. Price and he gave it to trustees for the Guild of All Souls, the present patrons.' In 1866, in the mandate for the induction of C. D. Goldie, the patrons are recorded as: Mary Ann [sic] Ansley of Houghton Co. Hunt[ingdonshire] widow [of Gilbert], Benjamin Frederick Ansley of 124 Englefield Road, Essex Road Islington Co. Middx Esq [wine merchant] & Gilbert John Ansley of St. Ives Co. Hunt[ingdonshire] Esq. [sons of Gilbert]. Cf. Charles Dashwood Goldie, Vicar of St. Ives with the Chapelries of Old Hurst & Woodhurst Annexed [Mandate for Induction Record], 1866, in Huntingdonshire Archives, AH26/239/7, https://discovery.nationalarchives.gov.uk/details/r/be10958d-2c8b-460e-bb5a-f2f94f813f29

33 *Clergymen Made Scarce*, p. 39.
34 Hunt's use of inverted commas here would seem to indicate that he intends the word to be understood humorously or deprecatingly. The expression *of the XY persuasion* was applied originally to religious affiliation or another (political or moral) conviction, e.g., *of the Jewish/Protestant persuasion*. In the course of time, *of the female persuasion* came to be used humorously and ultimately became a hackneyed (colloquial) phrase, amounting to a laborious way of saying 'female' or 'woman', e.g., 'America recently pilloried the misuse of "persuasion" in a list of British vulgarisms—those crimes against proper speech that arouse more antipathy to John Bull than all the indiscretions of his ambassadors and statesmen. A great deal of the responsibility must he fixed on his funny men. The joker of the 'eighties never lost a chance of saying that a woman was of the female persuasion...', *Irish Independent*, 1 December 1913, p. 4; cf. *The Illustrated American* 4, 1890, p. 308). See H. W. Fowler

overtones of male chauvinism, such that a woman should preferably not be involved in men's affairs.[35]

Hunt informs us about initial interest in the appointment:

> Several persons had applied to him [Fosbroke] for information as to its value, but he always declined to tell them. A clergyman who had just returned from India had written that very week offering £1,000[36] for immediate possession.[37]

The living was not a rich one, and the parson who took it was expected to be able to contribute to the parish from his own means. The ailing Fosbroke observed the process, concerned that the right man, a gentleman, should be presented:

> 'Make money out of this poor living,' he would often say and forgetting that he had once bought it himself, he would reflect on the patrons for not giving it up to the Bishop to appoint a man who would teach 'Church' doctrines as he had done. It might be bought by some 'wretched Evangelical' who would fraternize with the Dissenters and call their ministers his 'reverend brethren.' It might fall into the hands of some Rationalist or worse still, some one might buy it who was not a 'gentleman' and who might associate with people in business, that is s___bs [sc. snobs].[38]

This display of clerical and social superiority—what one might call snobbery in today's sense of the word—appears to have been commonplace amongst the Anglican clergy of the day; indeed, we have even seen elements of it in Hunt's own behaviour. High-handed conduct also comes to the fore in Fosbroke's treatment of the impending parish confirmation and his desire that Hunt should 'beat up'[39] candidates for it, which Hunt professes not to understand.

---

and F. G. Fowler, *The King's English* (Oxford: Clarendon Press; London; New York: H. Frowde, 1908), pp. 171f.; Henry Watson Fowler, *A Dictionary of Modern English Usage* (Oxford: Clarendon Press, 1926), p. 434; H. W. Fowler and R. W. Burchfield, *The New Fowler's Modern English Language* (Oxford: Clarendon Press, 1996), p. 591; OED, s.v. '4.c. *colloquial* and *humorous*. A group or collection linked by a shared characteristic, quality, or attribute. Esp. in early use in of the —— persuasion: of a (specified) nationality, occupation, inclination, etc.'

35 Cf. Hunt's chauvinist remarks about a rector's wife as 'Di-rector', above, 48.
36 Approx. £128,488 in 2020.
37 *Clergymen Made Scarce*, p. 35.
38 *Ibid*.
39 Cf. OED, s.v. beat, v.1: '27. figurative. With up in many constructions, as to beat up for recruits, to beat up the town for recruits, to beat up recruits, and elliptical, to

The 'excitement' of the situation made Fosbroke ill, and parishioners frequently asked about his health. Hunt relates: 'Then would follow, in an undertone, "Is the living sold?" Nobody knew. "Sad thing that the souls of men should be bought and sold," people would say—"Whoever bids the highest for the presentation will be thrust upon us, whether we are willing or not."'[40]

Hunt relates how there had been attempts to secure the living for him, as he had proved very popular in the parish. Financial considerations had nevertheless thwarted this. It emerges in this context that the patrons' price for the living was £1200:[41]

> One or two of the parishioners had offered a year ago to pay the patrons the sum required for the living that it might be given to me, but the offer was refused on the ground that I had no private income.[42] [...] By every law of equity and propriety the living of Ousebank should have been given to me. This was the all but universal wish of the people. The patrons had already refused it, though the £1200 was offered them. They wished it to be sold to someone who could spend something upon it. There was a measure of wisdom in this wish. The value of the living was not over £500 a year,[43] and there were three Churches which involved the necessity of keeping two Curates.[44]

Hunt rejected other attempts to obtain this preferment on his behalf out of a sense of probity, or at least a profession thereof, determining that any preferment he should gain should be on merit.[45] Such, however, was not to be at this time.

As we have seen, there were several factors at issue in the succession, including principally money and status. Churchmanship had until now

---

beat up'. More usual nowadays is *drum up*.
40 *Clergymen Made Scarce*, p. 35.
41 Approx. £154,187 in 2020.
42 *Clergymen Made Scarce*, p. 35.
43 Approx. £64,245 in 2020.
44 *Clergymen Made Scarce*, p. 38.
45 'A friend of mine in London would have bought it the week before Mr. Coldstream died, but my whole being recoiled at the thought of buying the presentation while Mr. Coldstream lay on his death-bed. The charge of the souls of a parish is responsibility enough in itself, without adopting underhand ways of procuring it. I reflected that after a few short years I should be as Mr. Coldstream is now, and if my work was not successful, how bitterly would I repent of having obtained a living in a way that certainly God never intended livings should be obtained. "No," I said, "I will take my chance of preferment. When it comes by merit, it shall be doubly pleasant; and if I do my work with a clear conscience, it will bring peace at the last"', *Clergymen Made Scarce*, pp. 35f.

not specifically raised its head. The people of St Ives appear to have been content with moderate or Broad-Church clergy, though there had been High-Church leanings: 'We had always passed in Ousebank for being a little high Church'.[46] Evidence of this at the time was the use of the surplice at All Saints', though probably not for preaching. Its use, particularly in the pulpit, was much detested by the Low-Church party as a badge of Popery.[47] Although Hunt had no objection to the use of the surplice in the pulpit, he thought the black academic gown 'the more appropriate dress when the minister appears as the instructor of the people'.[48]

At a time when St Ives had settled to a middle-of-the-road form of nineteenth-century Anglicanism, things were about to change drastically. We have seen how Fosbroke was concerned that the living should go to a gentleman and not a 'wretched Evangelical' or Rationalist, but adherents of other parties appear either not to have occurred to him or not to have troubled him.

The daily decline of Fosbroke is depicted sympathetically by Hunt, with some charming allusions to nature in the vicarage garden.[49] His death and funeral occurred in July, and immediately the thoughts of the parishioners turned to his successor: 'No sooner had we laid Mr. Coldstream in his last resting place than the whole parish was on the *qui vive* about his successor. "Is the living sold?" was everybody's question.'[50] Legally, the living could not be sold while it was vacant. Rumours were rife in the town. The three patrons were supposed to be in disagreement. Many, including Hunt, hoped that they would continue to disagree until, after six months, the presentation fell to the Bishop.[51]

---

46 *Clergymen Made Scarce*, p. 40.
47 See Chadwick, *Victorian Church* I, pp. 497–501; William Crouch, 'St. George's-in-the-East and St. George's Mission', in William Crouch, *Bryan King and the Riots at St. George's-in-the-East*, Chapter IV (London: Methuen, 1904), pp. 31–44, http://anglicanhistory.org/ritualism/crouch_king1904/04.html
48 *Clergymen Made Scarce*, pp. 38, 43.
49 *Clergymen Made Scarce*, p. 37.
50 Ibid.
51 I.e., Edward Harold Browne, Bishop of Ely, 1864–1873. Cf. 'Browne, Edward Harold (1811–1891), Bishop of Winchester', *Oxford Dictionary of National Biography*, https://doi.org/10.1093/ref:odnb/3672

9.2 Ritualism

One of the persons mooted to have bought the living was a local solicitor, Martin Hunnybun,[52] who was rumoured to have purchased it for his son, a curate of All Saints', Margaret Street, London. This church was a bastion of Anglo-Catholicism, a concept that, at the time, was alien to St Ives. Hunt comments, probably somewhat tongue-in-cheek:

> The town was petrified with horror. Men's faces turned pale, and even women shuddered at the approaching spiritual calamity. Then there were visions of priests clothed in albs and copes and chasubles; visions of incense and altars, acolytes and thurifers, lighted candles, holy water, rood lofts, altar screens, crosses, crucifixes, and mimic Virgin Marys.[53]

Such was not to happen at this juncture, since the solicitor was not minded to pay the amount asked by the patrons. A delay of several weeks then ensued. More rumours about the new incumbent spread abroad. Mary Anne Ansley, who had played the principal role among the three patrons, had offered the living to the Rev. Charles Dashwood Goldie:

> She [Mary Anne Ansley] was the acting partner in the firm. Through her astute wisdom the living had been *offered* to Mr. Goldwing.[54] She knew what she wanted, and where to apply for it. She wrote to *Sam. Oxon*,[55] and *Sam.* sent his favourite man.[56]

Mary Anne Ansley was, as Hunt wryly comments, the 'acting partner in the firm'. She is further described by Bateman Brown as a 'lay curate', by which her strong religious proclivities are emphasized.[57] One is

---

52 Hunt's whimsical pseudonym is 'Mr Sweetbread'. Mrs Eliza Hunt's annotation is not entirely legible—probably Honeybun or Honnybun.
53 *Clergymen Made Scarce*, p. 37.
54 'Goldie', Mrs Eliza Hunt.
55 Samuel Wilberforce, Bishop of Oxford, 1845–1870. Cf. 'Wilberforce, Samuel (1805–1873), Bishop of Oxford and of Winchester', *Oxford Dictionary of National Biography*, https://doi.org/10.1093/ref:odnb/29385
56 *Clergymen Made Scarce*, p. 39. See Yeandle, *Clash of Churchmanship*, p. 6.
57 The following assessment of the Ansleys, from the point of view of a principal dissenter and Mayor of St Ives, Bateman Brown, is a telling summary of personalities: 'A little prior to the events recorded above, the Squire of the Parish [of Houghton], Gilbert Ansley, who hitherto had been non-resident [in London], married a lady [Mary Anne Martelli] who had come from a parish in a distant part of the country [Hampshire], where her brother [Thomas Chessher Martelli] was a clergyman of considerable influence, and she was his lay curate. She found her lot now cast where

prompted to ask why she should have contacted 'Sam. Oxon.', i.e. Samuel Wilberforce, Bishop of Oxford (1845–1870), and also why Goldie was Wilberforce's 'favourite man'.

In the first instance, family connections are the clear reason;[58] in the second, patronage and diocesan associations were paramount. Mary Anne Ansley was born to Horatio Martelli and Catherine Holloway in Hastings, in 1817. The Martelli family came originally from Italy and would doubtless formerly have been Roman Catholic.[59] This may in part have influenced the Martelli descendants' Anglo-Catholic leanings. Mary Anne's brother, Horatio Francis Kingsford Martelli (1807–1870; Deputy Lord Lieutenant of Hampshire), who, in 1828, took his mother's surname Holloway as a condition of a very considerable inheritance from Thomas Holloway, his maternal grandfather,[60] lived in a regency mansion called Marchwood Park and funded the building of St John the Apostle's church, Marchwood (1839–1843), as well as the parsonage house and schools, which he also endowed.[61] The church was designed by the Irish architect John Macduff Derick (c. 1805/6–59), who also designed St Saviour's Leeds for Pusey (1842).[62] His Anglo-Catholic credentials were established. The brother of Horatio Francis Kingsford Martelli and Mary Anne Ansley was Thomas Chessher Martelli (1813–1859), a graduate of Brasenose. He was first vicar of Marchwood, the living being in the gift of his brother Horatio.[63] Wilberforce, a graduate of Oriel,[64] was at the time (1843) Archdeacon of Surrey (1839–1845).

---

the Squire, from his having been non-resident, was comparatively nobody, and two persons engaged in trade in the village were people of the most influence, and, more dreadful still, were Dissenters of an advanced sort', Bateman Brown, *Reminiscences*, p. 50, https://www.cantab.net/users/michael.behrend/repubs/brown_reminisc/pages/chapter_04.html

58 I am grateful to Mrs Bridget Flanagan for alerting me to the connection. See Flanagan, *A Commanding View*, pp. 16f.

59 The grandfather of Mary Anne and her siblings, Francesco Antonio Martelli (1721–1799), had originally come from Florence to London.

60 See 'Holloway v. Webber; Holloway v. Holloway', in *The Law Times*, xix (1869), 514–516.

61 Cf. E. R. Kelly, *Hampshire, Including the Isle of Wight*, ed. by E. R. Kelly. (County Topogr.), 1875, p. 218, https://books.google.co.uk/books?id=6wsHAAAAQAAJ

62 Cf. Phil Mottram, 'John Macduff Derick (c.1805/6–59): A Biographical Sketch', *Ecclesiology Today* 32 (2004), 40–52 (47).

63 BA 1841, MA 1844. Cf. *The Gentleman's Magazine, Early English Newspapers* (F. Jefferies, 1859), p. 540, https://books.google.co.uk/books?id=02Q3AQAAMAAJ

64 BA 1826, MA 1829.

Although Marchwood was in the Archdeaconry of Winchester, Wilberforce attended the consecration of the new church. The Oxford dimension was a further link. It is thus highly probable that Mary Anne, who, on account of her Italian ancestry, may have been predisposed to ritualist worship, was, together with her brothers, on friendly terms with Wilberforce and that this personal acquaintance with a leading High Churchman would make him the obvious person to whom to turn in the search for an appropriate ritualist incumbent at St Ives.

Hunt, it seems, cannot resist an ironic swipe at the decision to offer the living to Goldie, referring to Mary Anne Ansley's 'astute wisdom'. Although Hunt does not introduce the subject of evolution at this point, it may be noted that Wilberforce had become prominent for opposing Darwin's science. Wilberforce, like Hunt, was a keen amateur scientist. Hunt refers specifically to Wilberforce's opponent, Thomas Henry Huxley, later in *Clergymen Made Scarce*,[65] albeit in an analogy designed to demonstrate the differences between the Church of England and the Church of Rome. It is therefore highly likely that on this front, too, Hunt disapproved of Soapy Sam.[66] The answer to the question, why was Goldie Sam's favourite man, would seem to be that Goldie's parish, Colnbrook, was in the Diocese of Oxford, where Goldie had risen to some prominence.[67]

There appear, however, to have been further problems over payment of the sum demanded by the patrons, which resulted in Goldie's declining the offer at first:

> Her [Mary Anne Ansley's] plans were greatly disconcerted by Mr. Goldwing's declining. It was said that the wine merchant [Benjamin Frederick Ansley] would not forego his right, that if the living was to be given away, he thought it should be given to an old man, so that the presentation might be sold immediately after.[68]

---

65 *Clergymen Made Scarce*, p. 45.
66 The nickname is usually attributed to Benjamin Disraeli, who described Wilberforce's manner as 'unctuous, oleaginous, saponaceous'. Cf. Ian Hesketh, *Of Apes and Ancestors: Evolution, Christianity, and the Oxford Debate* (University of Toronto Press, 2009), pp. 30f. Other explanations also exist.
67 Goldie's name occurs in the local and national press with regard to his stipend at Colnbrook, from which it can be deduced that he was potentially a difficult character.
68 *Clergymen Made Scarce*, p. 39.

In due course, Goldie accepted the living:

> A few days later the news came that Mr. Goldwing had consented at last to take the living. The only barrier had been the wine merchant's objection, and that could only amount to £400.[69]

Goldie's entry into St Ives and his subsequent behaviour were quite unlike anything the town had seen before.[70] He had an unusual background, having been born in Paris in March 1825 and baptized apparently twice, once in London in 1825, then again in 1827 at the British Embassy Chapel, Paris. His father was from Dumfries in Scotland, his mother from Devon. The reason for their being in Paris at the time is unknown, but probably because of his father's occupation as an M.D. Goldie's six siblings were all born in India, where his father was in the Honourable East India Company Service. The family was well-to-do, of Manx origin, with high-ranking military and other important connections.[71] Goldie graduated from St John's College, Cambridge, where he had been a scholar.[72] He was second Senior Optime (i.e. second-best in the Upper Second class of the Mathematical Tripos) in 1847 and also a first-class cricketer, playing for the University, albeit as a stand-in, in 1846.[73] He and his wife had twelve children and employed five domestic servants

---

69   *Clergymen Made Scarce*, p. 40. Approx. £51,395 in 2020.
70   James Conway Walter, *A History of Horncastle from the Earliest Period to the Present Time* (Horncastle: W. K. Morton, 1908), p. 62.
71   Cf. Walter, *History of Horncastle*, p. 62: 'The Goldies were an old Manx family; Col. Goldie, his brother, of the Scotts [sic] Guards Regiment, being President of the House of Keys, the local parliament. Their residence in that island is 'The Nunnery,' near the town of Douglas, so called from the ruin close at hand of an ancient priory, said to have been founded by St. Bridget in the sixth century. Mr. Goldies' [sic] nephew is the present Sir George Dashwood Tanbman [read 'Taubman'] Goldie, Privy Councillor, K.C.M.G., F.R.G.S., &c, formerly of the Royal Engineers, but latterly holding various Government appointments, director of several expeditions in West Africa, having travelled in Egypt, the Soudan, Algiers, Morocco, &c., and attended the Berlin Conference in 1884, as an expert on questions connected with the Niger country, where he founded the Royal Chartered Company of Nigeria. His latest honour (1905) is the Presidency of the Royal Geographical Society, in succession to Sir Clements P. Markham, K.C.B., &c.'
72   Cf. *Crockford's* 1865, p. 248: 'GOLDIE, Charles Dashwood, Colnbrook Parsonage, Slough, Bucks.—St. John's Coll. Cam. 2nd Sen. Opt. B.A. 1847, M.A. 1850; Deac. 1848 and Pr. 1849 by Bp of Lin. P. C. of St. Thomas's, Colnbrook, Dio. Ox. 1852'; 'Charles Goldie (Cricketer)', Wikipedia, https://en.wikipedia.org/w/index.php?title=Charles_Goldie_(cricketer)&oldid=938240178
73   Cf. 'Charles Goldie', ESPN cricinfo, http://www.espncricinfo.com/england/content/player/13907.html

and a governess at St Ives.[74] Only the twelfth child was born at St Ives. His wife, Harriet, the daughter of Col. James Nicol, formerly Adjutant-General of the Bengal Army, was a beauty and a hostess, as Walter relates, describing Goldie in his curate days in Horncastle:

> We next take two of the well chosen curates of the Vicar, T. J. Clarke, who were contemporaries at Horncastle; Charles Dashwood Goldie of St. John's College, Cambridge, where he took Mathematical Honours in 1847, was ordained as Curate of Horncastle in 1848. An able preacher and indefatigable worker in the parish, he at once made his mark, not only in the town, but in the neighbourhood; he and his beautiful wife being welcome guests in many a rectory and vicarage. He was also a man of good social position and private means, and occupied a good house with large garden [...] Mr. Goldie being curate at the time when Holy Trinity Church was built presented the carved oak chairs within the communion rails. After leaving Horncastle he was appointed to the vicarage of St. Ives, in the diocese of Ely.[75]

It is not clear where Goldie first developed his ritualist leanings, whether in Cambridge, Horncastle, High Toynton, or Colnbrook, where he had been Perpetual Curate from 1852–1866, immediately prior to coming to St Ives. He had evidently come to the notice, probably in Colnbrook, Diocese of Oxford, of Samuel Wilberforce, the prominent High-Church Bishop of Oxford.

At any rate, he was known for his High-Church views. His reputation had gone before him: 'There were rumours afloat that he was a high Churchman—very high. 'It will never do in Ousebank' was the unanimous remark.'[76] Goldie's entrance on his first Sunday in church was altogether theatrical:

> Next morning the congregation were breathless to see Mr. Goldwing. He walked into the desk. Instead of reading the usual sentences, he shouted at the pitch of his voice the name of a woman who had come to be churched. The people were bewildered, and the woman's nerves if they were like other womens' [sic] must have had a shake. Mr. Goldwing went through the morning service part reading and part intoning. He had a rich musical voice of great compass, and sometimes it was really

---

74   Cf. the 1871 census; Descendants of Quintin Riddell, Probably Born Late 1300s, http://www.airgale.com.au/riddell/d15.htm#i33543
75   Walter, *History of Horncastle*, p. 62.
76   *Clergymen Made Scarce*, p. 41.

solemn. At other times, especially in the Litany, it degenerated into an effeminate whine like the cry of a sick girl.[77]

Goldie had made known his arrival in no uncertain terms. The bells had rung out on the Saturday previously, and he set about demonstrating to the congregation and town how he meant to go on. Hunt comments:

> He was no Jesuit introducing things by stealth. He was no man of half measures. He had a determined will and an unbounded confidence in his own ability to execute that will. He restored neglected rubrics and when there was no rubric he made one. The gown in the pulpit he discarded at once as illegal and unbecoming the priest in his ministrations to the people. He placed the women who came to be churched on a form before the desk—received the offering himself—carried it to the 'Altar,' and there presented it to Jesus Christ, ever present in the Holy Place. Before the act of baptizing he filled the font with pure water. The choristers and some other people laughed when they heard the splashing in the font. He carried the children into the centre of the Church to sign them with the sign of the cross, and to receive them into the body of the congregation [...][78]

Before a week had passed, Goldie turned his attention to the curate, to whom he sent a letter. The correspondence merits quotation in full:

> 'My dear Mr. _____ [Hunt]
>
> 'I enclose a notice to you in the usual form, which I should at any rate have sent in order that I might enter into fresh arrangements with you—as a matter of form. But I cannot but feel that this must be an actual notice and not a form. I have been honoured by the reception of two sermons preached by you in the Church of _____ [All Saints] since the late Vicar's death, and, according to my view, they are in points so lamentably deficient in the full statement of truth, and in some points so erroneous, that I feel it my duty either personally or by deputy, to supply your place in the pulpit during the next six weeks. I shall be glad to have your assistance in the reading desk and otherwise.
>
> 'I am the more sorry to say this, because I cannot but own the undoubted power the Sermons show; and I should be glad if the opportunity offers, to have some conversation with you, and to aid you (if it is not presumption in me to say this) in finding out the point, where, as it seems to me, you diverge from Catholic truth.

---

77 *Clergymen Made Scarce*, p. 40. See Yeandle, *Clash of Churchmanship*, pp. 7f.
78 *Clergymen Made Scarce*, p. 41.

'I hope that the fact of my acting thus will not in any way destroy our friendly converse during the short remainder of our connection.

'Ever yours truly,

'_____.' [Charles Dashwood Goldie]

Hunt had evidently displeased Goldie by the theology he had propounded in his two sermons, the subject of which was the sacraments.[79] They were evidently too 'Protestant' for him. In response to the preaching inhibition imposed, Hunt replies:

'My dear Sir,

'I have received your letter and the notice, the latter of which I have expected daily since Sunday. Indeed, I had no wish to remain in the Parish after seeing how distinctly you identified yourself with a party in the Church with whose peculiar views I have no sympathy in the world. No one will blame you for wishing to have a Curate of your own way of thinking, but to inhibit me from the pulpit is an arbitrary and uncalled for exercise of power, likely, I fear, to recoil upon yourself. This Parish has been virtually in my hands for nearly two years. I have been feeding the flock. I *know* the sheep and they *know* me. Not to allow me to preach a final sermon is to make me a martyr when I do not wish to be one. As to the sermons I did not cause them to be sent to you. I believe them to be so thoroughly in accordance with the doctrines of the Protestant Church of England, that I cannot well understand your objections. I had a letter yesterday morning from a friend of mine, a minister of the Episcopal Church of Scotland, and reckoned a High Churchman, who says, 'Without accepting, perhaps, all points in them. I certainly think you have put in clear and forcible terms some important views of your subject.' I should be glad to have a friendly conversation with you on the doctrine of the sermons. I should like to hear what a sensible man (and I believe you are a sensible man) has to say about what you call 'Catholic truth.' *There is no such thing* in the sense in which you seem to use the words. There are Catholic lies in abundance, Catholic errors and Catholic superstitions, which must be swept away with the besom of destruction. There are, I know, many earnest men who believe in what they call Catholic truth, but the religious sentiment is wild in its wanderings, and ought to be governed and restrained by reason. I have had much experience among men of all kinds of opinion and I have learnt to be tolerant towards all.

---

79   *The Two Sacraments. Two Sermons Preached in the Parish Church of S. Ives, August 5th, 1866, by the Rev John Hunt, Curate, Second Edition, With an Appendix* (St. Ives, Hunts: W. Lang, 1866).

'I will duly consider whatever you wish to say to me, and I shall promise that, on my part, nothing will arise, if I can help it, to promote anything but the most friendly understanding between us.'

'Yours very truly,

'_____.' [John Hunt][80]

Hunt, who, at thirty-nine, was just twenty-one months younger than the forty-one-year-old Goldie, must have felt insulted and belittled. His theology had been disparaged. His social status stood in question—as an unmarried Scot of humble origins, who had studied, as far as we know, for only one year at a university not commonly attended by English clergy, who had failed to achieve preferment, as against the father of eleven children from an old patrician family, a graduate of Cambridge and an accomplished sportsman, married to the daughter of a colonel. Perhaps social considerations did not play a part, but there was an obvious rift between the two men, and Goldie's bearing was disdainful. The references to friendship and the faint praise of each other's intellect would hardly make for harmonious relations. Either man was as discourteous as the other in respect of their differing theology and churchmanship.

Hunt counters Goldie's haughty condescension in part with Biblical allusions, but one can sense his feelings of wounded pride and inferiority. Although he is intellectually fully a match for Goldie, who, it must be remembered, was a man with an impressive academic record himself, albeit not a theologian, his position is of necessity one of submission.

Hunt was fatigued by the whole affair and appears not to have offered further resistance. A scandal ensued, of which the newspapers became aware. As with all scandals, good as well as bad can be the outcome:

> As I had only six weeks more to be in the Parish and was really so exhausted by long and incessant work as not to care about preaching much, this inhibition seemed to show a want of ordinary discretion. The Bishop was vexed about it. The newspapers paraded it, and as a consequence the people bought the sermons by hundreds.[81]

People began taking sides. Goldie continued with his high-handed, egotistical behaviour. We saw earlier how, as a curate in Hornchurch, he

---

80   *Clergymen Made Scarce*, pp. 40f.
81   *Clergymen Made Scarce*, p. 41.

'at once made his mark, not only in the town, but in the neighbourhood'. The same was true in St Ives, though here it was not because he was 'an able preacher and indefatigable worker in the parish',[82] but because of the confrontational way in which he set about introducing his ideas. Hunt's text gives a wry account of this, observing:

> Mr. Goldwing was determined to do what he thought right. He first did everything his own way, and then he made calls and wrote letters to appease those who were offended. He ignored the existence of the Churchwardens. The Sequestrator[83] never had the joy of presenting the *new surplice*. A sad fate awaited him. He was numbered with 'persons excommunicated, unbaptized, and who have laid violent hands on themselves.'[84] Many years ago he had committed the fearful sin of marrying his deceased wife's sister, and Mr. Goldwing denied him the benefit of those sacraments which are universally necessary to salvation.[85]

Public opinion at the time was greatly divided about this 'sin' in general. It was still illegal until 1907, when the Deceased Wife's Sister's Marriage Act was passed, and Goldie stuck to a rigid ecclesiastical interpretation, evidently denying communion to the unfortunate churchwarden.[86] Public opposition to Goldie grew rapidly. Tact was not in evidence on either side of the quarrel:

> The parish of Ousebank was soon in a ferment. The people could do nothing but growl. The walls were placarded with *No Popery*; and letters of all kinds, wise and foolish, filled the columns of the local paper. One morning I was sitting at my window which looked into the marketplace.

---

82 Walter, *History of Horncastle*, p. 62.
83 Mrs Eliza Hunt identifies him merely by his surname 'Wise'. This would appear to be Alderman Richard Relton Wise, listed in the 1871 census as 'Bank Manager, Crown St., aged 60'. Kelly's, for 1869 gives his address as 'The Pavement' (p. 268). On the sequestration process, see Philip Jones, 'Ecclesiastical Sequestration', Ecclesiasticallaw, https://ecclesiasticallaw.wordpress.com/2012/11/17/ecclesiastical-sequestration/
84 Cf. Henry John Hodgson and J. Steer, *Steer's Parish Law: Being a Digest of the Law Relating to the Civil and Ecclesiastical Government of Parishes, Friendly Societies, Etc., Etc.: And the Relief, Settlement, and Removal of the Poor, Nineteenth-Century Legal Treatises* (Stevens and Norton, 1857), p. 77, https://books.google.co.uk/books?id=iLEDAAAAQAAJ
85 *Clergymen Made Scarce*, p. 41.
86 See Deceased Wife's Sister's Marriage Act 1907, https://en.wikipedia.org/wiki/Deceased_Wife%27s_Sister%27s_Marriage_Act_1907; William McKee Dunn, *Is Marriage with a Deceased Wife's Sister Lawful?* (London: Rivingtons, 1883), https://en.wikisource.org/wiki/Is_Marriage_with_a_Deceased_Wife%27s_Sister_Lawful%3F

> I heard the stentorian voice of the town crier, 'This is to give notice,' he exclaimed in his lofty monitone [sic], 'that whoever enters a Dissenting place of worship commits an offence against God. These are the words spoken in the Parish Church of Ousebank on Sunday morning last, and he who said them is a liar and a fool.'[87]

Goldie, who was referred to as a 'high Ritualist',[88] was not to be deterred in his pursuit of this form of church service, and later in his incumbency he had many clashes with the congregation, especially at annual vestry meetings,[89] in particular with the longstanding parish churchwarden, Read Adams, the first Mayor of St Ives.[90] Goldie realized that to inhibit Hunt from preaching a final sermon before his departure would be unwise. Hunt describes his farewell presentation, even making some charitable remarks about Goldie:

> I left Ousebank in the midst of the excitement. It was announced to me that the long-intended presentation was at last to be made and it was intimated that the occasion would be a proper one for a parting address. Mr. Goldwing had the prudence to suspend his inhibition, and asked me to preach once more in the Church, which of course I was eager to do. There was not much wrong with Mr. Goldwing, except the poison of the 'pernicious nonsense.' Sacerdotal blood flowed in his arteries, and filled his veins to repletion. On the Friday evening a great multitude assembled in the town-hall. Thirty guineas[91] were presented to me in a long purse with dangling tassels. The Chairman made a flaming speech, he spoke of the 'talented preacher,' the 'great scholar,' and the respect which the inhabitants of Ousebank had for 'all that was great and good.' He quoted Shakespere, of course, and, in allusion to the Ritualists, the lines of Milton, beginning—
> 'Wolves shall succeed for teachers, grievous wolves.'[92]

---

87   *Clergymen Made Scarce*, p. 41.
88   E.g. *Bradford Observer*, 1 April 1875, p. 7.
89   See Yeandle, *Clash of Churchmanship*, pp. 11f. and passim.
90   Read Adams (1832–1889), who lived in Madeley Court in neighbouring Hemingford Grey, owned a wholesale grocery and tallow-chandlering business and was the first Mayor of St Ives, upon its incorporation in 1874. He was presented by the Secretary of State to the Prince of Wales in 1875 (cf. *The Morning Post*, 27 April 1875) and was generally well known. As Hon. Sec. of the Hunts. Protestant Association, he had many skirmishes with Goldie and others. Hunt expresses his admiration for his staunch Protestantism in the dedication to him of his edition of *Poems by Robert Wilde*, p. vi. See 'St Ives 100 Years Ago: Read Adams', St Ives 100 Years Ago, https://stives100yearsago.blogspot.com/2020/06/read-adams.html
91   Approx. £3,835 in 2020.
92   *Clergymen Made Scarce*, p. 41. The quotation is from Milton's *Paradise Lost*, xii, 508. The continuation of the passage makes clear the relevance of these words to the

The presentation was made on Friday, 19 October 1866.[93] Although Mrs Eliza Hunt did not reveal his name, we know from newspaper reports that the chairman was Read Adams. Whether Goldie was present we do not know. If he was, the occasion must have been embarrassing for him, but he was not a man to show embarrassment.

The booklet ends with the text of Hunt's address, which is printed in full in the Appendix. I do not propose to scrutinize it in detail, merely to pick out some of the main aspects. The opening paragraphs show Hunt's popularity amongst the townsfolk. Not only the churchgoers but also several Dissenters had contributed to the presentation. Whether this popularity was entirely due to Hunt or existed partly in opposition to Goldie it is hard to say, but probably elements of both are present. Regarding the 'testimonial',[94] Hunt displays a degree of modesty—it would be unfair to impute a hint of false modesty to him, but one cannot help wondering if the humility displayed is not an attempt to seize the moral high ground.

Hunt next turns his attention to a discourse on the lot of the curate. This theme has, of course, emerged repeatedly in the course of his booklet, but with exemplification far exceeding analysis. He now proceeds to analyse the unfortunate situation in which many a curate found himself at the time, elements of which we have traced in *Clergymen Made Scarce*, lamenting that 'The earnest curate, who has nothing but his own merits to depend on, has but few chances of promotion in the Church.'[95] He is clearly speaking *in propria persona*, though his comments are general. He has missed every chance of promotion in London and has just failed in St Ives to secure it, where his objective was almost within his grasp. He is

---

situation in St Ives: 'Wolves shall succeed for teachers, grievous wolves, | Who all the sacred mysteries of Heaven | To their own vile advantages shall turn | Of lucre and ambition, and the truth | With superstitions and traditions taint, | Left only in those written records pure, | Thought not but by the spirit understood.'

93 'Presentation of a Testimonial to the Rev. John Hunt.— The Rev. John Hunt, who has been curate of this parish during the last two years, being about to leave St. Ives, several his friends decided to present him with a testimonial as a token of their respect and esteem for the efficient manner in which he had performed the duties of his sacred office.' (*Cambridge Chronicle and Journal*, Saturday, 20 October 1866, p. 6). Cf. also *Cambridge Independent Press*, Saturday 20 October 1866, pp. 6f. For the full text, see Appendix, p. 192–195.

94 Here used in the sense of 'A gift presented to some one by a number of persons as an expression of appreciation or acknowledgment of services or merit, or of admiration, esteem, or respect', OED.

95 *Clergymen Made Scarce*, p. 42.

one of the most salient examples of a talented, published theologian who had not secured preferment and was still to wait twelve more years for his own incumbency. He draws attention to the social aspect, whereby it is primarily those whose family owns the gift of a living or who can buy the same who are able to succeed. The comparison of a successful career in the Church and the other professions is very telling: 'A man who has passed creditably at his university, can reckon upon success, or at least a competency in any other profession, but unless he inherits a family living, or speculates in the purchase of a presentation he has not the same chance in the service of the Church.'[96] He proceeds to put forward ways to remedy the situation regarding curates, proposing that they should be chosen and paid for by the congregation. Robust criticism is levelled at 'the clergy of the Established Church', namely that they 'will know before long that if they are to keep their position, they must pay more attention to the will of the people. They must cease to come into their parishes as hierarchical autocrats.'[97] Did Goldie know that this was aimed at him and hundreds of other parsons of all parties in the Church of England? Hunt's observations were prescient of things to come regarding church governance and power, but in Goldie, he and the congregation had encountered a new type of incumbent, who was convinced by his sincerely held belief in 'Catholic truth' and was prepared to fight a crusade in its defence. The Church was at that time in a state of some turmoil. There was strong opposition in places to the Ritualist movement. Clergy and churchgoers were beginning to be split on this matter at precisely this time.[98]

Hunt's account now turns, after a brief allusion to tensions within the parish and an exhortation to the congregation to show Christian charity in the matter, into a lengthy peroration on the merits and demerits of the 'Catholic Revival'. Here he sifts the wheat from the chaff, explaining what he sees as good in the movement and what he rejects. He scrutinizes the Church of Rome from an English Protestant viewpoint and takes issue with Dr Pusey on his desire for rapprochement with Rome. Alluding to evolution and his knowledge of anatomy, he demonstrates the differences between the Church of Rome and the Church of England, despite apparent similarities, further berating the Mariolatry of the Roman Church.

---

96 Ibid.
97 Ibid.
98 See Chadwick, *Victorian Church* II, pp. 308–327.

9.3 Beyond St Ives

It is clear that Hunt had been happy and successful in St Ives before Goldie's advent,[99] that his leaving was widely regretted and that his parting was performed with charitable sentiment. He sums up in the final paragraph, stressing the need for reason, reasonableness, and the necessity for the Church to mould the human material available to it into reasonable beings in its service:

> The Church is troubled. All its teachers are perplexed, from the Bishop who rides in his carriage, to the Curate who rideth on the top of an omnibus. We do not know whether or not we are sacrificing priests! One half of the clergy are surprised to hear that it is even supposed; the other astounded that everybody does not know it. Wisdom may be crying aloud in the streets, but it is in another sense that she is crying in the Church. Like Rachel, she laments there for her children, because *they are not*. Can we expect it otherwise, when no encouragement is given to men able and willing to do the Church's work; when, of the material that is available for the ministry, it is impossible to make anything better than innocent Evangelicals, or brainless Ritualists—preachers of platitudes, or performers of attitudes. Shall it ever be that in religion, as in other things, men will listen to the solemn voice of Reason?[100]

Here the open letter ends. It is a telling commentary on the state of the Victorian Church. Many of the ills observed therein would be corrected or lessened in the ensuing years; but the Church's influence and the faith of the nation would decline, too.

After leaving St Ives, Hunt was to serve another two curacies—at St Mary's, Lambeth, and at St Nicholas's, Sutton, in Surrey—before finally (twelve years later) obtaining preferment as Vicar of Otford on the recommendation of the progressive liberal theologian, Dean Stanley of Westminster.[101] In his fifty-second year, he had, by his own merits, achieved his goal through hard work, intellectual acuity, and hundreds of pages of published scholarship, which a man of no special talent, but with influence, might achieve after two years.

---

99 Cf. especially the dedication to Read Adams in Hunt's *Poems by Robert Wilde*: 'a memorial of the pleasant time which I spent as Curate of St. Ives', p. vi.
100 *Clergymen Made Scarce*, p. 48.
101 See Chapter 11 Postscript: John Hunt in Otford, p. 93.

10. Conclusions

John Hunt wrote *Clergymen Made Scarce* in order to highlight negative aspects of his career that he hoped might be rectified in future especially by an enlightened Bishop of London and afterwards, no doubt, by the Church more generally. As well as setting forth his personal woes, frequently with humour and irony, he hoped to provide a stimulus for reform. Indeed, the Church was in the midst of a slow process of reform, change, and upheaval. In the ensuing decades, some of the ills described by Hunt were addressed, but the wheels of change turned slowly, and it proved hard for many of those in authority to produce radical solutions to problems that would diminish their own power, wealth, and status.

Whether Hunt's open letter actually had any effect, or indeed was even read by Bishop Tait, is questionable and probably unlikely. The lowly status of a curate and the many demands on the Bishop's time probably meant that at best it might have been read by one of his staff. Owing to the negative publicity that Hunt's activities had attracted by the time of its publication, he was probably dismissed as a maverick or rebel who might potentially be dangerous to the wellbeing of the Church institution. The reforms of the Victorian Church and the progress of those reforms have been amply covered in the monumental survey by Chadwick, amongst others.

Hunt's booklet provides an insight at a personal level and from an individual's point of view into much that was amiss in the Church. It also allows us to extrapolate more generally a picture of the Victorian Church, its failing system of curacies, and the shortcomings of the system for obtaining incumbencies.

Probably the most salient feature of *Clergymen Made Scarce* is the lack of employment security enjoyed by curates and the haphazard nature of the employment market. Curates were regarded almost as a commodity to be traded. Their status was lowly, and they were expected to know their place. In society at large, they enjoyed a more respected position but were expected to adhere to certain societal norms of behaviour. They were not expected to step out of line or to be vocal about their lot. This applied particularly within the institutional Church. They had to fend for themselves in the job market, where the law of supply and demand operated, but where many other factors came into consideration. A would-be curate needed to be assiduous in seeking out employment, using every means available. Some curacies were obtained seemingly without much effort, others required many hours of searching in the press, letter-writing, visiting for interviews, preaching trial sermons, and taking trial services, before an incumbent might avail himself of a clergyman's services. Would-be curates had to suffer the inconvenience and indignity of unanswered letters, fictitious excuses for rejection, and even invalid, futile advertisements. The time and expense involved in travelling, especially to more distant locations, for interview were considerable.

Some curacies were naturally more desirable than others and attracted more applicants. The geographical location, the type of church building (old or new), the social makeup of the parish, the type of churchmanship, the character and reputation of the incumbent all played a role in making some positions more sought after than others. The aspirations of the curate, the work he was permitted or expected to do, the facilities provided, the degree of independence afforded him, the remuneration and accommodation offered him all contributed to the desirability or lack thereof, although these were not always apparent until after an appointment had been made.

The remuneration of a curate could vary greatly; benefits in kind were a further consideration. The salary was often low, but by the 1860s most were about £100 per annum; some indeed were merely on a par with the wages of a manual labourer. There were no allowances for clerical attire or accommodation. Board and lodging were occasionally provided, such as living in a large parsonage house, together with the incumbent and his family, but a deduction was then normally made from the curate's salary. Some curacies were offered on quite unattractive terms, even without a salary or in return for looking after and funding a household, including animals and servants, during an incumbent's absence. Good shooting, boating, and bathing were offered as an enticement in one case. Perhaps the greatest dishonesty was where a curate was persuaded to take services on the pretence that he might be offered employment, but in fact merely to provide unpaid cover for an incumbent's temporary absence.

Curates needed references from past employers, which could be vindictive or might contain anonymous assertions. Both here and in dealings with a potential new employer, the applicant was often subjected to scrutiny regarding his churchmanship. Sermons could be judged to be lacking in evangelical or catholic 'truth'. An applicant could be rejected for being a rationalist or serious thinker. In one case, a curate was required to be teetotal as well as an anti-Puseyite and an anti-Rationalist. The prejudice of those in authority was blatant and unchecked. Anyone who had not done the bidding of his master was unlikely to receive a positive testimonial. Not only must they satisfy the incumbent in question, but they were often subject to the prejudices of the society that paid their salary. In the case of evangelical parishes, this usually meant the Pastoral Aid Society, whose strictures regarding evangelical 'soundness' could be severe. Progressive theology was mostly frowned upon. Curates were not expected to have dangerous new ideas, such as questioning the account of the creation in Genesis. They were not expected to take issue with the debates of the day or to contribute to them. The most glaring example discussed in this book is the *Essays and Reviews* controversy. Most incumbents easily formed a negative opinion of the theology contained in it and were content to dismiss, and indeed condemn, it without having read it. They expected their curates to do likewise, which most did. Anyone who had read the book and had soberly evaluated its content was regarded with much suspicion and could face summary dismissal.

Dismissal could take place at the whim of a capricious incumbent for often spurious reasons. The curate often had no recourse to the bishop or other authority in the case of unfair dismissal. Bishops would almost invariably take the part of the incumbent in a dispute if they became involved at all.

There was a strict hierarchy of parish clergy. The incumbent frequently saw himself as an absolute ruler in his parish, which he regarded as his personal fiefdom. His wishes were to be obeyed by his curates, and in practice, he was subservient to no-one. An exception to this is seen in the case of rural parishes, such as Burley, where the squirearchy held sway and the incumbent was second in status after the squire. In such cases, the incumbent was required to do the squire's bidding.

Incumbents were frequently at pains to ensure that their curate did not outshine them in any way, and they took steps to prevent this. Many incumbents had obtained only a modest degree from Oxford or Cambridge but had given up all pretensions of scholarship subsequently. Nevertheless, they were arrogant about their education and the social status that it conferred. Those parish clergy who continued with scholarship and published serious works on theology were regarded mostly with suspicion. A curate was not expected to be acquainted with progressive theology, especially not of the continental variety. German theology in particular was denigrated as 'neology'. It was not seemly for a curate to show an acquaintance with German culture or the German language.

Although scholarship was little appreciated, social considerations weighed very heavily. An incumbent was, by dint of his calling, a gentleman. Such a gentleman was provided with a large house, in which he and his wife employed several servants and in which the family could live a gentrified life. To a gentleman's life belonged appropriate pastimes, which could range from an interest in nature to foxhunting and more. Some hobbies, such as the practical study of anatomy, demonstrated an excess of zeal, and opinions were divided as to whether these were an appropriate interest for a clergyman.

A suitable university education belonged to an incumbent's station in life. A curate who had graduated from Oxford or Cambridge had not only the ideal academic credentials, but more importantly had received an education alongside aristocrats and men of high standing, thus fitting him for his future role of leadership in society when he became an incumbent. Clergymen, more especially curates, who had not enjoyed such a privileged education were looked down upon. A strict educational hierarchy existed, in which, after Oxford and Cambridge, Trinity College Dublin was ranked, followed by Durham University and King's College London. Last came the theological colleges, such as St Bees, which turned out 'literates', on whom all other clergy were content to look down.[1] The Scottish universities, despite their venerable history

---

1   Cf. 'The Deficiency of Curates' (letter), in *The Times*, 10 September 1864, p. 12.

and academic strengths, appear not to have fitted into this pattern. No doubt their location in a different country, with a separate national church, contributed to this sense of otherness and perceived inferiority.

Although the concept of racism is scarcely appropriate in this context, there was a strong feeling that Britishness equated to Englishness and that people from Wales or Scotland were different. It was unusual for a Scotsman to enter the Church of England, even if Archbishop Tait was a very prominent example. Tait, however, was the child of a landowner and continued his education, after the University of Glasgow, at Oxford. He thus fulfilled the criteria of social status and university education, even if the land of his birth was 'wrong'. We have observed how speaking with a Scotch accent and not having a degree from an English university were genuine disadvantages. More important were social status and parentage. A man of lowly parentage would have a much more difficult career path.

The easiest route to preferment was through social connections, especially wealthy aristocratic heritage. A curate from the right background could gain preferment in two years. A man without the right connections, especially one who was deficient in other respects, could not expect to be recognized solely on his own strengths, such as intelligence, ability, and scholarship. These were potentially more of a hindrance than an advantage. To make a gentleman from such material was evidently considered a peculiarly difficult task.

The next easiest path to preferment—one open to all with the necessary means—was to purchase the advowson to a living. Wealthy parents or relatives furthered aspiring sons and nephews in this way. A friend might also act as an intermediary.

A curacy was essentially an apprenticeship with no fixed time limit. Indeed, some curates never succeeded in gaining an incumbency. It was not unknown for a man to serve numerous curacies for many years, although the norm was two years.

The death of the incumbent was a time of uncertainty for a curate, as the new incumbent was under no obligation to maintain his services. Especially if he differed in outlook from the incumbent, the curate might expect to be replaced.

Gaining preferment on merit was the exception.

11. Postscript: John Hunt in Otford

Although the purpose of the present work has been principally to highlight aspects of John Hunt's career as a struggling curate, it would seem appropriate now to look briefly beyond this stage in his life in a postscript that examines the remainder of his life and career as Incumbent of St Bartholomew's church in the village of Otford, Kent, a position that he achieved in 1878, at the age of fifty-one and in which he remained for twenty-nine years. Otford, near Sevenoaks, was a village of approximately 1,200 inhabitants. The living was in the gift of the Dean and Chapter of Westminster, and it was through Hunt's friendly relations with Dean Stanley, who, as a fellow progressive theologian, recognized his prowess, that he was presented to the living. The position of Vicar of Otford could hardly be described as one of prestige; the living is reported in the press in 1878 as being worth £210,[1] plus house.[2] The vicarage was a substantial three-storey building, with ample grounds; both house and grounds would have necessitated the employment of

---

1 Approx. £25,560 in 2020.
2 There are several brief press reports, which contain mainly identical wording, e.g.: 'None too soon Church preferment has come to the Rev. John Hunt, one of the most accomplished of clerical writers. Nearly a quarter of a century has passed since Mr Hunt took orders, and yet, while we have seen a perfectly unknown curate of two years standing presented to one of the best Crown livings in the east of England, Mr. Hunt has, until now, been allowed to go from curacy to curacy—Bishop Wearmouth, Deptford, Fulham, Hoxton, St Botolph's (Aldgate), St Ives, Hunts, St Mary's, Lambeth, and has never held benefice. He has now, thanks to Dean Stanley, been presented to Otford, near Sevenoaks, in the diocese of Canterbury. It is but a poor affair after all, for the tithes bringing in £666 a year [approx. £81,000 in 2020], are appropriated, and the vicar's gross income is only £210 and a house. The population, however, is small—under 1,200, and the supervision of parish will not interfere with Mr. Hunt's literary work. Otford is also sufficiently near to London for him often to run up and visit the British Museum Library. Mr. Hunt, who is a graduate of St. Andrews, first appeared as a writer in 1852 [...]', *Western Morning News*, Saturday, 26 January 1878, p. 2.

© 2021 David Yeandle, CC BY 4.0   https://doi.org/10.11647/OBP.0248.11

staff.³ It was a fitting residence for a gentleman parson, but the financial means to keep it running were scarcely extant on the Vicar's meagre stipend, which by 1898 amounted to a net income of £243.⁴

John Hunt found perhaps his ideal calling in the small rural community of Otford, where he was able to pursue his scholarly interests at a more leisurely pace. It is noteworthy that his major scholarship, with the exception of a second edition of his book on pantheism (1884), was completed before his arrival in Otford in 1878. Despite his waning scholarly activity towards the end of his life, he was awarded, in 1901, a Civil List pension of £100 per annum 'In consideration of his theological writings and of his straitened circumstances'.⁵ The straitened circumstances are to be explained partly by the paucity of his stipend at Otford and partly by his remarriage in 1899.

Whether he cherished a desire to rise higher in the Church's hierarchy cannot be known for certain. He rubbed shoulders with the ecclesiastical great and good, for example, while attending gatherings such as the Old Catholic Congress in Germany, but he appears to have been content, once settled in Otford, to live the life of a gentleman parson of the scholarly mould, with his books and his successive wives for comfort and companionship. He may well have perceived his career in similar terms to that of his mentor, F. D. Maurice, who, despite his outstanding scholarship and professorships, 'was almost forty years in orders, and never held any higher preferment than a church, of which the income was derived from pew rents'.⁶ Hunt appears to have been content to feed his flock as the 'poor man's friend', loved and respected by this small community.⁷

Two works, both local to Otford, deal with John Hunt's time as Vicar there and his involvement in local affairs. The earlier of the two is *John*

---

3   This Vicarage (built c. 1820), now called 'The Grange', still stands. Cf. 'The Grange, Otford, Kent', https://britishlistedbuildings.co.uk/101259017-the-grange-otford. A new, smaller, vicarage was built in 1924. Two servants are recorded as living at the Vicarage in the 1881 census.
4   *Crockford's* 1898, p. 692. Approx. £29,580 in 2020.
5   The value in 2020 is approx. £12,570. See 'Civil List pensions (London, 23 June 1902)', *House of Commons Parliamentary Papers Online*, (ProQuest Information and Learning Company, 2005); for a near-contemporary assessment of these Civil List pensions, see http://archive.spectator.co.uk/article/13th-july-1907/8/civil-list-pensions.
6   John Hunt, *Contemporary Essays in Theology* (London: Strahan, 1873), p. viii.
7   Cf. p. 216, below.

Hunt, the Poor Man's Friend, by Harold Hart (an unpublished typescript of 1958 in the Otford and District Historical Society archive),[8] which gives a brief overview of various aspects of Hunt's activities, mainly relating to his time at Otford. There are errors and misquotations in the work, which was not intended for publication in that form. *Otford in Kent*, by Clarke and Stoyel, published by the Otford and District Historical Society in 1975,[9] devotes much of Chapter 10 'Late Victorian' (pp. 215–236) to Hunt's actions in the parish and surrounding district, mainly from a secular point of view. The book, which is not without minor inaccuracies,[10] asserts: 'No one could have endeavoured to identify himself more thoroughly with his new home and its people than did this learned and dynamic Scotsman.'[11] This reinforces the assumption that Hunt was indeed content with his life and status in Otford, where he appears to have found his bucolic idyll. Hart notes: 'Hunt was a thinker and writer who loved a simple country life [...] [he] had a great zest for the style of life which he led'.[12] He was a mostly benign influence in the small community, able to exhort and admonish his flock, becoming a father-figure and person of respect, to whom his flock looked up with affection. Those who were not of his flock held him in less high esteem, especially when, from a position of moral superiority, he criticized and berated those who were wrongdoers in his eyes. Having worked himself into a position of moral, spiritual, and also secular authority, he could be high-handed and supercilious when he met with opposition. As chairman of the Otford vestry, which at that time held powers as a parochial church council and also a secular parish council, Hunt fought several skirmishes with local personalities. This was particularly the case with the introduction of a new water supply

---

8 For a transcription of the text and further details, see Appendix, p. 216. The work was begun by Hart's son, Roland, who was unable to complete it, with the result that his father did so (from a handwritten memorandum in the Otford and District Historical Society archive, initialled 'R.D.C.', presumably Reginald Dennis Clarke, 5/9/61).

9 Reginald Dennis Clarke and Anthony Stoyel, *Otford in Kent: A History* (Otford: Otford and District Historical Society, 1975). Hart's work was used in the production of this book.

10 E.g., 'he [Hunt] came to Otford at the age of 51, after a wide experience as curate and incumbent in a number of English parishes, mostly in the south-east' (p. 215).

11 *Ibid.* It is perhaps noteworthy that he identifies himself as English by the time he comes to Otford. Cf. p. 205, below.

12 Hart, *Poor Man's Friend*, p. 1.

and mains drainage system to Otford in 1885.[13] Hunt did not always emerge victorious but was usually outspoken, 'humorous, untiring and fearless', often displaying histrionics along the way.[14] After so many years as a curate of submitting, however unwillingly, to his superiors, the tables had turned, and the parson could now lord it over those of whose souls he had the cure and others with whom he came into contact locally. A comparison with the 'hierarchical autocrats', to whom he had earlier meted out stern criticism,[15] might easily come to mind, though this would perhaps be to do him an injustice.

Hunt's strongly held, often strict, views were communicated in sermons and addresses as well as through the pages of the Otford parish magazine and the local newspaper, the *Sevenoaks Chronicle and Kentish Advertiser*, to which he contributed several letters, and which frequently reported on his activities. He still published in periodicals and journals with a national circulation, but as we have noted, he was no longer moved to write long works of theological scholarship, having become more of an observer and critic of society and religion.

As part of the argument over the water and sewerage system, Hunt crossed swords with a local overseer, Benjamin Parish, who had the task of levying a drainage rate. Parish accused Hunt of 'wanting to underpay the rate-collector',[16] and a verbal skirmish occurred. Parish declared: 'You are very well paid for all you do. I could preach better sermons than you for £100 a year'. Hunt, who was not well paid, even if the work was not unduly arduous, was ready with an astute, witty retort: 'As I like to encourage lay preaching I will give you the pulpit next Sunday morning and see how you get on'.[17] It is not recorded whether Parish took up this offer. Matters came to a head when Hunt refused to pay rates on tithes, and Parish took out a summons against him.[18] Hunt's willingness to be obstinate to an almost extreme degree in pursuit of a cause in which he believed strongly is amply illustrated by this incident. He won the argument by proving from his research into the Tithe Commutation Act

---

13 See Clarke and Stoyel, *Otford in Kent*, pp. 215–219.
14 Clarke and Stoyel, *Otford in Kent*, pp. 218, 222.
15 *Clergymen Made Scarce*, p. 42.
16 Clarke and Stoyel, *Otford in Kent*, pp. 221f.
17 Clarke and Stoyel, *Otford in Kent*, p. 222, with reference to the Sevenoaks Chronicle and Kentish Advertiser of 3.11.1885.
18 Cf. *ibid*.

that the tithe payer and not the tithe owner was legally responsible for payment.[19] The case had national repercussions.[20]

In politics, as in theology, Hunt was a liberal, as noted publicly by Parish in the above dispute.[21] He encouraged working men to have a voice and to become involved in decision-making. He would preside at meetings of the Otford Working Men's Liberal Association.[22] His political involvement was, however, not partisan; he chose neutrality in political matters and was not a member of a party.[23] Hunt disapproved of the reforms of local government that were introduced in 1894, but he did stand for election as a parish councillor when the old system was no longer in force. The working men, whom he had encouraged and supported, disappointed him by not voting for him in large numbers, with the result that he was third from bottom in the poll and never again stood for elected office.[24] This was another of the ironies of Hunt's life, where his work for the benefit of others did not always result in reciprocal support for himself. Hunt joined in occasions of royal and national celebration, such as Queen Victoria's Diamond Jubilee (1897), but he may have harboured latent republican sympathies. Hart notes: 'speaking in 1898, on the reign of Queen Victoria, he expressed his opinion that the reign had been a prosperous one as well as a long one, and after mentioning railways, the telegraph, and other benefits to the public, remarked that the people of Britain were republicans in all but name.'[25] As Hunt's churchmanship became broader towards the end of his life, so his political activity waned, and his 'domination of village affairs came to an end in the mid-1890s'.[26]

A look through the pages of the *Sevenoaks Chronicle and Kentish Advertiser* in the 1880s and beyond shows how heavily Hunt was

---

19 *Sevenoaks Chronicle and Kentish Advertiser*, 2 April 1886, p. 5, and 27 July 1888, p. 8.
20 Clarke and Stoyel, *Otford in Kent*, p. 222.
21 *Ibid.*
22 Cf. 'On Wednesday evening, in very unfavourable weather, a fairly attended gathering of Liberals was held at the Vicarage, Otford, the promoters being the newly-formed Liberal Association, of which the Rev. Dr. Hunt, vicar of the parish, is president', *Sevenoaks Chronicle and Kentish Advertiser*, 14 May 1886, p. 6. This fairly lengthy article gives valuable insights into Hunt's political thinking.
23 Clarke and Stoyel, *Otford in Kent*, p. 222.
24 Clarke and Stoyel, *Otford in Kent*, pp. 225f.
25 Hart, *Poor Man's Friend*, p. 3; cf. Clarke and Stoyel, *Otford in Kent*, p. 233.
26 Cf. Clarke and Stoyel, *Otford in Kent*, pp. 225; 233.

involved in local affairs, e.g., as a member of the Diocesan Education Society, a school manager, a speaker at dinners and other gatherings, an exhibitor at horticultural shows, and more.[27]

One of the ways in which he sought to have a moral influence was through his strict Sabbatarian views. These were communicated to his flock in sermons and addresses as well as through the pages of the Otford parish magazine, which he introduced in 1891.[28] He wrote short articles on Sunday observance[29] and was a frequent contributor to *The Day of Rest*, an 'Illustrated Journal of Sunday Reading', published by Strahan, which was intended to provide wholesome reading material for a properly observed Sabbath. His tone could become acerbic when berating people for their failure to observe Sunday appropriately, as Hart notes, quoting from the Otford parish magazine: 'After thirteen years, your indifference to the services of religion has been to me a continual sorrow. The Sunday is spent in idleness, with no higher aspirations than belong to the cattle of the fields.'[30] Stern admonitions or disapproving looks were also meted out at the Old Catholic Congress to clerical participants who indulged in secular entertainment in a casino and feasting on the Sabbath.[31] Furthermore, he berated his parishioners for their moral turpitude, pointing to the number of illegitimate births in the parish and lax sexual morals.[32] He disapproved of excess, both regarding drinking and smoking, but he was not a teetotaller and allowed these pleasurable vices in moderation.[33] Parish accused him, in the exchange reported earlier, of wanting to 'Shut public houses on Sunday [...] and [...] deprive the working man of his Sunday beer'.[34] This, understandably, did not increase Hunt's popularity amongst some members of the village.

---

27 Cf. *Sevenoaks Chronicle and Kentish Advertiser*, 13 June 1884, p. 5.
28 Cf. Hart, *Poor Man's Friend*, p. 2; Clarke and Stoyel, *Otford in Kent*, p. 223. The magazine was entitled 'Otford Church and Home Magazine'.
29 E.g., John Hunt, *Should Museums, etc., be opened on Sunday? A lecture* [...] *Reprinted from The Day of Rest* (Sevenoaks: J Salmon, 1881).
30 Hart, *Poor Man's Friend*, p. 2. See also Clarke and Stoyel, *Otford in Kent*, p. 223, whose account varies slightly.
31 Cf. Hart, *Poor Man's Friend*, p. 6. Hunt describes these events in *Contemporary Essays in Theology*, pp. 427f.: 'I almost tremble to record how the Sunday evening was spent.'
32 Clarke and Stoyel, *Otford in Kent*, p. 223.
33 Cf. Hart, *Poor Man's Friend*, p. 3; Clarke and Stoyel, *Otford in Kent*, p. 226.
34 Clarke and Stoyel, *Otford in Kent*, p. 222.

Despite this sternness, Hunt was a man who showed warm Christian love towards his neighbour. His kindly nature led not only to the personal dispensing of charity to those in need, 'without regard to creed or character',[35] but also to the reorganization of Otford's charities, as recorded in his epitaph, putting them on a 'liberal foundation'. He gave an annual 'treat' to those villagers who were older than himself.[36] Although his simple trust in human nature led to people taking advantage of him on occasions, he strove continually for the good of humanity: 'in all matters appertaining to the Parish and its welfare he was always prepared to do his best for the general good'.[37]

Hunt travelled abroad frequently for both religious and more touristic reasons. This began before his time in Otford: the contact with foreign personages and clerics with a different, not always sympathetic, outlook from his increased his comprehension of human nature and spirituality. In 1904, he gave a lecture at Otford on his reasons for foreign travel, which was reported in the local press:

> The Vicar of Otford, the Rev. Dr. Hunt, gave an interesting lecture on his travels at the National Schools on the 4th inst. In the course of his remarks, the Rev. gentleman said:—'There are certain reasons why men travel—one is to see the country, another is to learn the language, and a third is to see something different from what they see at home.
>
> We English may be very great people, but we live in a small island. The world outside of us is very large. To see the manners and customs of many men, and many nations makes a man very learned [...]'[38]

Hunt was a competent linguist, with a particular penchant for German, which had featured in his publications and aided him in his theological research. He had cherished a strong pro-German bias for many years. He favoured Germany as the home of the Protestant Reformation and felt an affinity with its people. The same cannot be said of the French nation, to whom he felt a considerable antipathy, which he did not

---

35 Cf. Hunt's Obituary, p. 228, below.
36 Cf. 'On Tuesday the Vicar (Rev. J. Hunt. D.D.) gave his annual treat to all persons in the village who are older than himself. Five years ago, his seventieth birthday, there were 22 persons eligible and this year there were only 11', *Sevenoaks Chronicle and Kentish Advertiser*, 18 July 1902, p. 8.
37 Cf. Hunt's Obituary, p. 228, below.
38 *Sevenoaks Chronicle and Kentish Advertiser*, 5 February 1904, p. 8. The full text is reprinted in the Appendix, p. 204, below.

disguise. His negative remarks about the French were unrestrained, as was his adulation of the Germans.[39]

Hunt continued to travel abroad until the end of his life, including a pilgrimage to the Holy Land. Through contact with many diverse people and varieties of the Christian religion, he was able to gain a sympathetic understanding of those who were different, such as the Church of Rome, without falling prey to blind prejudice. His travels were also the occasion for humorous encounters and many anecdotes.[40] His somewhat forbidding outward appearance and bearing, with long white straggly beard, dark coat, and shovel hat, were the occasion for both respect and mirth.[41]

Hunt's literary outpourings were numerous; his theological works were long and contained much profound thought, but he failed to make a lasting impression nationally or internationally. Perhaps this had never been his ambition.

Although Otford was by no means a rich or prestigious living, Hunt was able to make a considerable impression on the church, village, and neighbourhood. The son of a humble tradesman, he became, by dint of his calling, a gentleman.[42]

After twenty-three applications for curacies and the like, ten appointments—many very short in duration—and thirteen rejections, he had eventually become his own master. His scholarship had made his name known far afield, and it is to be hoped that his experiences and example led in some small part to the much-needed reform of the Church. Although at times he may have been difficult in his social interaction with others, showing on occasion a supercilious bearing and an unwillingness to compromise, there is no doubting his deep faith, strong intellect, and Christian charity.

A man 'more sinned against than sinning', he deserved better in this world than was meted out to him. Yet, he settled down to a life of

---

39 For examples, see Hart, *Poor Man's Friend*, pp. 5f. and *Contemporary Essays*, Chapter xiii 'A Visit to Munich'.
40 Cf. Hart, *Poor Man's Friend*, p. 7; Clarke and Stoyel, *Otford in Kent*, pp. 224f.
41 Cf. Hart, *Poor Man's Friend*, p. 7; Clarke and Stoyel, *Otford in Kent*, p. 224.
42 Cf. Nicholls, 'Social Expectations', p. 157: 'Formerly "the approved method of converting tradesmen's sons into gentlemen", a clerical career had to compete with a multitude of professions which provided an easier path to genteel status, and a better pecuniary reward.'

pastoral care, scholarship, and domesticity in Otford, where his position in society allowed him to show his 'rare simplicity of nature' and 'rich humanity',[43] whilst remaining true to his roots as 'a level-headed, rugged kind-hearted Scotsman'.[44] Outpourings of grief and affection were very much in evidence at his funeral, and touching tributes, such as that from his curate, John Martin, show that this 'Christian scholar and sage, who was in heart as a little child',[45] was much loved and greatly revered in this small, rural community. Inscriptions on his tombstone in the graveyard of Otford Church further attest to the affection and esteem in which he was held: 'The poor man's friend' and 'He loved the sheep and the sheep loved him'.[46] For all his learning and scholarship, he had found his niche in the gentle Kent countryside, where he could truly show his worth.

11.1 Transcription of Hunt's Epitaph in Otford Church

To the Glory of God
& in Memory of
the Revd John Hunt, D.D.

Vicar of Otford for 29 years.
Born at Bridgend, Perth, on the 21st January 1827,
he died suddenly at the Vicarage, Otford, on the 12th April 1907.
During his incumbency he did much to place the charities of Otford
on a liberal foundation, & was lovingly called the poor mans friend.
For his 'Religious Thought in England' & 'Pantheism'
his name was held in honour far outside the limits of his own parish.
A writer of strong intellectual force
& one of the deepest philosophical thinkers of the church,
he rested his soul on the truth that God is love.
He possessed a rare simplicity of nature & withal a rich humanity
as a preacher of religion, he was ever
loyal to what is written.
& his faith was based on the divinity of Jesus Christ.
He left a deep impress on men.

---

43 From the memorial in Otford Church. See below.
44 Words from Hunt's Obituary, p. 228, below.
45 Words from John Martin's wreath. See Appendix, p. 231.
46 Clarke and Stoyel, *Otford in Kent*, p. 234. For photographs of the tombstone in Otford churchyard, a simple cross, see https://billiongraves.com/grave/John-Hunt/24910974.

102 A Victorian Curate

And his teaching lives on in the hearts of his people
as a precious heritage
Nature had so endowed him that all who knew him said this was a man!

———————

This tablet was erected by parishioners and friends[47]

———————

Fig. 4 John Hunt in old age in Otford, c. 1905, courtesy of Mr Edwin Thompson, Otford and District Historical Society.

---

47 For a photograph of the original, see https://www.findagrave.com/memorial/33393484/john-hunt.

12. Chronological Table of John Hunt's Life

Date[1]	Age	Curacy	Event
1827			Born in Bridgend, Perth (21 January)
1837	10		Queen Victoria ascended the throne (20 June)
1845	18		Eliza Meadows Shepard Thorp (Hunt's first wife) born in St Ives, Hunts.
1847	20		Matriculated at St Andrews University
1848	21		Completed Latin 1 and Greek 1 at St Andrews
1851	24		Private tutor, later newspaper editor in Preston
1852	25		*Select Poems: from the German*
1853	26		*The Spiritual songs of Martin Luther, translated by John Hunt*
1855	28		Ordained deacon
1855	28	1	Arrived as Curate, Deptford St Andrews, Bishopwearmouth, Sunderland [Bulmer]
1858	31		Margaret Allen Foote (Hunt's second wife) born in Cupar, Fife
1859	32		Left as Curate, Deptford, Sunderland
1859	32	2	Arrived as Curate, St Philip's, Arlington Square, Islington [James Sutherland] March*
1859	32		Applied to St Paul's, Lisson Grove [Keeling] (July)

---

1 Many of the dates are only approximate or estimated, based mainly on the information given by Hunt in *Clergymen Made Scarce*, which is not always clear. These are indicated by an asterisk. The calculation of Hunt's age is potentially a year different from that given, since many of the events are recorded in the sources by year only. The names of the incumbents are given in square brackets.

1859	32		Applied to St Mary's, Battersea [Jenkins] (July)
1859	32		Left as Curate, St Philip's, Arlington Square September*
1859	32	3	Arrived as Curate, St John's, Walham Green [William Garratt] October*
1859	32		Left Walham Green December*
1859	32		Refused to sign *Essays and Reviews* petition December*
1859	32		Applied to the War Office and Indian Army December*
1860	32		Applied to Burley on the Hill, Rutland [Jones] (January)
1860	33	4	Arrived as Curate, Edmonton [Tate] January*
1860	33		Applied to All Saints', Norfolk Square, Paddington [Steventon] March/April*
1860	33		Applied to St Mary Magdalen, Old Kent Road, Bermondsey [Snape] March/April*
1860	33		Left Edmonton March/April*
1860	33		Unemployed for three months April–June*
1860	33		Applied to Trinity Church, St Giles-in-the-Fields [Samuel Garratt] April–June*
1860	33		Unspecified application April–June*
1860	33		Applied to St Jude's, Southwark [Cruse] April–June*
1860	33		Unspecified application 'no salary' April–June*
1860	33		Applied to 'H. L.', Christ Church, Chelsea [Robinson] April–June*
1860	33		Applied to St George the Martyr's, Southwark [Allen] April*
1860	33		Applied to St James's, Pentonville [Courtenay] April–June*
1860	33		Applied to Stoke Newington [Jackson] April–June*
1860	33	5	Arrived as Curate, Christ Church, Hoxton [Kelly] September*

12. Chronological Table of John Hunt's Life

1863	36		Left as Curate, Christ Church, Hoxton September*
1863	36	6	Arrived as Curate, St Botolph's, Aldgate [Roberton] (September)
1864	37		Anatomy scandal at St Botolph's, Aldgate (November)
1864	37		*Punch* articles (November/December)
1864	37		Left as Curate, St Botolph's, Aldgate (November)
1864	37		Applied to an unspecified 'Evangelical parish' (November/December)
1864	37	7	Arrived as temporary Curate, Swallow near Caistor, Lincolnshire (December)
1865	38	8	Arrived as Curate, All Saints', St Ives, Huntingdonshire [Fosbroke/Goldie] (January)
1865	38		First Edition of *Clergymen Made Scarce*
1866	39		Yate Fosbroke, Vicar of St Ives, died (6 July)
1866	39		Charles Dashwood Goldie inducted as Vicar of St Ives (25 August)
1866	39		*The Two Sacraments: Two Sermons*
1866	39		*An Essay on Pantheism*
1866	39		Left as Curate, All Saints', St Ives (October)
1866	39		Period covered by *Clergymen Made Scarce* ended
1866	39	9	Arrived as Curate, St Mary's, Lambeth
1867	40		Second Edition of *Clergymen Made Scarce*
1870	43		*Poems by Robert Wilde with a historical and biographical preface and notes by John Hunt*
1870	43		*Religious Thought in England* vol. I
1870–72	43–45		First journeys abroad, including the Old Catholic Conference in Cologne, Germany
1871	44		*Religious Thought in England* vol. II
1873	46		Married Eliza Meadows Shepard Thorp at St Mary's, Lambeth (2 September)
1873	46		*Contemporary Essays in Theology*
1873	46		*Religious Thought in England* vol. III

1874	47		Left as Curate, St Mary's, Lambeth
1876	49	10	Arrived as Curate, St Nicholas's, Sutton
1877	50		Goldie accused of ritualism at St Ives
1878	51		Left as Curate, St Nicholas's, Sutton
1878	51		Arrived as Vicar of Otford, Kent
1878	51		Proceeded D.D. at St Andrews
1884	57		*Pantheism and Christianity* (revised edition of *An Essay on Pantheism*)
1886	59		Goldie died at St Ives
1890	63		Eliza Hunt died at Otford, aged 44
1899	72		Married Margaret Allen Foote
1901	74		Queen Victoria died; Edward VII acceded
1905	78		John Martin appointed Curate of Otford until 1907
1907	80		Died (12 April)
1908			Margaret Hunt married John Martin

Appendix
Documents and Press Quotations

Text of Clergymen Made Scarce

CLERGYMEN MADE SCARCE.

Five Years' Experience as a Curate in the Diocese of London.

A LETTER

TO THE

RIGHT HON. AND RIGHT REV.

THE LORD BISHOP OF THE DIOCESE.

BY

A PRESBYTER.

SECOND EDITION,
WITH A POSTSCRIPT, CONTAINING TWO YEARS'
FURTHER
EXPERIENCE IN THE COUNTRY.

'Make the greatest fool in the family a parson, that is, if he will let you.'—Punch.

'Nisi Dominus frustra.' Unless ye be a lord's son, ye need'na come here.—Scotch Translation.

'Si *Ecclesia* negat, facit indignatio versum
Qualemcunque potest.' —Juvenal.

PRICE ONE SHILLING.

LONDON:

HALL & CO., 25, PATERNOSTER ROW

1867.

[Page 2 is blank in the original.]

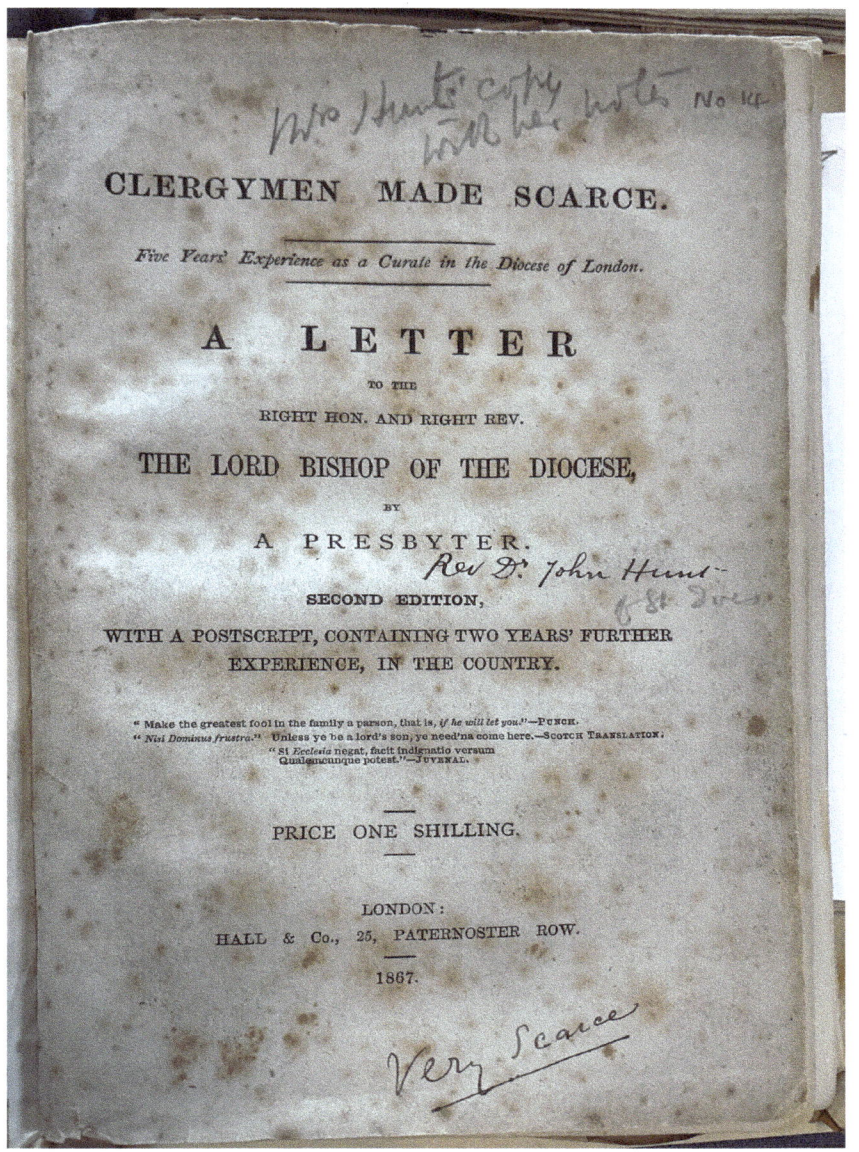

Fig 5. Eliza Hunt's copy of *Clergymen Made Scarce*, courtesy of the Norris Museum, St Ives.

[3] LETTER, &c.[1]

My Lord,

Lucius Apuleius the Getulian, as your lordship knows, wrote the fable of the Golden Ass. He wished to show that wisdom might sometimes exist even under an asinine exterior, and that there might be observing eyes where people did not expect to find them. Were I to call myself the Golden Curate, it would seem self-laudatory if not egotistical, I shall therefore keep in check the spirit which has suggested the comparison.

I mean to write my experience of five years as a Curate in the Diocese of London. After the example of St. Augustine, Rousseau, and other holy and unholy men, I might call it my 'Confessions,' but I prefer the term experience. In the last century, this was the favourite word with the English Methodists and the Scotch Metaphysicians, it is still the watchword of all the true friends of religion, science, and progress. He that does not build on experience builds on an unstable foundation. Goethe says:—

> 'Grey, dear Friend, is all theory,
> But green is the golden tree of life.'

But why should I trouble the world with *my* experience? I answer because I represent an oppressed race—a race that is fast dying out because of oppression. Curates are men who rarely speak for themselves.

---

1   The original, occasionally old-fashioned, spelling and punctuation have been preserved in this transcription except in the case of obvious errors, which are indicated in footnotes, with a square bracket after the emendation, followed by the original, e.g., fn. 3: 'Neander!] Neander! Extra space before punctuation marks has been removed. Inverted commas, which are inconsistent in the original, have been standardized. The original pagination is marked in square brackets. The manuscript annotations of Mrs Eliza Hunt are contained in footnotes relating to the words that she underlined. A few annotations are not easily legible. Her spelling and punctuation have been preserved. Brief elucidations and corrections are given in round brackets. The annotations were made with an ink pen. The ink, which may originally have been black, now appears brownish. The title page is annotated 'Rev D^r. John Hunt' beneath 'A Presbyter', and at the bottom of the page 'Very Scarce' has been written. These would appear to be also in Mrs Hunt's hand. The annotation 'Very scarce' may refer to the rarity of the booklet and also be a pun on the scarcity of clergymen. I am grateful to Ian Dobson for this suggestion.

It is dangerous for every oppressed class to speak, but for them most dangerous of all. Their policy is in silence and submission. In the marvellous unfolding of events, a singular opportunity has presented itself to me to set before your lordship some of the difficulties that beset every Curate who is really in earnest to fulfil the duties of his calling as a Minister of Christ—an opportunity apparently so providential that I believe I now write under a divine impulse, and that with such facts as are in my possession, were I to be silent I should be wanting in what is due both to God and man.

A few words concerning myself before I came to London will help to explain what follows. From my earliest youth theology has been the study of my life. I never had a thought of any calling but the one I have followed. I was educated in a Presbyterian sect, and matriculated at a Scotch University. Difficulties as to some doctrines of the Westminster Confession, which always appeared to me without a foundation in the Holy Scriptures, presented a barrier to my admission to any of the orthodox communities in Scotland. I came to England full of one doctrine, compared with which every other seemed [4] of small importance,—this doctrine was that 'Christ had tasted death for every man.' I found the Prayer Book full of this momentous truth, and waiving all other considerations I united myself to the Church of England.

The late Bishop Maltby admitted me to Holy Orders. His examining Chaplain said that I had passed the best examination of all the Candidates, though there were present men who had stood well at Oxford and Cambridge. The curacy to which I was ordained was a Parish in the suburbs of a large town in the North of England. The Parishioners numbered 10,000. They were entirely of the working class—ship carpenters, bottle makers, glass makers, keel-men, and colliers. It was a curacy that men had generally taken for the sake of a title, and left as soon as they obtained priest's orders, and often before that time. The Incumbent[2] was in ill-health, so that almost the entire management and working of the Parish devolved on me. It was just the work I had coveted, and I felt that with such freedom as I enjoyed, if something were not done the fault would be mine alone. By means of Lectures, Reading Rooms, Schools, &c., I won the confidence of the

---

2 W H Bulmer. Bishops wearmouth Sunderland (William Henry Philip Bulmer, Deptford St Andrew's, Bishopwearmouth)

working men, and, by assiduous visiting, the affections of the whole parish. The apparent prosperity of my work was a wonder to all the Clergy in the neighbourhood. I did not leave when I was made priest, I remained four years with no interest at heart but that of this Parish. With the Incumbent I lived on the best terms. He was a Calvinist of the extreme evangelical school, I a devout believer in Arminius and Wesley; but this never interrupted our harmony, beyond an occasional disputation, in which we always tried to remember that we were Christian Ministers. During the four years I remained here many changes took place in the Episcopal Bench. Among them your lordship came to the Diocese of London. The whole nation soon heard what the new Bishop of London was doing. It seemed to put into us a yet newer life. We studied his plans and tried to imitate them. One of his Diocesan Missionaries preached one summer evening at our Church gate, and made a deep impression on many of the working people. Why, we asked, did no Bishop think of this before? I looked back on the four years which I had spent here with no counsel and but little experience. I thought if I could only be under the Bishop of London what an amount of good I might be able to do. I would cry aloud in the streets. I would assemble the multitudes in the public places. I would feel and make it felt that times of refreshing had indeed come upon the land. It could not be long before I would have a Church and District to myself. A vision passed before me like what the prophets must have seen when they foretold the ingathering of nations, and the final reward of 'the teachers who are to shine as the firmament, and as the stars for ever and ever.' I thought I was called to London, and to London I came. I preached my 'farewell' sermon as the custom is in the country. The congregation wept audibly each time I repeated the words of my text. 'And now, brethren, I go bound in the spirit to Jerusalem, not knowing the things which shall befall me there.' Indeed I did not know them and could not know them, nor could [5] I by any possibility conceive them. I knew indeed that I was to be a Curate, but as yet I knew nothing of a Curate's trials.

My first Metropolitan Curacy was in the north of London. For convenience sake, I shall call the Incumbent the Rev. Simon Arlington.[3]

---

3 James Sutherland Arlington Square Islington (St Philip the Evangelist's, Arlington Square, Islington)

He was a man advanced in life, and had been a Curate until within a very few years of the time when I first knew him. This, one would have expected, might have made him have sympathy for Curates, but, no, on the certain principle that the persecuted are in their turn the greatest persecutors, this Incumbent was about the worst into whose hands I could have fallen. He was a man of meagre abilities, but of considerable craft. He bustled about among the people, was expert in gossip, and supremely in his element in the management of soup tickets. The Church was new. It was his first Incumbency; I was his first Curate, and he displayed the senile vanity of an old man just elevated into position. He called on me as soon as I arrived, and we took stock of each other. I agreed to read prayers in the morning and preach in the evening the following Sunday. This was by way of trial, for we had not yet concluded any engagement. He called on Monday, to say that he and the congregation were well satisfied, and that he wished to offer me the curacy. I recommended my remaining a month on trial, but he thought that quite unnecessary, I had better get licensed at once.

The poor people among whom I had laboured in the north collected about £20, to present me with an expression of their gratitude for my four years' ministrations. They asked me to decide how the money should be expended. My greatest want was a few more books, and it was agreed that the money should be spent in books. I selected 35 volumes, chiefly in theology. Among them were the complete works of Archer Butler, Neander's Church History, some volumes by Mr. Maurice, and Kingsley's Sermons. I had just arranged them on a table, when Mr. Arlington called. They were handsomely bound, and garlanded with a profusion of ribbons in the shape of book marks, with crosses suspended, the work of such young ladies as were in the congregation. They caught Mr. Arlington's eye, and I told him the history of the trophy now before him. 'Very gratifying,' he said, 'very gratifying!' Looking closer, he read 'Maurice's Theological Essays,' and exclaimed, 'Maurice! Neology!' He looked at another volume, 'Kingsley! Neology!' at a third, 'Neander![4] Neology again!' I said I had not read them, which was quite true, and this seemed to remove all suspicion.

---

4   'Neander!] Neander!

I accepted the Curacy. My next business was to see the Bishop. It is always interesting to see a man of whom you have heard much, especially a man that will probably be spoken of in the middle of the next century, and it is more interesting if there is a probability of your own name being mentioned incidentally in his biography. I went to *London House* anxious to let the Bishop know that a zealous Evangelist had come to the Diocese. I really considered my coming to London an event of importance, and expected a conversation with the Bishop on the subject of the work I had undertaken. In my rustic [6] simplicity, I had supposed Rome to be like Mantua. It did not enter my head that a man who is Bishop of almost half a world, could not have time for such conversations as I expected. I was introduced with six other curates. We took some oaths, kissed a book, signed a paper, and departed. The Bishop's lawyer exacted a sovereign out of my small funds for a bit of paper, which he called a licence. I suppose it was of some use, though I have not yet had time to enquire into the necessity of this expenditure of Curates' money. I had seen the Bishop, and left with the curious sensation that the sight of him had cost me a sovereign.

Next day my new Incumbent called, to arrange as he said about the work of the Parish. I was to read the prayers morning and evening, and begin an afternoon service, and he added, 'Sometimes you may have the privilege of preaching in the evening.' Privilege of preaching! I said to myself. Is not preaching to be the work of my life? Is it not the work for which I was ordained and for which I have just been licensed? And is it now to be a *privilege* only occasionally granted by this man! I added mentally, I won't[5] be long here, that I know. However, I was licensed, and in ordinary fairness I ought to stay a year. I said to Mr. Arlington 'I am a believer in systematic Pastoral Visitation; I shall begin at once and go over the congregation.' 'Oh, no,' he answered, 'the congregation is mine, not yours, I will visit the congregation.' A District was assigned to me, which consisted of Misery Lane, Poverty Corner, Starvation Street, and a few similar streets, terraces, and even parades, for so they called them. The population of my district was reckoned at 4000. I was to labour in these streets without a room of any kind in which I could hold a meeting. My work was simply that of a district visitor. I could not invite these

---

5   won't] wont

poor people to Church, for even if they had been willing to come, we had not pews for people who could not pay pew rents, and if I had taken pews for them and got them to come, even in the best clothes they had, the officers at the Church would have warned them off. It was not a rich congregation, but what it wanted in wealth it had abundantly in pride. After a few weeks, Mr. Arlington asked me to take a Sunday Evening Lecture in a City Church for a friend of his who was unable for his work. This was a very interesting service. The congregation consisted of the Beadle, Organist, and Pew-openers, with a few big boys and girls who played at 'Hide and Seek' in the organ gallery. I preached to the pews of this Church for four Sundays, but as I did not like being sent away from my own Parish, I intimated to Mr. Arlington that as his friend had a salary for the Lectureship he might pay a substitute. Mr. Arlington said sharply, that I could have the money if I liked. I reminded him that the society which payed my salary as his Curate, did not allow me to take money for preaching in other churches, but that I would be satisfied if the money were given to the funds of that society. The business was settled by sending a cheque for £1.1s. to the 'Pastoral Aid' and declining any further service from me as Substitute City Lecturer. [7]

During four months I had preached in our own Church about four times, and this Mr. Arlington granted as a favour, mingled perhaps with a feeling that I should not be idle on Sundays. He had been a non-preaching Curate for nearly twenty years, and now that he had got a Church and congregation to himself he could not endure that another should share the public ministrations with him. It was evident that I was in his way. He manifested this sometimes by taking the whole service himself, and leaving me to sit in a pew. He had an idea which afflicts many vain preachers, that the congregation were not satisfied to see any but himself, either in the pulpit or the desk. I endured this, intending to complete my year's service. But one Saturday Mr. Arlington entered my lodgings. He had a face which betokened that he had something to say, and he began with those conciliatory phrases which are the sure indication that something disagreeable is to follow. I wondered what it could be. I thought of all the sins I had committed since I came[6] to London, and I tried to remember if there was one really cognisable as

---

6   came] come

a public offence, 'I am very sorry, and it is a matter of great trouble to me' he proceeded to say, 'but a deputation from the congregation waited on me yesterday to state that your reading is so bad, that they will not endure it longer.' He added, that there was no objection to my preaching, only to my reading. The natural amendment which suggested itself to me, was, that he should read and I would do the preaching. I remarked that the information he brought me was very strange. I had come one Sunday on trial, and had offered to stay a month in the same condition that they might all be perfectly satisfied. I proposed to resign the Curacy, but he would not hear of that.[7] He wished that I should confine my labours to visiting the poor, and on Sundays I could sit in the communion and *read the Epistle*. The novelty of the proposition made me smile. He wished to confer upon me the dignity of a Bishop or a Dean, to sit enthroned, so that the congregation might behold me—and strange infatuation! I refused the honour. My absence from Church was a subject of inquiry. I told the story in a good humoured manner, shielding Mr. Arlington as well as I could, but the result was an excitement in the parish. Pews were threatened to be given up, hard words were spoken, and the people asked indignantly who were the deputation that waited on Mr. Arlington. When pressed he denied the deputation. It was finally reduced to the Churchwarden's wife and one or two old ladies, Mr. Arlington's special admirers.

The complaint was that I read with a Scotch accent. I had often heard Scotch preachers in England, and wondered that they had not rid themselves of this very uninteresting mark of the country of their birth; but I was not aware that I had retained a trace of it. We are never supposed to know the breadth of our own speech. I have heard two Irish Curates retort on each other in the wildest Hibernian, that they were far too Irish for this Country, and each say for himself that he was not a bit Irish at all. I mentioned Mr. Arlington's visit to a Scotch lady, a member of our congregation, expecting she would enter [8] a protest against the 'Deputation' ladies, but instead of that she answered my remarks by exclaiming with the most execrable Aberdeen intonation, '*That aboa-minible Scootch awksent, I was six years in London myself before I could get quit of it.*' The most curious of all was, that Mr. Arlington was himself a north

---

7 that.] that

countryman, and with a voice that might have frightened Bushmen or Andemaners.

As the excitement increased, Mr. Arlington became more distant. I felt it was desirable both for him and myself that I should get another curacy. How to set about that I did not well know, but I had a faint idea that curates and curacies should be in the Bishop's hands, or at least in the hands of some authorized person or body. I thought the Bishop might know what vacancies were in the diocese. Accordingly, I repaired to *London House*. I waited here from 11 o'clock till 2. A multitude of Rectors and Vicars had come by appointment to see the Bishop. When they had finished, his lordship came and asked if I wanted to see him, adding that he had no time, as he had to address a meeting in St. James' Hall at half-past two. He looked tired, and I felt that to inflict upon him any account of my paltry grievances would have been cruelty. When he learned who I was, he said that he had lately had a visit from my Incumbent, and that he was just about to write to me. He asked what was the matter, and I answered that the matter was too contemptible to be mentioned. I wished to leave as soon as possible. 'Very well,' he said, 'get another cure,' and in the agitation of the moment I omitted to ask the question for which I had come. Next day I was served with a legal notice, countersigned by the Bishop, to leave at the end of six months. I was sorry the Bishop had been a party to this, for I had given notice to leave at the end of three months, so that this notice was a studied insult on the part of Mr. Arlington.

This was in the month of July, about the time when the Clergy begin to be scarce in London. I had now my first experience in the way of looking out for a Curacy. I advertised in the *Record*, and had a multitude of answers. The incumbent of a Church in the[8] North West asked me to come and preach on trial. I selected what I considered at the time my best sermon. The subject was the craving of man for an object of worship. The whole sermon was a commentary on the words of St. Augustine, 'Thou, O God, hast made us for Thyself, and our souls are restless till they find rest in Thee.' I had scarcely got into the vestry, when the Incumbent thanked me for the 'very remarkable sermon' as he was pleased to call it. A young man just from Oxford read prayers,

---

8   Lissom Grove. Name forgotten (James Keeling, St Paul's, Lisson Grove)

he was pleased to say that he had learned more from this sermon than from anything he had ever heard at Oxford. It was about settled that I was to take this Curacy. We adjourned to the Parsonage and entered into further conversation about the subject of the sermon. One sentiment was quoted as being very striking. I inadvertently remarked that Mr. Maurice had expressed some fine thoughts on that point in one of his Theological Essays,—'Mr. Maurice!' said the Incumbent, 'Do you agree with Mr. Maurice?'[9] 'On that point,' I answered, 'I certainly do.' This [9] effaced the good impression I had made, for a Curate to agree with Mr. Maurice, even when Mr. Maurice is right, is at least suspicious.

Another application was from a Vicar in the South West. He wanted Temporary Duty taken in a School Room. Some factories had risen in the Parish, and brought an increase of working people. I offered to take permanent charge of the District. It was just what I was looking out for. 'They are all infidels' said the Vicar. I remembered that I had read all the Sceptical books that had been written for the last 200 years, both in France and in England. I remembered, too, that I knew the thoughts that were troubling working men's minds, and the causes of these thoughts, and I felt in myself that this was just such a District as I ought to have. 'We never know,' he continued, 'where we are to find infidelity now,' and, as I thought, changing the subject, he asked if I had read Robertson's Sermons. I quickly answered that I had, and that they were wonderful sermons: 'Infidelity' he replied, 'nothing else. A lady came to me yesterday with a volume of them, wanting me to read a passage which she said was very beautiful, but I soon showed her the error that was in it.' 'What do you think of Kingsley?' he continued. I said that Kingsley was a very eloquent writer, I did not much admire his sermons, at the same time mentioning some that were really worthy of Kingsley, a very original sermon on the Trinity, another on the 104th Psalm, and one of rare beauty on the Transfiguration. He is, I said a man that seems to know everything, and to know it well. He has taught some great lessons in his novels. 'A young puppy,' said the Vicar 'nothing but a young puppy. I knew him when he was a boy and his father before him.'

---

9 Maurice?'] Maurice?

With a Vicar who could not appreciate Frederick Robertson's Sermons, I could have no sympathy in the world. Long before the conversation ended, it was evident there was to be no engagement. He[10] asked me to take some luncheon. In the dining room I met his wife and his bevy of daughters. There was plenty on the table, but I had great difficulty in getting any of it. The young ladies were about to have a drive. They gabbled and helped each other, but paid no attention to me. Why should they? I was only an 'Arab' Preacher come to beg a month's employment from their Papa. The 'Evangelical' Clergy when they have the means, are generally as 'worldly' in spirit as those who have fewer pretensions. Charlotte Brontë records that the Principal of the School at which Jane Eyre was educated, used to address the daughters of the poor clergy on the sin of dress, accompanied by his own blooming girls, flounting [sic] in all the finery of fashion. The sin of dress, if there is such a sin, must be a very venial one, and there can be no sin in young ladies having a drive, but I thought a man who wished to convert working men from infidelity, should teach his family to bridge the distance between the grades of society, especially that between a Clergyman who has a benefice and one who has not.

The third application was also from the South West. As it resulted in an engagement I shall give the Incumbent a name,—the Rev. Peter[11] [10] Walham. He came to my lodgings in a cab late one Wednesday night. We had some pleasant conversation; I greatly liked the man, perhaps because he was such a contrast from Mr. Arlington. He gave a good account of his Parish, and said I should make a profitable exchange in leaving this densely populated part, to come and live in his semi-rural Parish in the West. He intimated that there were a few good families in the neighbourhood, humorously adding that there were also some unmarried ladies; but he would not raise my hopes in that way, as I might be disappointed. It was agreed that I should preach next Sunday morning. The day following, he wrote that he and his congregation were well pleased with my sermon, and that the Curacy was at my service; but as the salary was paid by the Pastoral Aid Society, he could not conclude an engagement till he had placed my name before their Committee. As however he wanted to leave Town immediately, he would

---

10   Jenkins Battersea (John Simon Jenkinson, St Mary's, Battersea)
11   William Garrat Walham Green (William Garratt, St John's, Walham Green, Fulham)

make a temporary engagement for four or five months. Having been in the service of the Pastoral Aid Society ever since I was ordained, I did not for a moment anticipate any difficulty in that quarter. Mr. Walham was unusually generous. Though about to leave me in sole charge of his Parish, he asked no references. It was quite enough that I was licensed in the Diocese, and that he and his congregation had heard me read and preach. I told Mr. Arlington that I had got another Curacy, and I would be glad to know when he would release me. He was not disposed to give me permission to leave for the next three months; but he said at last, that he would be satisfied if I found a substitute. With some trouble I found a substitute; but Mr. Arlington, of course, would not have him. However, I was free. Mr. Arlington was chagrined at my success in getting a Curacy so soon, and specially annoyed that no reference had been made to him. I did not know which to admire most, my own dexterity, or Mr. Walham's good-nature. Next Sunday I was in my new Parish. A man has a strange joy when he feels he has escaped from an enemy. Time will never efface the memory of those mellow autumn days when I took up my residence in Mr. Walham's Parish. Never was the sun so beautiful to my eyes, nor the blue sky above me so radiant of promise. But my hopes were short lived. The Pastoral Aid Society demanded a reference to my last Incumbent. I wrote to the Secretary, that there had been some unpleasantness between us, and it would be desirable not to refer to him. My letter was never even acknowledged. I called at the office and saw the lay secretary. I wished the reference to be made to the Incumbent with whom I had been four years in the North. The lay secretary, who spoke to me with an air of authority, answered, *that nothing would do but a reference to my last Incumbent*. Mr. Walham then wrote to Mr. Arlington. He gave me a testimonial which was on the whole satisfactory. He certified among other things that I was an 'able preacher and a diligent student;' but the cunning man knew the crotchets of this Society, and added not on his own authority, but that some one had said that my sermons were not thoroughly 'Evangelical.' This was enough, with such a Society, to settle the matter against me. Mr. Walham remonstrated with Mr. Arlington, that he must know what would be the effect of such words as [11] these, and asked him to write a testimonial without adding remarks that would defeat the object. Several letters passed; and at last Mr. Walham wrote to me from Brighton that the Society had confirmed my appointment to the Curacy. My opinion of Mr. Walham was now at its height. He had taken high ground, and fought my battle manfully. This cloud had been dispersed, and I began to work earnestly in the Parish. I was in sole charge and free to do almost whatever I wished. I began classes and lectures of different kinds; I visited the schools and the homes of the poor, while on Sundays the congregation visibly increased. All went on smooth for about two months, when, one morning, I had a letter from Mr. Walham, saying, that the Pastoral Aid Society had confirmed my appointment *only for three months!* and that he would give me three months' notice from the date of his letter. We have heard a great deal in England about Jesuits. I began now to think if there was not something in the very nature of things which made Jesuit morality a necessity in the very existence of the Clergy, and societies constituted by the Clergy. I had to leave this Curacy. I could not help myself. A thousand voices will ask, Where was the Bishop? Why did you not apply to him? I could not, I had never been licensed. It was a manœuvre of Mr. Walham's never to have licensed Curates. My predecessor had been there four years, and had never been licensed. I indeed wished that I could have told the matter to the Bishop. I often walked among the trees around Fulham Palace, and by the foss along the river's side, and thought it sad that I could not speak to him. As Bishop there was perhaps no case to demand his interference. If with a licence in my former Curacy he could only help the Incumbent to insult me, what could I expect here without a licence? I had no access to him in any way. He did not know me when I met him—he did not even know my name. One day he preached at our Church, and spoke kindly to me in the vestry—asked if I had been out of Town for a holiday in the summer, supposing I was the Curate that had been there for years. Mr. Walham took care not to inform him that I had just come, and that I was to be under the Episcopacy of the Pastoral Aid Society. As the time approached for me to leave, the parishioners became anxious. Three different gentlemen called to ask if I would sanction a Petition being got up and presented to Mr. Walham for me to remain. I refused to move in anything of that kind, and told them the matter did not rest with Mr. Walham, but with a Society which paid the Curate's salary. The Parishioners never knew where the Curate's salary came from. The Church was unendowed. Mr. Walham was a man of property, and for that reason had been appointed. It had always been supposed that he paid the salary himself. It was then agreed to raise the salary in the Parish, and dismiss the Society; but that was an amount of lay interference not to be tolerated. The Churchwardens were deputed to ask if Mr. Walham would receive a petition of the kind proposed. He not only peremptorily refused, but immediately accused me of raising a disturbance in his Parish. No charge could have been more unjust. I vindicated myself, and we remained apparently friends till the close of my time there.

In my efforts to find another Curacy, Mr. Walham allowed me to [12] refer to him. Indeed, I had no other to whom I could refer. I believe he wrote fairly. One of his letters I happened to see. It stated honestly that my ministrations had been highly appreciated by the Parishioners. It gave as the reason that my style of preaching was figurative, and that the sermons were full of illustrations. And it added as a further explanation, that the appreciation was in some measure due to 'Scotch predilections on the part of some.' In allusion to this, I said to him pleasantly one day, 'I did not know, Mr. Walham, that your Parishioners were troubled with "Scotch predilections".'[12] He made an apology, and said he would not put that in again.

In this Parish I had made some genuine[13] friends, whose friendship remains till this hour. Defeated in their efforts to retain me among them, they manifested anxiety to do what they could for me in any other way. Some, who had Indian connections, suggested that an Indian chaplaincy might be easily obtained. On inquiry, it was found that an Indian chaplaincy was not to be had; but it was said at the War Office that I might easily get an appointment in our own army. Military life had never presented any attractions for me; but I remembered that soldiers were men; and when it was mentioned that earnest Clergymen were much needed in the army, it appeared that I might have a field of usefulness even there. I applied to Lord Herbert, who referred me to the Chaplain-General. This gentleman offered to put my name on the list; but he added that it was quite useless, as I could not get an appointment during this century. He would be a long time in his grave before they came to the last man now on the list, for an army chaplaincy. Among other applications, I wrote to the Secretary of the Colonial and

---

12 predilections".'] predilections.'
13 The word is underlined, possibly in a different hand, but without elucidation.

Continental Society, asking employment on the Continent of Europe. I mentioned, perhaps inadvisedly, that I had thoroughly studied the Roman Catholic Church, both on its good and its bad sides; that I was well acquainted with German Theology, from the Wolfenbüttel Fragments to the latest development; that I knew Kant and all the ramifications from Kant. These I then thought, and still think, are the proper qualifications for an English Clergyman on the Continent; but I had an immediate answer as pompous (the writer is now an 'Evangelical' Bishop) as it was prompt, to the effect that there was no vacancy in their Society that would suit me. A well known Bishop has said in a book, called 'Dangers and Safeguards,' &c., 'A very general impression seems to prevail, that the very fact of a writer's showing any acquaintance with the Theology of Germany, may be taken as an *a priori* indication of unsoundness.'

About this time I had an unusual adventure in the country, in answer to an advertisement in the *Record*. I had a letter from a Clergyman in[14] _____shire; he wanted me to take charge of his Parish for three months. He asked me to come at once and see the place. I might put two sermons in my pocket, and preach on the Sunday. It was a rural village, ten miles from a Railway Station. After a long ride, on a cold January day, I found the Vicar's coachman waiting [13] with a conveyance to drive me from the Station to the Village. We got into a familiar conversation on the road, when he told me among other things that his master was 'the finest gentleman in England,' and 'the missus too was as nice a lady as ever breathed;' and after a little time he whispered, 'Let me give you a bit of advice—Sir, tomorrow morning you must not begin the service until the squire[15] comes in; some Clergymen as I bring this way go wrong there, and the squire does not like it.' 'A squire!' I said, 'you have a squire too, have you?' We arrived at the Vicarage in time for dinner. I found the Vicar and his wife such as the coachman had described them. We passed the evening in agreeable and profitable religious conversation. Next morning we went to Church. I had forgot all about the squire; but I believe he arrived a few seconds before I began to read 'When *the wicked man*,' &c. I had brought two sermons with me: one on the 'Rich man that pulled down his barns to build greater,' and another on the 'Barren Fig Tree.' I had selected these as most likely to suit a congregation of

---

14 Rutlandshire John Jones
15 George Finch

simple farmers, I did not know when I wrote them that *this* squire was in existence. The first was preached in the morning. I drew a picture, in the introduction, of a man who had managed his estates well—a man who was a pattern to all his neighbours for prudence and foresight in the business of life, but who was yet so imprudent that he neglected the life to come. Yea, he was not half so prudent as his neighbours gave him credit for. He had never made a will—he had never once supposed the possibility of his two loving sons disputing about the inheritance after he was gone. I had unwittingly drawn the portrait of the squire. There he sat in his pew, and his two sons beside him, just the careful prudent man I had described. As I went on, the farmers looked to me and then to the squire, to the squire and then to me, as much as to say 'That's the thing for him—Give him some more of it.' As we walked back to the Vicarage after Service, the old Vicar said, 'I fear the squire and his lady will not like your sermon, this morning. Lady Louisa knows the truth. They like the 'Gospel,' and not sermons against covetousness.' I said that Christ's own parables surely contained the Gospel. I had taught what the parable taught, nothing more nor less. The afternoon sermon pleased him better, as the intercession of the vine dresser gave me an opportunity to speak of the atonement and the mediation of Christ. Next morning I engaged to take the duty for three months. I wished to return to London immediately; so we had an early dinner, and completed all arrangements for my residence in the Parish. The carriage was at the door. The footman had my carpet bag in his hand. I had said 'Good bye' to the Vicar's lady. At this moment, the squire was announced. I will not be surprised, I said to myself if a change should come over the spirit of this dream. The vicar withdrew for about ten minutes; then he came into the dining room with a £5 note in his hand, trembling from head to foot. 'My dear friend,' he began, 'here is five pounds for you; the squire did not like your sermon yesterday morning. I am very sorry, very sorry; but I hope [14] you will get a better Parish than mine.' It happened that I preferred the five pounds to the engagement, so that my sorrow was greatly mitigated. I expressed the usual regrets, and departed with an ineffaceable remembrance of the squire and his lady, who liked the 'Gospel,' but hated sermons against covetousness.

It seemed to my friends that I was doomed to misfortunes. They could not understand how a preacher who had pleased them so well, was not accepted wherever he offered himself. They were sound Church of England people; but they began to think there must be something wrong in a Church, which made it difficult for such as me to get employment. They proposed building a Dissenting Chapel. There was an unusually good opening in the Parish; but I was not disposed to become a Dissenter. I had been brought up a Dissenter, and though I had no priestly notions about the divine institution of Bishops, or the sin of schism, yet I had taken to the Church of England advisedly with a full consciousness of its short comings. I suggested that before long, a new Church would be wanted in the Parish. The population was rapidly increasing. It would be better, I said, for us, as Churchmen, to apply to the Bishop, and see if any funds were available for such an object. Three gentlemen made an appointment with his lordship. Considerable sums had been promised, but the whole expense was greater than they could undertake at once. The Bishop however did not lose the opportunity; a site was secured, and there is now a probability of its being built with the aid of the 'Bishop of London's Fund.'[16]

Before this scheme of a new Church was matured I had left Mr. Walham, to take charge of a Parish[17] six miles north of London. We apparently maintained our friendship to the end. On the last day, he called with a petition for me to sign. It was the Clerical protest against the 'Essays and Reviews.' He asked me, to sign it as a matter of course—all the Clergy were doing it. He had not read the book, but that was no matter. He was surprised to find that I had read it six months since, before there was any noise about it. I looked over the names on the petition, and pushed it from me with a smile politely contemptuous, remarking that it was not at all in my way to sign papers of that kind, and Mr. Walham was confirmed in his suspicion, that my gospel was not the soundest in England. The charge which I had now undertaken came in answer to an advertisement in the *Record*. The Vicar wrote on a Friday for me to come and take his duty on the Sunday. Next day he wrote that his congregation were so well pleased with my sermons, that he wished I would take charge of his Parish for six months, expressing a regret that he had engaged a permanent Curate and could not therefore offer me his Curacy. I seemed to be on my feet once more. For three months

---

16   Fund.'] Fund'
17   Edmonton (probably All Saints', Edmonton)

everything went on well. The congregation was very large—every seat occupied. It was remarked that during my time there, the masculine side of humanity was better represented than it had ever been before. The Parish was a favorite residence of gentlemen whose business lay in the city. There were here, as might be expected, many [15] reading intelligent people. The 'Essay and Review' mania had reached its height. The book was in the hands of many. It was the subject of conversation in every party, and especially if either of the Curates was present. I expressed my judgment of it freely, taking each Essay by itself, showing what I approved and what I did not approve. I alluded to the subject in a sermon, taking a considerably more favourable view of the 'Essays,' than the Bishops had done. I was not aware that violent feeling existed on the subject. I had weighed the book calmly, and wished others to do the same. There was truth in it that we needed—truth, some of it unpalatable indeed, but it was necessary for truth's own sake that it should come out. My remarks brought me anonymous letters, expressing amazement and disappointment, that one whose ministrations they so much esteemed, should see any good in such a book. The Vicar too wrote that I must leave at once. The other Curate,[18] an ignorant man from St. Bees, next Sunday denounced the 'Essays and Reviews' as the most atrociously infidel book that had ever been published. The Vicar came home, and he preached 'Essays and Reviews' till every servant girl in the Parish was reading 'Essays and Reviews.' The Curate of course had never read the book, and the Vicar made a vow he never would read it; but if his congregation wanted to go to hell, that, he said, was the book for them to read. It gave me great pain that I had been in any sense the cause of all this raving. I felt I had made a mistake, but it was done in innocence. I never could realize that religious people could be angry about a religious inquiry; least of all that Clergymen, the science of whose profession is theology, should be angry about theological Essays, displaying such ability and learning, as ought to make the Church glad that such gifts are still consecrated to her service.

I had not a licence in this Parish, and for the same reason as before, I could not appeal to the Bishop. I was again afloat in search of a Curacy. Mounting my Rosinante (the *Record*), I set out in quest of

---

18   John Goodwin

new adventures. My first application was from a Clergyman[19] in the neighbourhood of Oxford Street West. I had an interview with him, and after some preliminary conversation, he asked, 'What do you think of Mr. Maurice?' I looked at him with eyes that said 'You impertinent vagabond,' and answered that 'I knew nothing against Mr. Maurice.' 'But I mean, what do you think of his doctrines?' 'Which?' I said. 'Well, any of them.—He has written a book against Mr. Mansel.' I went on to say that on that subject, Mr. Maurice was certainly in the right. Mr. Mansel's doctrine makes religion impossible. Besides, he does not prove his own thesis. The Lectures are full of learning, much of the reasoning is sound, until he comes to the point he undertakes to establish. There he fails signally. It is true we cannot comprehend the Infinite, but it does not therefore follow that we cannot know God, or that justice with God can be different from justice with men. I further compared Mr. Mansel's Lectures to Bishop Warburton's 'Divine Legation,' an immense display of reading and a clear intellect at work, but breaking down at the very point where [16] strength was most required. I scarcely knew if this pleased him or confounded him. He went on to ask what I thought of Mr. Maurice's view of the Atonement. I said I was not quite sure what it was. I had to complain of Mr. Maurice as an obscure writer; but if he did not differ from Robertson or Kingsley on that subject, I would agree with him. At the mention of Kingsley, the Incumbent was a little agitated, and hastily seizing a volume of his sermons from a book shelf, read a passage about the popular view of the Atonement, denouncing it as a gross misrepresentation. I admitted that the picture was overdrawn. In the popular theology there was a great deal of phraseology which seemed to represent that the Father had to be appeased by the Son, but it was merely in the phraseology, which we should remember was figurative as language taken from things human and applied to things divine must be. If some of the expressions used by St. Paul were to be pressed literally, he might be accused of misrepresenting the Father. I did not believe that such expressions as price, propitiation, and penalty were used by orthodox divines in that literal sense, which Mr Kingsley seemed to suppose. It might be with some very extreme men, but not with all,—not even generally. I quoted as an instance Dr. Guthrie, who

---

19 Steventon Paddington (Edwin Henry Steventon, All Saints' Church, Norfolk Square, Paddington)

distinctly says that 'God did not love us because Christ died for us, but that Christ died for us because God loved us. The tree of Calvary had its roots in the love of God.' I believe Kingsley was himself right on the Atonement, but not right in his estimate of other people's views of it. The Incumbent then went on to 'Essays and Reviews,' which he seemed to have read; but it was evident from the beginning that we were not to make any engagement.

I had another application[20] from the South East. The letter carried the motto *Timere vel mutare sperno*. I had an interview, and was asked to read Prayers next Sunday. As I had not left my other Parish I could not do this without giving up my emolument for the Parish I was now in; so it was agreed that I should have two guineas for my work. If my testimonials were found satisfactory I was to engage for three months. Before Sunday came I had another letter, saying that my referees had been written to, and I would not be wanted on Sunday. I wrote back that as I had made a *bona fide* engagement, and had given up another in consequence, I must therefore insist on coming. At the end of my letter I wrote in large characters *Timere vel mutare sperno*. I suspect that Mr. Walham informed him of my refusing to sign the petition. His morning sermon seemed specially written for my benefit. The subject was the teaching of the Holy Spirit. The preacher maintained that the Spirit never taught, except through the Bible. We had just prayed in the Communion that our hearts might be cleansed through the inspiration of that Spirit, and now we were taught that inspiration was confined to a printed book. Why this difference between the Pulpit and the Communion? The book itself gives no authority for this bibliolatry. I had been so used to hear nonsense from the Pulpit, that I had ceased to be angry at anything I heard there, yet I wished we had enjoyed the freedom of a Jewish Synagogue, in the old time, that I might [17] have cried out in the words of Theodore Parker, '*My Brother Men, God is not dead*.' But this would have been a mistake, for the congregation only consisted of women with a sprinkling of feminine men.

As the three months' engagement was to depend on my testimonials, and I knew that Mr. Walham had done me justice until I refused to sign the 'Essay and Review' protest, I trusted him still, and reckoning

---

20   Snape Old Kent Road (Alfred William Snape, St Mary Magdalen, Old Kent Road, Bermondsey)

that this engagement was certain, I resigned my other Parish at once, where I could have stayed a week or two longer; and in consequence was thrown out of employment altogether. Three months were spent in advertising, corresponding, having interviews, and preaching trial sermons. I generally advertised in the *Record* twice a week, and had about a dozen answers to each advertisement. The working of the Curate system was revealed to me during these three months as I hope it never was to another before me, and I trust for the sake of the Church of England, it will never be so revealed in the experience of another after me. In most cases the Curacies were filled up before a second letter was written; and often, after long correspondence, some unexpected friend had turned up to take the Curacy. I was often in doubt if the men really wanted Curates, or if they were only answering my letters for the sake of increasing the Post-office revenue. One man[21] sent for me in great haste, wishing his duty taken at once. I found him in his school room holding a prayer meeting, at the end of which I presented myself. He happened to be a relation of Mr. Walham's, but they were not on terms of friendship, and when I mentioned the name it was enough. Another had me to preach—kept me a week in suspense, and then said he had changed his mind as to having a Curate at all. A third[22] said, he did not understand my sermon on the craving of the soul for God, and pronounced it 'lacking in the fulness of Evangelical truth.' Many of the letters were great curiosities. One man wished 'A Curate willing to spend and be spent for Christ, for there was no salary.' Another who only gave the letters H. L.,[23] to be left at a Publisher's in Paternoster Row, asked twelve questions, numbered by so many figures; besides the usual interrogations as to my age, university, if my blessedness was single or double, I was to certify whether or not I was 'Anti-Puseyite, Anti-Rationalist, and a Teetotaler.' I was to hear again if my answers were satisfactory. The letter ended '*Yours truly in Jesus, H.L.*' I answered 'X.Y. is of opinion that H.L. is half-cracked, and would recommend him if he is *in Jesus*, to walk in the light and not in the darkness.' In the course of my long experience in Curacy

---

21 Garrat Little Queen Street (Samuel Garratt, Trinity Church, St Giles-in-the-Fields)
22 Krus St. Judes, Lambeth or Southwark (Francis Cruse, St Jude's, Saint George's Road, Southwark)
23 Robinson Chelsea (William Woolhouse Robinson, Christ Church, Chelsea)

hunting, I met H.L.[24] again, and with his true name. It happened that a member of Mr. Walham's congregation, whom I never knew, but who had been one of my devoted disciples, migrated to H.L.'s parish. She gave him such an account of my 'gifts and graces' as a gospel preacher, that H.L. was persuaded he had at last discovered the man he had been long seeking. He wrote to me, but I had just entered on a Curacy, and could not accept his offer. He wished, however, as he had heard so much about me, that I would come and preach for him. I gratified him thus far, and in return he [18] volunteered a criticism on my sermon. The doctrine was all sound, but I had omitted to mention the Holy Spirit until near the end. Now, Charles Simeon had taught him at Cambridge forty years ago that a sermon should consist of an exordium, then a prayer to the Holy Spirit, three heads, and an application.

During the first few weeks of my advertising, I was introduced to the Rector[25] of a large Parish, not far from London Bridge. This Rector was a kind of an Ishmael among the Clergy. I found him a somewhat vehement, but withal a clear headed sincere man. He often invited me to his house, and we had long conversations on all subjects relating to theology. Starting as I had done from Arminian ground, he understood me better than any of the Clergy I had met in London. We differed entirely in our judgment of certain writers and certain books, but he considered that my own views were sound, and offered me a Curacy under him. The salary of this Curacy was also paid by the 'Pastoral Aid.' I had taken the precaution to call at the office of this society; to know if they had really rejected me; and the Secretary said that they would confirm my appointment to one of their Curacies, if Mr. Walham gave a satisfactory testimonial. As I had that in my possession, I trusted the Secretary, and the Society. My name was placed before the Committee. I was objected to because I was reported to have said to some one in Mr. Walham's Parish, that the world was not made in six days *out of nothing*. The Rector told them bluntly that they were a set of fools to object to any man in the present day because of his mode of interpreting the first chapter of Genesis. Every child knew the facts which geology had revealed concerning the making of the world. The case was deferred for a week, and I believe would have been passed, but meantime I had

---

24 H.L.] H.L
25 Hugh Allen (Hugh Allen, St George the Martyr, Southwark)

visited the Parish of the 'Essay and Review' mania, and stayed a night with the Curate to whom I mentioned in the most friendly and confiding way, what was pending in Fleet Street. He told the Vicar; and between them they sent a dispatch to the Society that I was one of the rising infidels, who were to be crushed by every possible means.

About this time I chanced to call one day with a friend on the Principal[26] of an important 'Evangelical' Institution. My friend had been studying some of the Eastern Languages, and their conversation turned on this subject. The Principal, whom I had never seen before, addressing himself to me, asked if I too was a linguist. I said I had not yet had time to give much attention to *oriental* literature; but that I had lately been greatly interested in the study of the Hindu Philosophies. From this we quickly passed to Philosophy in general, and the Principal asked what I thought of Mr. Mansel. I answered that I thought very highly of Mr. Mansel, but I did not agree with the subject of his Bampton Lectures, for we certainly could know God. 'Only through the book,' said the Principal. 'God has revealed Himself only in the book.' 'The revelation in the book,' I answered, supposes in man the capacity which Mr. Mansel denies. The highest revelation of God is in the spirit of a man—'The inspiration of the Almighty gives him understanding.' 'But,' said the Principal, 'the heathen did not [19] know God. St. Paul condemns Greek Philosophy as insufficient for this knowledge.' I said that the heathen had this knowledge, and St. Paul testifies that 'When they *knew* God they glorified Him not as God.' We were here in danger of confounding *knowing* with *comprehending*, and to clear up this ground I went on to say that in the sense of comprehending we could not know God. The Infinite must ever be beyond us—in the words of Fichte, 'After thousands upon thousands of spirit lives, we shall know Him as little as we now do in this house of clay.' In this sense, God is as much unknown to us as to the old Greeks. We may still inscribe on our temples and our altars, 'To the unknown God!' At these words the Principal started from his seat, his form agitated with passion, he exclaimed, 'You are an Atheist! and I order you at once to leave these premises, that they be not polluted by your presence.' I wished him to remember that we were Christian Ministers, and that we ought, above all things, to keep our tempers. I

---

26 Thomas Green Church Missionary College Islington

wished to show him in what sense we could know God; and if I could have got an opportunity, I would also have shown, that as a follower of Mr. Mansel, he was pledged to the words for which he had called me an Atheist.

This conversation, combined with what had taken place at the Pastoral Aid Society, brought me into great mental trouble. I asked myself if I was really honest in advertising in the *Record*, as Evangelical. I re-examined the leading doctrines of Christianity as set forth in our standards, and I was convinced that I had departed from none of them. I had rejected many religious phrases which were continually in the lips of 'Evangelical' preachers, and I did not speak about inspiration as they did. But the last was no new thing with me. I had rejected the popular view of inspiration as untenable by any educated man, as soon as I knew the history of the formation of the Canon of Scripture. I concluded, however, that the word 'Evangelical' had come to be used conventionally in an improper sense, and I therefore ceased to use it in that sense.

As most of the Curacies that came through the *Record* were under the Pastoral Aid Society, I was advised to try the *Guardian*, and also the Curates' Registry at Whitehall. It is scarcely possible, one would think, for a Clergyman to be in a more humiliating position than that of advertising, or hanging on at a Registry Office for employment. I never forget the feeling of degradation that came over me when I was first reduced to these expedients. It appears, however, that as yet the Bishops have been able to devise nothing better for Curates and Curacies than a Registry Office. This at Whitehall boasts the sanction of Canterbury, York, London, &c. No complaint can be made against this institution in itself, but it is necessarily subject to all the evils of every Registry Office. The Incumbents who are always in want of Curates, because they do not know how to use them, have their names there from year to year, and are continually supplied with fresh Curates. The Curates who fall into the hands of these men in the natural order of things lose caste with the Bishop and the beneficed Clergy. They get the reputation of dangerous men. In [20] most instances the Curacies entered here are filled up before the entry is a week old. One Incumbent,[27] whose name I took from this Registry, refused to see me, and sent an angry message that he

---

27 Courtney St. James Pentonville An Irishman (Anthony Lefroy Courtenay, DD, St James, Pentonville)

had ordered the Secretary to take his name off these books two months ago. This is just possibly true, but generally Incumbents do not seem to trouble themselves about informing the Secretary that they have got what they wanted. In the *Guardian*, I was introduced to an entirely new class of men. I had hitherto conscientiously avoided this class, as I had always looked on High Churchmen as a generation of simpletons. They had built Churches and kept them clean. They had abolished square pews in prominent places for the rich, and free benches in obscure corners for the poor. This exhausted the catalogue of their merits. My first *Guardian Advertisement* brought me 36 answers. The variety was infinite, but most of them had small salaries. High Church has no 'Pastoral Aid' to raise the salary to the orthodox sum of £100 per annum. The worshippers of the Bible have been more zealous, than the worshippers of the Prayer Book. One man offered the charge of his Parish and Rectory, with the use of the domestics, on the condition that I boarded them. I was to take his duty and pay his household out of my private income. Another offered the use of an unfurnished room, a garden, and a cow. Some of them were very genial, reminding you of the jovial times the Clergy had in the last century, when such as *Sterne* could retire to *one* of his favourite livings to play his fiddle, and finish *Tristram Shandy*. One offered 'good shooting, capital boating, and bathing.' He added that he wanted a man of a good moral character, as the last Curate had disgraced the parish. With one I entered into correspondence, and was finally refused, because I had not graduated at an English University. This indeed was the case with some of the most desirable Curacies that turned up. I felt this too as a hardship, it was not fair that I should be classed either with the 'literates,' or the 'illiterates,' of the Church. I was not an ignorant man, and I knew I was not. I had sat at the feet of Sir David Brewster, I had learned Metaphysics from Ferrier, and other sciences from other great doctors eminent in their day. It was too bad that I should be classed with men from the Clerical Colleges—institutions whose very existence is one of the greatest scandals of the Church. I had an interview with one Incumbent[28] who would have nothing but a University man for his Curate. He was an M.A. of Cambridge. It was about the time of the Prince of Wales' marriage. He was very wroth that it should be permitted in

---

28   Henry Kelly Christs Church (Henry Plimley Kelly, Christ Church, Hoxton)

Lent. I asked if he knew the custom of the Catholic Church before the Reformation as to marriages in Lent. 'Reformation,' he said, 'was there *any Lent before the Reformation*?' I was thankful for once that I was not an M.A. of Cambridge.

One *Guardian* application was from a High Church Rector[29] in a fashionable part of London. He asked that I might preach on trial, as the congregation paid and selected the curate. 'High Churchism for ever.' I said, 'if this is to be the practice.' It was some miles from my lodgings, but I was there in time on Sunday morning. The [21] Church was one of the finest in London, the congregation perhaps one of the wealthiest. The Rector was absent. I did my best; but when I had finished there was no guinea, no dinner, not even a glass of wine. The Rector's wife passed through the vestry, and bowed as she passed. Outside, the gay congregation rolled away in their carriages. It began to rain, and like Cowper's nightingale,

> 'That all day long
> Had cheered the village with its song,'

I began to feel 'the keen demands of appetite.' A Curate friend, also in misfortune, was with me. We journeyed on through the wet and remembered what 'David did, and they that were with him, when he was an hungred, how he entered into the temple and did eat the shew bread, which was not lawful for him to eat.' We, having concealed the badges of our profession, went into a temple of another kind, and there did eat such things as could be obtained; this we did in the company of some cabmen and omnibus drivers, for no other room was available. I never heard from the Rector again. Long after I was told, on good authority, the whole affair was a swindle, no Curate was wanted. The Rector for certain reasons had to be out of the way, and by this device he got his duty taken without expense, for two months. This Rector once preached a charity sermon at a Church where I was taking duty, in a poor neighbourhood, about a mile and a-half from his own parish. His subject was the luxuriousness of the Greeks to whom the Apostles preached. The inhabitants of Pergamos he described as having been very luxurious. In his youth he might have been eloquent, but his speech

---

29   Thomas Jackson Stoke Newington

was now impeded by the amount of adipose tissue that had collected in the vicinity of the submaxillary, and the *os hyoides*. Like a swimming pig about to commit involuntary suicide he kept screaming out '*Lux-u-rious* inhabitants of Pergamos.' About £5 was collected from these very poor people. Next day an innkeeper presented the Churchwardens with an account for 10s. 6d.—the fly fare for conveying the obese Rector from his Rectory and back to it again.

I will conclude my curacy hunting adventures with one that got into the newspapers at the time and which I have omitted in its proper place. It was in the days of my *Record* advertisements. I had given the address, 'A.B. to be left at the *Record* Office.' One evening, about a week after it appeared, I was sitting in a friend's house in Lambeth. I had left orders at my lodgings that the letters were to be sent to me. The Curate who accompanied me in my last adventure was engaged at a chess table. I had more congenial employment in discoursing with an old lady, a follower of Edward Irving, on unfulfilled prophecy. A letter was put into my hand which ran thus:—'Mr._____, Abbey Road, St. John's Wood, wishes to see A.B. at five o'clock this evening.' It was now past seven. I told my chess friend that I had had an answer to my advertisement and must leave immediately. He put aside his 'kings' and 'bishops.' I postponed the discussion of Ezekiel's [22] 'wheels' and Daniel's 'little horn.' We mounted an omnibus and passed over Westminster Bridge towards Regent Street, into Edgware Road, thence to St. John's Wood. I sent in my card, and was shown into a sitting room. A gentleman entered, to whom I rose and bowed. He was followed by his wife, a grave lady, to whom I also bowed with all the politeness I am possessed of. They seated themselves, so did I. The gentleman taking his pen in hand began his interrogations. 'Are you an Englishman?' he said. 'No,'[30] I answered, telling him to what country I did belong. The lady muttered, 'My dear it is of no use.' 'No, it is not, but let us ask a question or two.' 'Where were you last?' 'In the parish of E_____,' I replied readily. The lady again mysteriously interposed, 'My dear, it is of no use, he does not know his place.' Rather perplexed, and my sensitiveness a little wounded, I said, 'I beg your pardon, but I do not understand you.' 'Why,' said the lady, 'you don't know your place as a servant, you sit down without being asked.'

---

30 'No,'] 'No,'

The tide of my indignation was swelling fast, I thought of all the insults I had of late received, but this seemed to crown them all. During the two months I had been in search of a Curacy I had got a good many knocks on the head from unfeeling and fickle Incumbents that wanted Curates, but now I thought surely I have come to the last step of degradation, anything after this. And then these Incumbents' wives! What mischief do they not make! If this gentleman is the Rector of a parish, evidently his wife is the Di-Rector. Shall not I as a Curate protest against this monstrous government of women? Shall I not assert the equality of all members of the priesthood? Whilst these thoughts were overwhelming my mind, taking up the lady's word servant,' I exclaimed almost with vehemence, servant! servant! I am a clergyman.' 'Clergyman,' cried the lady, 'clergyman!' said the gentleman. 'There must be a mistake somewhere. Pray sir, what did you advertise for?' 'For employment in the duties of my profession,' I replied. 'Oh!' he rejoined, 'my letter was in answer to a footman's advertisement, a thorough indoor servant.' Here it is in the *Record*. 'Address A.B.' Suddenly the lady's gravity and the gentleman's perplexity, and the floods of my wrath all yielded and gave place to mutual apologies, not unmingled with merriment at the odd mistake that had brought us together.

After long toil and great waste of money I obtained a Curacy. It was in the Parish[31] adjoining Mr. Arlington's. The Incumbent took me without references, because he knew that I had been in the next parish. But a new difficulty arose, I had none to sign my testimonials for a licence. I applied to Mr. Walham and the Vicar of the old Parish out of which Mr. Walham's was originally formed. This Vicar[32] was a sensible man and had always been friendly to me. He was ready to sign if Mr. Walham signed, but Mr. Walham returned the testimonials saying that the Bishop would require some account of me for the nine months I had been in London before I came to him. That surely was not his business. I sent his letter to the Bishop, and his lordship generously gave me a licence without troubling any of them. My [23] new Parish had great disadvantages. At one time the Church had been in the hands of an extreme High Churchman, and was made a kind of rendezvous for the High Church people in the surrounding Parishes. The ceremonies

---

31 Christ Church Hoxton
32 Baker Fulham (Robert George Baker, All Saints, Fulham)

which attracted these people, drove away all the parishioners, who took their revenge by building a Wesleyan, and an Independent Chapel in the vicinity of the Church. That Incumbent was removed, and all the fantastical High Church people left with him, so that the new Incumbent had no congregation. The first morning I preached, we had not thirty people. After a time we got a tolerable evening congregation, but the difficulties in this parish were too many and too great for a Curate to overcome. One of these was the prejudice created by the former Incumbent. The boys watched at the church doors and cried, even after *me*, 'Pusey, Pusey, Pusey!' and mewed like cats and kittens. I began my work with a course of lectures to working men; they were well attended, and at the first lecture I announced that I was to hold two Bible lectures every week, inviting the people to come. I had not been many minutes in my lodgings when the Churchwarden came to prohibit the lectures being held in that school room. I told him, as Churchwarden, he had nothing to do with the school. It did not matter, he would prohibit the lectures. The Incumbent would not fight for me, and so I had to yield. I remained in this Parish two years, and of my own account left it to take another.

It was some time in September 1863, when I entered on my duties as Curate of one of the City[33] churches. The parishioners were 'Jews, Infidels, Turks, Heretics,' and other Dissenters. Those who attended the Church were a few shopkeepers and their families. Those who were of the Church, but did not attend it, were a multitude of paupers. As an old City parish it had immense charities, and as it consisted of many small tradesmen, it abounded in men eager for public offices. I took an inventory of the Parish, and drew up my plans for work. A Curate who has plans generally requires considerable tact to persuade his Incumbent to sanction them. I thought I could succeed, and began warily by proposing lectures for the working men. It was objected, that there were no working men in the Parish except day labourers. There was besides a more serious objection, no school room was available. We had five schools in the Parish, but it happened that they were managed by committees of shopkeepers, who excluded the Incumbent, or admitted him only as one of themselves. I saw at once that my work

---

33 St Botolphs Aldgate

here was to be limited to visiting the sick and relieving the poor. For the last I had but small means, as these shopkeepers had seized on the management of all the Parish charities. After I had been there about nine months, I wrote to the Bishop asking Missionary employment. I began to be sad when I thought of my life passing away—so much to be done—so much that I could do—and no prospect of realizing the object for which I had come to London. I was certain the Bishop could put me in the way of getting the care of one or two streets in some wretched locality, where I could work without the interference of any paltry Incumbent. The Bishop's Chaplain[34] [24] referred me to the Secretaries of two societies. One of them had nothing to give. With the other I had a long correspondence. Before offering my services to this society, I wished distinctly to understand their work. I had believed that it consisted chiefly in street preaching. I did not object to preach in the streets, but I had not cultivated the style of preaching generally practised by street missionaries, and was disposed not to press my application. The Secretary however informed me, that after this the Society's agents would be settled in parishes and not migratory as they had been before, and on this information my application was renewed. I had to preach a sermon in the East End, by way of trial. It was a dark night in the beginning of October. The wind was high and the weather cold, but a considerable number of men gathered in the light of a gin palace window and listened attentively while I discoursed of the joys of religion. Next day the Secretary[35] informed me that the members of the Subcommittee were of opinion that my voice was not strong enough for preaching out of doors. It was also intimated that what I had said, though very excellent in itself, and very suitable in a church, was not exactly what they wanted for a street audience. About this time the Ecclesiastical Commissioners cut off the half of our Parish to form a new District. In consequence of this, the Incumbent did not require me any longer, and wished me to look out for something else before the expiration of six months. A fortnight after, he reduced the six to three. This mattered nothing, so long as I had him to refer to as last Incumbent, ready, and even anxious, to help me in getting another charge. The Bishop was in Scotland, and

---

34   Hon. Freemantle (William H. Fremantle, Chaplain to the Bishop of London)
35   Joseph Bardsley (Joseph Bardsley, Secretary of the London Diocesan Home Mission)

I was anxiously waiting his return, to let him know the result of my application to the two societies. Meanwhile an event occurred which changed all our relations. During these years I had been in London, as I could not do all I wished, either in Preaching or in Parish work, I did not lose the advantages which London offers in the way of books and lectures. As a Clergyman coming continually in contact with the poor, the sick, the depraved; and as a student of theology, seeing that nearly all theological questions impinged on the question of nature, I felt it my duty to include among my studies, anatomy and physiology. I attended Lectures at St. Bartholomew's Hospital, and cultivated the acquaintance of all the medical men in our Parish. I kept these studies as secret as I could, till a Churchwarden,[36] one of the officious small tradesmen of the parish dragged them to light. A coroner's jury, consisting of sixteen of these small shopkeepers, condemned my studies, and brought down on themselves and the whole of the Parish authorities, the ridicule of the public press, including the sarcasms of *Punch*.[37] No sensible person could find any fault with anything I had done, but the Incumbent inhibited me from acting as Curate of the Parish. I appealed to the Bishop for protection. I had heard it mentioned as one of the Bishop of London's failings, that he never took the side of a Curate, but I did not believe it. His lordship judged the matter with considerable impartiality. He had no power to overrule the Incumbent's inhibition, but he exacted from the In-[25]cumbent[38] a promise that he would be my referee as heretofore, and that he would say nothing of any cause of difference between us, unless *asked*, and then he was to refer to me for an explanation. The Incumbent took the first opportunity of breaking the promise. *Unasked*, he alluded mysteriously to something which I would explain. I was once more helpless, and but for the voluntary service of a neighbouring Rector, I would have had difficulty in getting a Curacy either in London or any other place. The decision in Bishop Colenso's

---

36 David King
37 1864 'Curates made scarce' 'Times' leader. The Anatomist Curate' &c. (The first reference is possibly a misremembering of the title of the *Punch* article, entitled 'Clergymen Made Scarce', of 17 December 1864, p. 25. The second may refer to any of several leaders in *The Times* in 1864, in which the supply and situation of curates are discussed. The reference to The Anatomist Curate probably relates to the *Spectator* article of 19 November 1864, pp. 1324f.; see 14.3, p. 181.)
38 James Roberton (James Matthew Roberton, St. Botolph's without Aldgate)

case has demonstrated to the world that the Church of England is an ecclesiastical body without Church Government. The case of every Curate in the kingdom would prove the same thing. Every rightminded man will rejoice that the state has protected Bishop Colenso from the arbitrary persecution of the Metropolitan of the Cape; but that state which shields Bishops and Incumbents, leaves Curates unprotected. The law only enables the Incumbent to kick the Curate, and gives the Bishop the power to help the Incumbent to do it more effectually.

I made but one effort more to obtain a Curacy in London. It reached the stage of an interview, and is too good to be omitted. The Clergyman was an 'Evangelical' Rector of the purest species. 'What are your views?' he asked almost as soon as I was seated. My answer was, 'I agree with the Bishop of London.' '*Bishop of London!* Have you read his address at the Philosophical Institution in Edinburgh?' 'Yes,' I said; 'and it is the best thing the Bishop of London has written.' 'I don't understand it,' rejoined the Rector. 'I don't know what the Bishop means. What have we got to do with science? When I was ordained, the Bishops were content to know the road to heaven. *Jesus Christ knew nothing about Science.*' The naiveness of the last sentence was really charming. I told the Rector that M. Renan had said the same thing, and that Jesus' idea of the kingdoms of this world and the glory of them was derived from some insipid *Rue de Rivoli*, built by the Romans in Cæsarea Philippi. The Rector said he had never read Renan, but he was delighted to hear that he had been quite as original as the eloquent Frenchman.

After this eventful experience—this battling simply to be allowed 'to spend and be spent for Christ,' I speak seriously, many will ask if I am not sick of the Church, and of religion, too? Most men would have renounced both, I have renounced neither. My words, like those of the Abbé Lamennais are still *Les paroles d'un Croyant*. Frederick Robertson marks it as one of the characteristics of Jesus that He never despaired of humanity, though no man suffered more than He from the baseness and the hypocrisy of men. And Mr. Renan has a grand thought. He supposes that when Jesus came to Calvary, and His great soul was clouded with sorrow, a half repentant feeling may have crossed His mind that He was suffering too much for such a worthless race. Such a feeling may indeed have crossed the mind of Jesus, but it could only have been a momentary temptation. The true spirit has within it a perennial spring of faith. We that do live, live by faith. [26] We walk by faith. In faith we follow the *'Noble Initiateur.'* In the beginning I likened myself to the priest of Isis, but I checked the comparison. I again check it in the end. Apuleius wrote a fable, I have written the truth. Apuleius was at last delivered from his ass-hood; my curate-hood remains.

I am, my Lord,

Your Lordship's obedient Servant,

A PRESBYTER.

POSTSCRIPT.

There is no special reason why this Postscript should be addressed to the Bishop of London. The events it records took place in another diocese. The facts, however, concern the whole Church and therefore every Bishop in the Church. What concerns all Bishops must be of special interest to the Bishop of the Metropolis.

Notwithstanding the apparent egotism of this letter, nothing but a deep sense of duty would ever have allowed the writer to publish it, and nothing but the same sense impels him to write again. We do not make all the circumstances of our lives; most of them are made for us. It is our business to use them as best we can, so to serve our day and generation, that when the night cometh, wherein no man can work, we may lay our heads down to sleep with the peaceful assurance that we have not lived in vain.

It is difficult, indeed, to determine how far we are the children of destiny, and how far our own character and acts create the circumstances of our lives. We seem carried on to do certain things by an impulse apparently irresistible, and when they are done we wonder what end they can serve. And yet how often after years have passed away do we see the necessity that these things should have been done, yea that they *should have been done by us*, and that they were worth our doing even if we had spent ourselves in the performance of them. There is a Wisdom teaching and guiding us all, shaping our ends, and making us the servants of a Divine Will in adversity as well as in prosperity.

After immortalizing the Churchwarden and the Coroner's Jury of the City Parish, I was compelled for a time to leave London. It is necessary always that a Curate be a man *of whom not much can be said*. It is with Curates as it is with young ladies, the more *unknowing* they are the more likely it is that some Rector will give them employment. I again had recourse to that valuable periodical the *Record*, and I should say here that it is the best medium for Curates and Incumbents to make known their wants. It is cheaper than the *Guardian* and the people in the office are vastly more civil.

Before leaving London I had difficulty in deciding between two Incumbents, both of whom were anxious to secure my services. A man's destiny seems to hang on a very slender thread. Both these Incumbents were in urgent want of temporary assistance, and both concluded an engagement by the same post. I chose the one with whom I was first in correspondence. How different the course of events had I decided on [27] the other! In December 1864, I was in the wolds[39] of Lincolnshire. I saw in the farmers' houses newspapers in which were copied *Punch's* articles concerning the Rev. _____ who had been dismissed his curacy for studying anatomy. Knowing the public prejudice against dealing in bones, and being unwilling that these simple people should know why I was temporarily banished from London, I borrowed all the papers with the intention of never returning them. There was nothing remarkable in this Parish, except that the people were nearly all Methodists. The population was very small. The church stood much in need of repair. Religion seemed to have left the old fabric and taken up with the chapel. I do not know if the original chalice and patten were lost, but I had to administer the sacramental bread from a cheese plate of very ordinary earthenware. Here I enjoyed myself on a farm for six weeks, among the ducks, the geese, and the sparrows. Here I meditated on the past, and formed plans for the future, and here I wrote the letter of which I now publish a second edition.

I again advertised, and again came in contact with two Incumbents, not knowing which of the two to choose. One was an 'Evangelical.' He wrote so smoothly; his letters were so full of religion, of prayers and blessings, that much as I distrusted men who put religion in their letters,

---

39   Swallow near Caster (Caistor)

I thought he was sincere, and decided for him. Some men have such a gift of using religious phrases, that they can deceive the very *elect*. After the engagement was about concluded, he wished me to meet him in London. A journey from the wolds of Lincolnshire and back again, implied an expenditure not only of time, but of about £2 10s. in money. Now, the most 'Evangelical' being in the world[40] must know that £2 10s. is a very large sum for a man who lives on £100 a year, and that before expending the £2 10s., he will naturally wish to be sure that for the next year he is to realise the £l00. I wished to know who was to bear the expense of my coming to London? This settled the business suddenly. The Incumbent had recourse to the usual excuse—the very night he arrived in London, he had met an old friend who was willing to take his curacy.

The other application came through the *Guardian*. The letter was short; it simply said that a clergyman was wanted, to take the duty for a few Sundays in the Parish Church of _____, the remuneration £1 1s a week, and live in the house with Mr. and Mrs. _____. The letter seemed written by a female hand. There was no Christian name, only the initials, so that I was in doubt about prefixing *Reverend*.

It was some days before I had a letter again, but one came by the same post which brought the final letter from the other correspondent. The scope of it was that the writer, who turned out to be the Curate, was leaving for another curacy, and must find some one to take his place for the next six weeks. If I chose I might enter at once on the duty. My new parish I shall call the parish of Ousebank.[41] The Vicar, with the greatest respect for his memory, for he has now 'crossed that bourne whence no traveller returns,' I shall call the Rev. Mr. Coldstream.[42] I left the wolds about four o'clock in the morning, and arrived at Ousebank about five in the evening. During this long journey I filled my imagination with conjectures about my new parish. What like is it? What kind of people are the parishioners? What new friends shall I make? How shall I get on with the Vicar? What sort of a man is he? These and many such questions were asked by the way. I was coming to this Parish with an accumulation of experiences. I knew all the rocks on which I had

---

40   in the world] in world
41   St. Ives Hunts.
42   Yate Fosbroke

split before. I resolved to say but little, and when I did speak to speak to some purpose. I was to hold my mouth, as it were, with a bridle. I resolved to be familiar with only a very few people, if with any; to avoid controversy, to show no acquaintance with the [28] writings of heretics, especially the Rationalists, to let no one know that I knew more than other people; but to do my work as a clergyman, both in the pulpit and in visiting the people, humbly, reverently, and honestly, not as seeking the praise of man, but the approbation of a good conscience, and the joy of doing good.

At the hour already mentioned, an omnibus landed me at the Vicarage of Ousebank. The Vicar and his lady gave me a hearty welcome. Before many minutes I was quite at home with them. I was a stranger indeed, but one or two clergymen in London had written high testimonials. 'Very flattering indeed,' said Mr. Coldstream, 'very flattering.' I remembered what Erasmus once said 'You have many ignorant theologians now-a-days, but the like of me you do not meet in the course of ages.' I remembered, too, that Sleiden boasted 'there was more learning in one hair of his head than in all the Universities;' and I recalled the story of Richard Bentley when Master of Trinity. Some one told him of the prodigious learning of Mr. Walse. 'Yes,' said Bentley, 'a very learned man, he will be the most learned man in England *when I am dead!*' I cannot deny that at the time I had the spirit of these great men, but I kept silent.

Next morning we went to Church. The Church was a beautiful building and had been recently restored. It had eight or nine richly stained windows. The spire was the very perfection of symmetry. Mr. Coldstream was proud of his Church, and proud that it had been restored during his Incumbency. Do you preach '*extempore* or do you read?' he said, when we got into the Vestry. 'I am doctor of both laws,' I answered, 'and will do which ever you wish.' This was rather boastful as I had only begun to preach without the *M.S.*, and was doubtful of my success. I made a running exposition of a Psalm. At the end I alluded to my coming to Ousebank, concluding with the words, that whether my stay there was to be long or short, I was determined to know nothing among them but Jesus Christ and Him crucified. They were words sincerely spoken. Christ as 'very God,' the incarnation of the Divine Word or Wisdom; Christ as 'very man,' the human manifestation of the

God-head—uniting humanity to Divinity—was to be the theme of all my sermons. I kept my resolution perhaps better than most resolutions are kept. 'Will you preach again in the evening?' said Mr. Coldstream, after dinner, 'and I should like it *extempore* again!' I willingly complied with his request. In the evening the congregation was much larger than it had been in the morning, and I preached what I considered one of my great sermons. Mr. Coldstream was delighted. He could scarcely express his joy. He wished me to take the preaching entirely, and he would read the prayers. Did I not think myself a happy man? The lines had fallen unto me in pleasant places. I praised that wonderful Providence which by so many apparent accidents had brought me to such a Goshen as this. Next day Mr. Coldstream called upon several of the parishioners, and after dinner he opened the subject again. 'There is a great opinion of your talents abroad in the town!' he said, suddenly, 'Your sermons, yesterday, are the subject of conversation everywhere. It is not a large salary that I am able to give, but the people speak of adding something to it, if you will take the Curacy permanently.' He said also, that as he had been in ill health for some time, he would be glad if I stayed. I answered that 'I would *think* of it seriously and give him an answer before long.'

The Parish of Ousebank had many attractions, but it had also some disadvantages. It was a quiet old-fashioned country town. It had no gentry, but the tradespeople were well-disposed, simple, industrious, and, perhaps I may say, with some qualifications, [29] intelligent. There was an honest independence about them,—I might call it pride, but that word would express more than I mean. There were many efforts after caste—everybody tried to be above everybody, and nobody seemed good enough for nobody. Excepting the representatives of the professions, they were all people in business, so that one or two trying to form a class above the others, could not succeed. 'We are all tinkers and tailors,' said the richest man[43] in Ousebank, to me, one day, 'and there is no use of any one trying to set himself above another.' But Ousebank had another disadvantage. It was emphatically a Dissenting town. There was but one Church, while there were seven or eight meeting houses, and the meeting houses were not small places which held only a few people,

---

43   Mutton (Frederick Mutton 'Money lender & news vendor', 1861 England Census Class: RG 9; Piece: 979; Folio: 23; Page: 5; GSU roll: 542731; Retrieved from Ancestry.com. He left c. £12,000 in 1872, approx. £1,387,680 in 2020.)

but large buildings, with congregations numbering three, four, and five hundred. One of them, indeed, was called the Free Church, a fine Gothic building, with a tall spire, and stained-glass windows, erected at an expense of £5000, and dedicated by local wit to the gentleman who was the chief contributor, whom they canonised on the occasion of the dedication. Ousebank was England in miniature—Young England. To study the great empire in all its political and religious bearings, it was only necessary to examine this interesting microcosm. You might walk from the one end of it to the other in seven minutes. At the west-end stood our beautiful Church, surrounded by the churchyard, which was washed by a wandering branch of the stream. Towards the east stood the new fabric. These two Churches represented the two opposing forces in the English nation, not merely Church and Dissent, not merely Conservativism and Liberalism, but the landed interest and the interests of trade. The estates had been divided and subdivided, till the present owners of the land were all, for their position, poor. The trading class, on the other hand, were comparatively rich. The new aristocracy was stronger than the old, or, to speak more correctly, the *meal*ocracy—for the richest men were millers—was too powerful a rival for the landocracy. The schism between them was wide and deep. There were but few Church people in the town—that is, people who went to Church from principle. The intelligence and wealth of the town, such as they were, were nearly all on the side of the Dissenters.

 Mr. Coldstream had been Vicar of Ousebank for nearly thirty years. He was an old-fashioned clergyman, and was proud of his office, not so much for the office itself, but because an English clergyman was equivalent to an English gentleman. A clergyman of the Church of England and an old English gentleman were to him nearly the same, and each was the ideal pre-eminently of all that was great, good, and desirable in this mortal life. His ancestors had been clergymen since the days of Charles I. They had stood by the Stuarts in adversity as well as in prosperity. His father was an eminent scholar, but Mr. Coldstream himself had no pretensions to learning. It was enough for him to be a 'gentleman.' He was not without talents. But after his ordination he abandoned study of every kind, and devoted himself to enjoying the world. Like Sydney Smith he could boast of invitations 'to brilliant dinners out while but a curate.' Not that he was guilty of possessing any of Sydney Smith's abilities, but he was an agreeable, fair spoken man, of handsome exterior, and as Diderot said of Madame Guyon *'formed for the world.'* Fellow curate forty years ago with Mr. Close at Cheltenham, while Mr. Close preached against the vanities of the fashionable world, Mr. Coldstream was the delight of the ball-room. He had on the whole been prosperous in life, though his early hopes of preferment were never realised. He had promises of livings from Lords and Dukes, and Bishops, but none of them were ever fulfilled. Once he had almost grasped a rich piece of Crown pre-[30]ferment, but the Whigs coming into office his hopes were blighted. Weary of trusting men who forgot their promises as soon as they were made, he resolved to be independent. One day he stepped into the office of a London trader in Church benefices. The next presentation to the Vicarage of Ousebank was put up to auction. It was knocked down for £600. He was the bidder, a friend was the buyer.[44] Thirteen months after the purchase the living was vacant. Mr. Coldstream was as little fitted to be Vicar in a Dissenting town as a man could well be. He had bought the temporalities and the spiritualities of Ousebank. Dissenters were interfering with *his* rights. They were *his* Parishioners, and it was their duty to submit to him in all things. His first movement was to embroil the Parish in a Church rate contest. He was beaten ignominiously. The Dissenters celebrated their triumph with a banquet, and Mr. Coldstream was made to feel that Dissent was the presiding genius of the town. This was all old when I went to Ousebank, but the memory of it still lived. Mr. Coldstream hated the Dissenters heartily, and had but little sympathy with the Parishioners in general. He was a 'gentleman,' 'born a gentleman,' and had always 'associated with gentlemen.' The Parishioners were only tradespeople, or, to use his favourite word (not, however, applied to them), s—bs. Into these two great classes he divided mankind. There was no doubt in his own mind to which of them he belonged. How often in the town and gown riots, when he was a student, had he given it to the s—bs.

Mr. Coldstream and I worked together for nine or ten months with great harmony. He was genial, kind-hearted, and good-natured. He was also arbitrary and self-willed, but his good qualities went a long way to atone for his failings. Where he took a dislike he could hate with a

---

44 Father-in-law (Joseph Pain)

fearful hatred. He delighted to be on good terms with everybody, and it was a joy to him to do a kind act or say a kind word to any one. At first he used to express himself in amazement at my abilities. He looked upon me with a kind of awe. Every Sunday night he thanked me for the good I had done to his people. He spoke of my sermons as containing emphatically *'the* Gospel.' This admiration met an answer among the Parishioners, some of whom said, that till I came to Ousebank the 'Gospel' had not been preached in the Parish Church since the time of the Reformation; no compliment, by the way, to Mr. Coldstream.

A kind of puzzle after a time arose in the Parish as to what party in the Church I belonged. I gave them no clue. I had preached practical religion. Mr. Coldstream began to be not entirely satisfied, because I did not sometimes preach what he called 'Church doctrines.' He saw my favourite authors lying about, but their names were all unknown to him. One Sunday morning he found me in the garden absorbed in 'Stanley's Lectures on the Jewish Church.' He expressed surprise that I should read the works of *'that infidel,'* especially on Sunday. He had read of Stanley in some Church paper and knew that he was no good. He told me of some Dissenting lady who was always speaking with approbation of sermons by a Mr. Robertson, of Brighton, and how earnestly he had warned her to take care what she read. I answered him that ROBERTSON sermons were very orthodox, and promised that some day he should read them. I asked if he remembered my preaching on a certain text. He answered 'Yes, and it was one of the best sermons you have preached in Ousebank. Many persons have mentioned how much it has been blessed to them.' 'Between you and me,' I said, 'that sermon was Frederick Robertson's, I sometimes preach other people's sermons just to see how my own stand beside them.' 'I don't care whose it was,' said Mr. Coldstream, 'it was a good *gospel* sermon.' [31]

Nearly a year had passed without anything but the most agreeable words passing and the most friendly feelings existing between Mr. Coldstream and myself. A time, however, came, when he was convinced that I was not 'a sound Churchman.' He could detect heresy, even under my orthodox phrases. I did not believe the Bible. He was not sure that I was quite sound on the Divinity of Jesus Christ. I explained away the atonement, original sin, and everlasting punishment. He did not quite understand it all himself, but he had read that these were the errors of

Stanley, Colenso, and the like of them, and of course they must be my errors too. The beginning and the end of Mr. Coldstream's theology was Apostolical Succession and Baptismal Regeneration. He questioned me very closely on these two points, and of course I believed them with all my might *in my own way*. It was only in his own way that Mr. Coldstream believed them too, for though he cut out the Dissenting ministers from apostolical grace, he allowed it to the Presbyterians, especially those of the Established Church of Scotland, because they belonged to a State Church, and were a respectable kind of men. He did not attach any definite idea to Baptismal Regeneration, but he knew that it was the doctrine of *all good Churchmen*.

    I scarcely know where Mr. Coldstream got his first suspicion of my heterodoxy. I cannot conjecture any other source but the monthly meetings of a Clerical Dinner Society. These little meetings of the Clergy are always dangerous to a Curate, if he has any doctrine different from his Vicar's. He is not allowed the same freedom of speech as an Incumbent. His words are marked, and they are canvassed all the more freely because he is a Curate. I would say to all Curates, if they are not mere puppets, 'Keep away from clerical meetings.' The Clergy in the neighbourhood of Ousebank were estimable men. It was a pleasure to meet them. They were mostly, as to doctrine, of the 'Evangelical' school, but not extreme—not narrow in their views. One or two were decidedly High Churchmen, and one at least was an avowed disciple of Mr. Maurice. I was always listened to with attention, except when I took the side opposed to Mr. Coldstream. Once or twice he rudely interrupted me, and spoiled the harmony of our meeting by peevishly showing his authority, but I overlooked it. He was an old man, in feeble health, and I calmed him, as I often had to do, with smooth words. The questions discussed at these meetings brought out a man's sentiments, if he had any. On one occasion the subject was, 'How to deal with Dissenters in our parishes.' It was a pressing parochial question, because the Dissenters in most of these parishes were more numerous than the Churchgoers. We were nearly all agreed that the Dissenters had done their work more zealously than the Clergy, and that was the reason why they were more numerous. And we also agreed with the conclusion, that those who had done most work ought to have most success. Some who were present told stories of the irregular lives of the past Rectors and Vicars of some of these parishes. Mr. Coldstream, who always defended the past generation, stood up bravely for the memory of their predecessors in office. He could prove that they were all 'perfect gentlemen,' with the exception of a former Vicar[45] of Ousebank, who was said to have frequented taverns and indulged in beer and tobacco. As to the Dissenters, they were dishonest, worthless people, whom no one could trust. They had no religion—they were nothing but conceited politicians—opponents of the Established Church for love of faction—haters of order, and despisers of that which is good. On another occasion, the subject was—'What is the Gospel?' Some defined the Gospel to be the Church, and preaching the Gospel setting forth the Church system through her ministers and sacraments. Mr. Coldstream could not go in for this. He thought that preaching the [32] Gospel was preaching the Bible—setting forth the inspiration and infallibility of the sacred writings, and the necessity of human reason bowing to their teaching. When it came to my turn to speak, I explained preaching the Gospel as declaring the good news of God to man, telling men that God *is* their Father, and that He sent His son to manifest His infinite and everlasting love. I was interrupted with questions about the wrath of God, the reconciliation, and the atonement. I explained wrath as referring to justice, not to any passion in God, for He is without *passions*. By the very constitution of things, the wrong doer suffers; and from this fact we, by personification, ascribe wrath to God. Reconciliation and atonement must be understood in the same way. They proceed originally from God, and not from another coming between God and man. St. John says expressly, 'God *so loved* the world, that *He gave his son.*'

A year had passed away. I had ceased to attend the Clerical meetings. I avoided coming in collision with Mr. Coldstream on theological questions. When he did drag me into discussion I spoke mildly. If he railed or tried to be sarcastic, which he sometimes did, I never returned railing nor tried to be sarcastic with him. I would sometimes suffer myself to be beaten, or would answer by saying *Good Night*, promising, goodnaturedly, to renew the subject some other time. Then he would put away his peevishness and answer with equal good nature, 'I wish you were a better Churchman.' By the end of the year, that is

---

45 Smith (Rev. Thomas Smith, d. 1802)

about the beginning of 1866, the Parishioners, who had intimated to Mr. Coldstream that if I staid in the Parish they would do something equivalent to adding to my salary, resolved on fulfilling their promise. Several of them met together and agreed as to what they should do and how they were to do it. I soon heard of what was going on. In a small town nothing is long a secret. Mr. Coldstream heard too and he busied himself about it in his own way. At dinner, there was present the Curate[46] of a neighbouring Parish. Whether he was asked to open the subject or whether he did it of his own simple innocence, I have no chance of ever knowing. But before the soup plates were half empty, 'I hear,' he said, addressing me, by name,' there is to be a grand testimonial presented to you.' 'Indeed,' I exclaimed, 'I am glad to hear it.' 'No doubt you are,' said Mr. Coldstream, sarcastically. 'A purse of gold!' said the guileless Curate. 'Very sensible people,' said I, 'I did not give the Parishioners of Ousebank so much credit for good sense.' 'After being only a year in the Parish,' said the Curate, simpering, with a sinister look, 'and some of us have been working here for many years, without a sixpence beyond our salaries, and these not large.' There are moments when a man ought to say things and there are other moments when it is dignified to be silent. The latter appeared to me most becoming. I tried to change the conversation by remarking 'that on former occasions when presentations had been made to me, I had objected to taking money. But that I had found the things purchased of so little use afterwards, that I had now resolved always to accept a money presentation when the people were pleased to offer it.' I soon learned that Mr. Coldstream had been through the Parish in the morning, showing his indignation that *his Parishioners* should interfere with *his Curate* or anything in *his Parish*. He had been to the very persons who first spoke of it on my coming to Ousebank. He gave them to understand that if they went on with the presentation they were no longer in his favour. He told the Churchwardens that their office was being usurped; and moreover he told everybody that his Curate had a large salary—larger than he had ever given before, and larger than any Curate in the County. One or two of the first movers were frightened, and I persuaded the others to defer it till some future time. The large salary was nominally £120 a year [33]—actually £1 1s.

---

46 Brown. (Possibly Thomas Brown, curate of Hemingford Abbots)

a week, and live in the Vicarage. I was nearly as well off as the young priest in the Book of Judges, who had ten shekels of silver by the year and his victuals, with an annual *suit of clothes*, and I felt as keenly as he did how much better it would have been to be priest to a whole tribe than to the house of one man.

For several years I had been engaged in writing a work which required wide reading and deep study. It was the prosecution of this work which called forth the unequalled wisdom of the coroner's jury, who pronounced the study of human bodies inconsistent with the study of divine laws. I explained in a letter to one of the morning papers that this was the object for which I had studied anatomy, and remarked incidentally that no publisher would look at my work; to which the Editor[47] of the *Publishers' Circular* had the impertinence to reply that there was enterprise enough in Paternoster Row to publish any work worth publishing, either in science or theology, or both combined. I had written to all the large publishers in London. With only one could I get an interview. When I explained to him the object of the work, he looked at me as if he had found a curiosity. Reading my name on my card he said, 'You may be a very great man, but I really never heard of you before.' He told me plainly that a book on such a subject by a man without a name, would not pay its own expenses, however great its merits. I was determined that the book should be published, and at Ousebank, I began to collect the names of subscribers. Mr. Coldstream took a great interest in the publication, and persuaded many of his friends to add their names. Several of the parishioners did the same. And with the help of Archbishops and Bishops, Deans and Archdeacons, Masters of Colleges, and Professors of Theology, it was at last published. From January 1865 to July 1866. I sat in my arm chair in the attic at the top of the vicarage with but little interruption, musing on many things. The window looked over an expanse of fields. An old fir tree stretched its branches almost to the panes. The sparrows had built their nests and hatched their young ones under my eyes for two springs in succession. I was surrounded by books and pictures, botanical specimens, stiffened insects, and skeletons of bats, birds, and mice. My studies in anatomy

---

47   Thomas Longman

were confined to the lower animals. I never touched human bones, except in the churchyard.

When Mr. Coldstream was convinced of my heresies, he was doubtful not only about the book, but about the man altogether. In fact, he would not have minded had I quietly left the parish. It did not suit me to do this, and had he taken any steps to bring it about, the Parishioners would have been up in arms. On my first coming to Ousebank, Mr. Coldstream used to marvel at the multitudes of people who came to Church. I do not know that the congregation decreased much. In the evening, it was always large from my first Sunday to my last. The people said that the increase was entirely in my time. Mr. Coldstream now began to say, that the same congregations had frequented the Church since it had been restored. He took latterly to preaching in the mornings, that he might be sure there was some 'Church doctrine' taught to the people. His sermons were generally denunciations of reason. He railed against the pride of the human intellect. He did not quite understand 'Catholic truth,' nor 'the universal consent of the Fathers.' When he preached on the Bible he was 'evangelical,' when he preached on the Church, he was 'a good Churchman.' In his zeal for the 'Church' and the Bible, he enunciated some curious doctrines which I hope were peculiarly his own. While the cattle plague was raging, the most stringent resources were adopted to check it, or as some said, 'to stamp it out.' *'Stamp it out,'* Mr. Coldstream would say emphatically, 'poor human reason talks of *stamping out* Almighty God when He visits us for our sins. Then I would tell him how many diseases science had expelled and how the physician's [34] daily life was a warfare with disease. But did not science imply reason, is not the use of reason Rationalism? I could not deny it. In the 'good Churchman' department Mr. Coldstream was once *sold*. He preached on the wreck of the London, and praised the mysterious Providence which had provided a duly appointed minister to exhort and pray with the passengers in their last hours. They were not left to the care of a schismatical teacher. They had the consolations of one properly ordained by the successors of the Apostles. On Monday, after dinner, the usual time for our conversations, I said, 'You referred yesterday morning in your sermon to Mr. Draper, I suppose?' 'Yes,' said Mr. Coldstream, 'it was very providential that he was on board.' 'And do you reckon Mr. Draper among the duly appointed? He was a Wesleyan minister.' 'No, he was a Church Clergyman.' 'You are certainly wrong,' I said, 'he was the representative of the Australian Methodists sent over to the English Conference.' I then told him that Dr. Wooley was a properly ordained Clergyman, and that like a true successor of the Apostles, he encouraged the people to work the pumps, not, I suppose, that he objected to praying, but he saw that the vessel was sinking through having too much water in it, and the appointed way of diminishing the water was by means of the pumps. There was something in that truly *Apostolic*.

My last theological conversation with Mr. Coldstream originated from a report of a Chairman's speech at a meeting of the Congregationalist Churches in the County. The Dissenters will persist in using learned words whether they understand them or not. If they have not learning substantially, they are determined to have it at least phenomenally. The Chairman of the Meeting wished to show that he had made some progress in Bible Criticism, and at the same time that he was as orthodox concerning the Bible as his innocent ancestors had been. So he said that the Bible was the very word or *Logos* of God, 'notwithstanding the imperfections of the containing volume.' The concluding part of the sentence, it is to be hoped, was made for him by the newspaper reporter. Mr. Coldstream and I were both immensely amused at this display of learning and liberalism exhibited by our Congregationalist neighbours. 'The Bible,' said Mr. Coldstream, 'is not the *Logos*, it is the *Rema* of God.' I said it was neither the one nor the other. *The Word of God* in the New Testament is a phrase generally applied to Jesus Christ. Mr. Coldstream took this for a challenge and undertook to prove that the Bible calls itself the word of God. 'Never,' I replied, 'I'll prove it from Cruden's Concordance,' said Mr. Coldstream. 'He is a Dissenter,' said I, 'I'll prove it from Dr. Angus's Bible Handbook,' said Mr. Coldstream. 'Another Dissenter,' said I. 'It does not matter,' said Mr. Coldstream, 'what he is, he proves that the Bible calls itself the word of God.' I told him that the thing was simply impossible. None of the writers of the books in the Bible seem to have known that they were all to be collected into one volume, so that they could not speak of them as a whole under any name whatever. The passages which Mr. Coldstream quoted, had, of course, no reference to the subject. At last he said, 'Now I have you.' There is a verse which says, so mightily grew the Word of God and prevailed.'

'Yes, certainly,' I said, 'I had quite forgotten that passage. It undoubtedly refers to the growth of the Bible—what orthodox theologians call the formation of the canon.'

Mr. Coldstream's health began considerably to improve. The physicians had told him unanimously, that he had a disease of the heart, which might cut him off any hour. He was warned by them not to continue to preach, because the excitement was dangerous. He would not follow their advice. He did not believe he was so ill as they said he was. About the middle of May when the chesnut trees were in blossom, [35] he celebrated his birthday. I drank his health after dinner; an honour which always pleased him. I wished him many returns, and he thanked me in the kindest manner. He said he intended to live some time yet, and he added 'I'll make the value of the next presentation to this living fall in the market.' This was in allusion to something which had greatly annoyed him ever since his last illness. The patrons had been advertising the sale of the living. Several persons had applied to him for information as to its value, but he always declined to tell them. A clergyman who had just returned from India had written that very week offering £1,000 for immediate possession. Mr. Coldstream answered, that he had taken a new lease of life, and that the Vicarage of Ousebank would not be vacant with his consent for some years to come. 'Make money out of this poor living,' he would often say and forgetting that he had once bought it himself, he would reflect on the patrons for not giving it up to the Bishop to appoint a man who would teach 'Church' doctrines as he had done. It might be bought by some 'wretched Evangelical' who would fraternize with the Dissenters and call their ministers his 'reverend brethren.' It might fall into the hands of some Rationalist or worse still, some one might buy it who was not a 'gentleman' and who might associate with people in business, that is s—bs.

Our Bishop had given notice of a confirmation. Mr. Coldstream duly exhorted all godfathers and godmothers to think of their spiritual children. He also invited all persons wishing to be confirmed to come to *him* at the Vicarage, and he would give them the necessary instruction. From forty to fifty young persons applied, and were formed into classes. Mr. Coldstream taught them assiduously two or three nights in the week. I noticed that he looked sullenly at me as if he meant that he was doing something which I ought to be doing. At last it came out. He reproached me with not having a class of candidates for confirmation. I answered that he had not given me one, and, as he had asked the young people to come to the Vicarage to him, it was altogether unlikely that they should ask for me. But Mr. Coldstream answered that I ought to go through the Parish and *beat up candidates for the Confirmation*. 'Beat up candidates for Confirmation' I exclaimed 'I do not know what that means, I never did such a thing, and I never will. We should present to the Bishop such persons as we *know* are prepared to receive confirmation, and not go through the parish to *beat them up* a few weeks before the Bishop comes.' This conversation made the subject disagreeable. We never either of us alluded to it again.

The excitement connected with the preparation for the Confirmation made Mr. Coldstream ill. He preached the second Sunday before it took place. Next Sunday he was unable to be at Church. The physicians said positively he must never preach again. I met Mr. Coldstream daily at dinner, and saw that he was getting worse. After a time he ceased being with us at dinner, and refused to see visitors. The physicians told him plainly to be ready for the worst—he would never survive this attack. He might rally for a week or two, but his end was certainly near. He never gave signs of even a temporary recovery. 'How is the Vicar?' was a question I had to answer a dozen times in a morning, if I walked into the town. 'No better,' was the invariable reply. Then would follow, in an undertone, 'Is the living sold?' Nobody knew. 'Sad thing that the souls of men should be bought and sold,' people would say—'Whoever bids the highest for the presentation will be thrust upon us, whether we are willing or not.' One or two of the parishioners had offered a year ago to pay the patrons the sum required for the living that it might be given to me, but the offer was refused on the ground that I had no private income. A friend of mine in London would have bought it the week before Mr. Coldstream died, but my whole being recoiled at the thought of buying the presentation while Mr. Coldstream [36] lay on his death-bed. The charge of the souls of a parish is responsibility enough in itself, without adopting underhand ways of procuring it. I reflected that after a few short years I should be as Mr. Coldstream is now, and if my work was not successful, how bitterly would I repent of having obtained a living in a way that certainly God never intended livings should be obtained. 'No,' I said, 'I will take my chance of preferment. When it comes by merit, it shall be doubly pleasant; and if I do my work with a clear conscience, it will bring peace at the last.' It was now the beginning of July, and the sun was burning in his fiery chariot. The trees were laden with their most luxuriant foliage. The flowers which shared Mr. Coldstream's chief care were arrayed in their gayest robes. Two longbills had built their nest in the corner of the portico above the stone pillar. The birds sat on two iron chairs in the garden. Mr. Coldstream, who had a real love of nature, sat watching them for many days, leaning on his stick with the silver head. 'For seven and twenty summers,' he said to me, 'ever since I came to this vicarage, a pair of longbills have built their nest and reared their young in this garden.' When he was unable to be with us, I daily watched the longbills till I saw the little heads rising above the nest eager for their food. Every day Mr. Coldstream was getting worse; every day the little longbills were growing in wisdom and stature. I had reckoned that Mr. Coldstream's spirit would depart just about the time when the longbills would be able to fly. 'A very bad night—as bad as it could well be,' was the answer to my inquiry concerning him, one morning. 'He cannot get over the day,' was the answer next morning. 'He is still alive, and that is all we can say,' was the answer the third morning. All that day the Messenger was expected, but he did not come. Next day, about one o'clock, Mr. Coldstream took leave of his friends—asked the doctor at what time he should go—was told it could not be long, and, in five minutes more, the great change had come. The servant came to my study, her eyes suffused with tears, and told me that 'Master was gone.' After an hour or so, I walked into the garden, full of those solemn feelings which all thoughtful men have when one we have known well has left this world for ever. I looked up to the corner of the portico, but I could see no heads rising—no mouths open for the insect morsel— they were mute and still. The poor little longbills were all *dead in their nest!* The angel of death had spread his wings over our dwelling. He had breathed as he passed, and his breath was cold and chill. Four days after, we followed in the solemn procession, and laid Mr. Coldstream in the vault by the river side. On the day of the funeral there was a great cricket match between the local players and the eleven of England. The shops were all shut, that the people might go to the cricket-field. The closing of the shops served both objects. It was in some respects as Mr. Coldstream would have ordered it. He never deeply sympathised with his parishioners, and he would not have wished them to come and mourn for him unless they really regretted the loss of him. He would have said, 'My day is past; I was a happy man while I lived. It is your day now. Enjoy yourselves while life and health and strength endure, and leave the terrors of the land of darkness to me.'

The week of Mr. Coldstream's death was a week of deaths in the Parish. The mortality was greater than it had ever been any week before in my time. There was the feeble old man with whom I used to have a friendly talk at the Churchyard gate; he took ill at night and was dead next morning. There was the young man who inherited disease from his profligate parents; after weeks of suffering, his frail emaciated body at length yielded to the destroyer. There was the poor boy in the workhouse, whose history no one knew; and who was unable, even with the assistance of the Board of Guardians to make good his claims to a longer existence. And then there was old [37] Sally, who for nearly half a century, kept a 'public' in the back lane. She could not read, and yet she was intelligent. How eagerly did she drink in the words of Jesus which I read to her from the gospels, especially from St. John's! How deeply she felt the blessedness of that 'peace which the world can neither give nor take away.' '*In the world ye shall have tribulation.*' 'That,' she said, 'I know is true, but He has also promised '*In Me ye shall have peace,*' and He has said '*Be of good cheer I have overcome the world.*' The day after Mr. Coldstream's funeral, a very old woman was announced as wishing to speak with me. I went to the kitchen door. She intimated that she had something to say which she wished no one to hear. I walked with her under the chestnut tree in the back garden. With that peculiar delicacy which is sometimes found in the poorest and most uneducated people, old Sally had charged her that no one should hear the message but myself. 'It was her last wish,' said the old woman, 'that I should come and tell you, she said, sir, the last thing she said, sir, before she died,' and the tears trickled down the old woman's withered cheeks, '*Tell him I died happy, and I bless the Lord he ever came to my house.*'

'Did Mr. Coldstream say anything about religion?' a poor man asked me the week after he was buried. 'Not to my knowledge,' I answered. 'When he knew that his last hour was come he felt that then his business was to die.' What he had written he had written. A high profession of religion, anything beyond what he felt was repugnant to him. He often told me, that in his former illness, a zealous Evangelical clergyman[48] in the neighbourhood wished to pray with him, but he declined on the ground that he was Parish Priest in his own Parish. He vindicated this doctrine under divers forms. Towards a fragmentary High Churchism his leanings were decided.

No sooner had we laid Mr. Coldstream in his last resting place than the whole parish was on the *qui vive* about his successor. 'Is the living sold?' was everybody's question. The answers were various, as they generally are when nobody knows the right answer. It was the general wish of the town that the presentation might lapse to the Bishop. All believed that the Bishop would appoint a man suitable for the place. 'It is sold,' said a gentleman to me knowingly, as I walked into the town one morning, sold at the eleventh hour. The bargain indeed was not completed a few hours before Mr. Coldstream's death. Even yet all the legal documents may not be drawn up, but *it is* settled, I have it on the best authority.' 'And who is the buyer?' was my question. 'Mr. Sweetbread the lawyer,'[49] whispered the gentleman, 'he has bought it for his nephew.' This was told me as a secret, but like all secrets in Ousebank, every body in the town had it as a secret. At first Mr. Sweetbread had bought it for his nephew, then for his son-in-law,[50] and last of all for his son, so report ran in its labyrinthine maze. Mr. Sweetbread's son was Curate of All Saints, Margaret Street, London. The town was petrified with horror. Men's faces turned pale, and even women shuddered at the approaching spiritual calamity. Then there were visions of priests clothed in albs and copes and chasubles; visions of incense and altars, acolytes and thurifers, lighted candles, holy water, rood lofts, altar screens, crosses, crucifixes, and mimic Virgin Marys. Their fears were soon allayed by a report that Mr. Sweetbread would not give the amount required by the patrons, so that the *ante mortem* negotiations could not be completed by *post mortem* arrangements.

One of the Churchwardens was appointed Sequestrator.[51] He was a very worthy man—could afford to keep a conscience and, when he liked, to have a will of his own. By the advice of his lawyer he took

---

48 Mc Gee Holywell (Robert James McGhee, Holywell)
49 Honeybun (Martin Hunnybun, solicitor, High St, Huntingdon)
50 son-in-law] son-in law
51 Wise (Alderman Richard Relton Wise, Bank Manager)

possession of all the Registers in violation of the Act passed in the reign of her present majesty, that they are to be in the keeping of 'the Vicar, Curate, or officiating minister.' They were, perhaps, as safe in his keeping as [38] in mine, and I was glad to be free from the responsibility. The office either of Churchwarden or Sequestrator, is a thankless one, and not without its cares and troubles. The Sequestrating Churchwarden of Ousebank performed his duties with such a solemn sense of right, and such unwearied assiduity as to be a pattern for all succeeding Churchwardens and Sequestrators. He looked after the Curate, the Clerk, and the Sexton, the Church, and the Churchyard. He was careful about the fees and the expenditure, and all matters relating to the incoming and the outgoing. Everything was so managed that the new Vicar, whoever he might be, would walk comfortably into his Church and find everything in proper order. A few weeks before Mr. Coldstream's death, I had pressed upon him to persuade the Churchwardens to provide me with a respectable surplice, as the one I wore was really disreputable. He prevailed, but instead of giving it to me he wore it himself. After his death, Mr. Sequestrator ordered it to be removed from the Vestry, as the Parish could not afford that the Curate should wear the *New Surplice!* It must be preserved for the *New Vicar*. No expectant mother ever provided so assiduously for her coming child, as the Sequestrator of Ousebank Vicarage for the Vicar that was to be.

By every law of equity and propriety the living of Ousebank should have been given to me. This was the all but universal wish of the people. The patrons had already refused it, though the £1200 was offered them. They wished it to be sold to someone who could spend something upon it. There was a measure of wisdom in this wish. The value of the living was not over £500 a year, and there were three Churches which involved the necessity of keeping two Curates. Moreover, two of the Churches were in a sad state of dilapidation, and the inhabitants of the hamlets in which they were placed, even the farmers and owners of the land were all Dissenters. The schools also were too small for the town, and moreover the restoration of the Parish Church had been left incomplete for want of funds. It is true, that there was willingness and wealth among the tradespeople, but they required humouring, and it was not becoming that the support of the Church should be left to them. A Vicar who could do what was wanted without their help would be independent of them.

How common this notion is in the Church I need not say. How injurious it is I need not prove. When the Church resolves to be independent of the trading community, it resolves to be independent of the nation.

Several weeks passed with no prospect of the vicarage of Ousebank being filled up. It was said that the patrons could not agree among themselves. A few days after Mr. Coldstream's death, clergymen were frequent visitors to the town, looking over the church and the churchyard, like ravens in search of food. One came with authority to look at the vicarage. He also attended the service on Sunday. 'I saw him,' said one. 'I saw him,' said another; 'he is the man; the living has been offered to him.' '*Offered!*' exclaimed an astute lady,[52] *sub rosa*, which means under the rose. Nobody comes into this living who does not satisfy the patrons with the *wherewithal*.' I rebuked her for being so scandalous. That gentleman *declined* the living. The reason why is unknown to me and to most other people.

'I have been introduced to the new vicar,' shouted a tradesman with great glee, as I passed through the chief street in Ousebank, the week following that in which I rebuked the scandalous lady. 'Don't tell me that,' I said, 'till you are sure about it. I have heard of new Vicars till I am sick of hearing of them.' In truth, I did not want to hear of a new Vicar. I shared the general hope, desire, and prayer of the whole parish, that the patrons might quarrel till the six months of vacancy passed, and so the presentation might fall to the Bishop. We all had faith in the Bishop. He was a man of prudence and discretion. Whether his own views were 'high,' or 'low,' or 'broad,' [39] no one could tell. In fact, he was a mixture of all the three. He had been claimed by each party, and again sneered at by them all as a most inconsistent man. He had been educated in a very narrow school of High Churchism. His mind was great enough to see the weakness of it, but not strong enough thoroughly to break away from it. He was a great harmoniser of discordant views, but he harmonised to the satisfaction of nobody. He was, however, a good working Bishop, and had the esteem and confidence of the whole diocese. The new Vicar, of whom the tradesman spoke, was said to have a private income of £2000 a year, and a public outgoing of two-and-twenty

---

52   Mrs. Theed (possibly Elizabeth, wife of William Vipan Theed, gentleman farmer in Hilton, a village close to St Ives; cf. 1861 England Census, Class: RG 9; Piece: 980; Folio: 52; Page: 2; GSU roll: 542731. Retrieved from Ancestry.com)

children. The Primitive Methodist butcher and the particular Baptist grocer, had their ledgers already filled with expectations. Even the heart of the barber, who shaved all the week in the back street, and *preached the word* in the outlying hamlets on the Sunday, leaped for joy at the thought of such an importation of gentry into the town. Both the income and the family had been greatly augmented by the fertile imaginations of the Ousebankians. No writer, either on the sublime or the ridiculous, could reduce to systematic rules the principle on which the people of Ousebank invented a story—Given at the west end of the town a penny, in half an hour's time at the east end, it is a pound. Sir Walter Scott, Cervantes, or even the author of the 'Arabian Nights,' could not surpass them in raising a 'baseless fabric,' and sometimes, it must be admitted, a base fabrication. The new Vicar, as yet, was a myth, and the stories of his appearing at intervals in the town were like the legends of angels' visits. He gave away sovereigns as if they were sixpences. He had thrown some gold to the sexton to put the churchyard in order before he was inducted. He was to rebuild the schools and the dilapidated churches. He was to double the salaries of all the officials in the parish. He was to buy up all the Dissenters and their meeting houses, to banish heresy and schism, and to establish the Church of England in Ousebank on a foundation that should never be moved. With the advent of the Rev. Mr. Goldwing, the *golden* age was to begin. Expectation was on its tiptoe. It was the consulship of Pollio—the birth of the long-expected was at hand, when even the very cradle should bud and blossom.

But these hopes were suddenly cast down. Mr. Goldwing[53] also *declined* the living. This amazed, confounded, perplexed everybody. Had he not agreed to accept it? Had he not been introduced by one of the patrons to several of the parishioners as their future Vicar? How and why does he now decline? We did not know, we could not even conjecture. A century ago, perhaps, the living of Ousebank was in the gift of the owner of the estates. As the estates came to be subdivided among the different branches of the family, the living had to be sold that the claims of each might be satisfied. The patrons at the present time were three in number. The first was our squire, a man of great integrity—a man who would not have sinned one jot against his conscience for all

---

53 Goldie (Charles Dashwood Goldie)

the wealth in the world. He wished heartily that a law were passed to prevent the sale of livings under any circumstances. The second patron was a wine merchant in London. He declared without any reserve that his sole wish was to turn his right into money. His share in the living of Ousebank was a part of his ancestral inheritance. That inheritance was now but small, and he could not afford to lose any of it. The third patron was of the 'female persuasion.' She was the acting partner in the firm. Through her astute wisdom the living had been *offered* to Mr. Goldwing. She knew what she wanted, and where to apply for it. She wrote to *Sam. Oxon*, and *Sam.* sent his favourite man. Her plans were greatly disconcerted by Mr. Goldwing's declining. It was said that the wine merchant would not forego his right, that if the living was to be *given* away, he thought it should be given to an old man, so that the presentation might be sold immediately after. [40]

A few days later the news came that Mr. Goldwing had consented at last to take the living. The only barrier had been the wine merchant's objection, and that could only amount to £400. On Saturday evening the bells were ringing. It was the new Vicar taking possession. There were rumours afloat that he was a high Churchman—very high. 'It will never do in Ousebank' was the unanimous remark. Next morning the congregation were breathless to see Mr. Goldwing. He walked into the desk. Instead of reading the usual sentences, he shouted at the pitch of his voice the name of a woman who had come to be churched. The people were bewildered, and the woman's nerves if they were like other womens' must have had a shake. Mr. Goldwing went through the morning service part reading and part intoning. He had a rich musical voice of great compass, and sometimes it was really solemn. At other times, especially in the Litany, it degenerated into an effeminate whine like the cry of a sick girl. In the evening he preached on the good Shepherd knowing his sheep. Everybody felt that whatever his peculiar views might be, he had come there with head, heart, and hand, ready for work. We had always passed in Ousebank for being a little high Church. But Mr. Goldwing surprised us all. He was no Jesuit introducing things by stealth. He was no man of half measures. He had a determined will and an unbounded confidence in his own ability to execute that will. He restored neglected rubrics and when there was no rubric he made one. The gown in the pulpit he discarded at once as illegal and unbecoming the *priest* in his ministrations to the people. He placed the women who came to be churched on a form before the desk—received the offering himself—carried it to the 'Altar,' and there presented it to Jesus Christ, ever present in the Holy Place. Before the act of baptizing he filled the font with pure water. The choristers and some other people laughed when they heard the splashing in the font. He carried the children into the centre of the Church to sign them with the sign of the cross, and to receive them into the body of the congregation. No matter how loud they screamed. No matter, though the whole congregation twittered, and put their hands on their faces to hide the excitability of the facial nerves. Mr. Goldwing had his duty to perform. He had a rubric, real or imaginary, to keep. When the children were baptized, he said they had received a new nature, pure as that of the angels, and he appealed to parents if they had not seen how the seeds of grace bore fruit in the baptized children, and how much more gentle and good and holy they were than the unbaptized.

During the first week of Mr. Goldwing's Incumbency I received from him the following letter:

'My dear Mr. _____

'I enclose a notice to you in the usual form, which I should at any rate have sent in order that I might enter into fresh arrangements with you—as a matter of form. But I cannot but feel that this must be an actual notice and not a form. I have been honoured by the reception of two sermons preached by you in the Church of _____ since the late Vicar's death, and, according to my view, they are in points so lamentably deficient in the full statement of truth, and in some points so erroneous, that I feel it my duty either personally or by deputy, to supply your place in the pulpit during the next six weeks. I shall be glad to have your assistance in the reading desk and otherwise.

'I am the more sorry to say this, because I cannot but own the undoubted power the Sermons show; and I should be glad if the opportunity offers, to have some conversation with you, and to aid you (if it is not presumption in me to say this) in finding out the point, where, as it seems to me, you diverge from Catholic truth, [41]

'I hope that the fact of my acting thus will not in any way destroy our friendly converse during the short remainder of our connection.

'Ever yours truly,

'_____.'

The sermons referred to were two sermons on the two sacraments. They were as innocent as two sermons could well be. They had been written half a dozen years before, preached one afternoon to a few servant girls in the north of London, and laid aside as not worthy to be preached again. I immediately wrote to Mr. Goldwing:

> 'My dear Sir,
>
> 'I have received your letter and the notice, the latter of which I have expected daily since Sunday. Indeed, I had no wish to remain in the Parish after seeing how distinctly you identified yourself with a party in the Church with whose peculiar views I have no sympathy in the world. No one will blame you for wishing to have a Curate of your own way of thinking, but to inhibit me from the pulpit is an arbitrary and uncalled for exercise of power, likely, I fear, to recoil upon yourself. This Parish has been virtually in my hands for nearly two years. I have been feeding the flock. I *know* the sheep and they *know* me. Not to allow me to preach a final sermon is to make me a martyr when I do not wish to be one. As to the sermons I did not cause them to be sent to you. I believe them to be so thoroughly in accordance with the doctrines of the Protestant Church of England, that I cannot well understand your objections. I had a letter yesterday morning from a friend of mine, a minister of the Episcopal Church of Scotland, and reckoned a High Churchman, who says, 'Without accepting, perhaps, *all* points in them. I certainly think you have put in clear and forcible terms some important views of your subject.' I should be glad to have a friendly conversation with you on the doctrine of the sermons. I should like to hear what a sensible man (and I believe you are a sensible man) has to say about what you call 'Catholic truth.' *There is no such thing* in the sense in which you seem to use the words. There are Catholic lies in abundance, Catholic errors and Catholic superstitions, which must be swept away with the besom of destruction. There are, I know, many earnest men who believe in what they call Catholic truth, but the religious sentiment is wild in its wanderings, and ought to be governed and restrained by reason. I have had much experience among men of all kinds of opinion and I have learnt to be tolerant towards all.
>
> 'I will duly consider whatever you wish to say to me, and I shall promise that, on my part, nothing will arise, if I can help it, to promote anything but the most friendly understanding between us.'
>
> 'Yours very truly,
>
> '_____.'

As I had only six weeks more to be in the Parish and was really so exhausted by long and incessant work as not to care about preaching much, this inhibition seemed to show a want of ordinary discretion. The Bishop was vexed about it. The newspapers paraded it, and as a consequence the people bought the sermons by hundreds.

Mr. Goldwing was determined to do what he thought right. He first did everything his own way, and then he made calls and wrote letters to appease those who were offended. He ignored the existence of the Churchwardens. The Sequestrator never had the joy of presenting the *new surplice*. A sad fate awaited him. He was numbered with 'persons excommunicated, unbaptized, and who have laid violent hands on themselves.' Many years ago he had committed the fearful sin of marrying his deceased wife's sister, and Mr. Goldwing denied him the benefit of those sacraments which are *universally* necessary to salvation. The parish of Ousebank was soon in a ferment. The people could do nothing but growl. The walls were placarded with *No Popery*; and letters of all kinds, wise and foolish, filled the columns of the local paper. One morning I was sitting at my window which looked into the marketplace. I heard the stentorian voice of the town crier, 'This is to give notice,' he exclaimed in his lofty monitone [sic], 'that whoever enters a Dissenting place of worship commits an offence against God. These are the words spoken in the Parish Church of Ousebank on Sunday morning last, and he who said them is a liar and a fool.'

I left Ousebank in the midst of the excitement. It was announced to me that the long-intended presentation was at last to be made and it was intimated that the occasion would be a proper one for a parting address. Mr. Goldwing had the prudence to suspend his inhibition, and asked me to preach once more in the Church, which of course I was eager to do. There was not much wrong with Mr. Goldwing, except the [42] poison of the 'pernicious nonsense.' Sacerdotal blood flowed in his arteries, and filled his veins to repletion. On the Friday evening a great multitude assembled in the town-hall. Thirty guineas were presented to me in a long purse with dangling tassels. The Chairman made a flaming speech, he spoke of the 'talented preacher,' the 'great scholar,' and the respect which the inhabitants of Ousebank had for 'all that was great and good.' He quoted Shakespere, of course, and, in allusion to the Ritualists, the lines of Milton, beginning—

'Wolves shall succeed for teachers, grievous wolves.'

I accepted the presentation and said,—'Mr. CHAIRMAN, LADIES, and GENTLEMEN, 'I am proud to receive the testimonial which you have been pleased to present. In looking over the list of subscribers, I find, with but few exceptions, the names of all the principal Church going people of the town, and also those of several Dissenters. It is true that some of the subscriptions are small, but since I knew that the testimonial was in contemplation, it has been my wish that it should be made up of many small sums rather than of a few large ones. It is more gratifying to me to find that my services have been appreciated by the whole Parish than only by a few persons in the Parish. Indeed, I expressed a wish that no one might be allowed to give more than 2s 6d, but this was overruled by those who had the management of the testimonial. It is at my own request that it is presented in money rather than as something which would be merely an ornament. Not that I am in want of money, but because money is one of the most useful things in the world. I shall not tell you how it is to be spent. It shall be kept till some great occasion requires it, that I may, with greater gratitude, remember your gift.

'I cannot let this opportunity pass without speaking of the propriety of such gifts to Curates when they do their work satisfactorily in a Parish. The earnest curate, who has nothing but his own merits to depend on, has but few chances of promotion in the Church. This, it is well known, is one of the greatest evils of the Church, and one which deprives it of the services of many able men. Indeed, it has come to this, that the Bishops cannot find a sufficient number of educated men in England to supply the ranks of the Clergy. A man who has passed creditably at his university, can reckon upon success, or at least a competency in any other profession, but unless he inherits a family living, or speculates in the purchase of a presentation he has not the same chance in the service of the Church. If he has preaching talents, he may get a competency as a Dissenting minister, but in the Church the chances are, that he spends the best part of his life as the stipendiary servant of some beneficed clergyman. To devise remedies for this must be left with those who have the government of the Church, but, in the meantime, it is the duty of the people to do what they can to lessen the evil. They should not wait till the vicar of a parish encourages a presentation to the curate, nor should they leave it to those well-disposed gentlemen, the churchwardens, who have generally such a large development of the phrenological conformation, which is supposed to be connected with the quality of caution, that but for this as a good heavy ballast, they would never be able to move through life at all. The gods, according to a Pagan poet, gave different qualities to different kinds of men, and, I suppose, when all these qualities were disposed of, they came at last to churchwardens, and told them that their safety lay in fear, for the gods had nothing else to give them. The people should do what they can when they think it is right, without consulting officials. It would be well if in every parish, where there is a Curate, the parishioners would unite to provide his salary, and claim in return a voice in his election. If you cannot choose both your ministers, it would be some satisfaction to be able to choose one. The clergy of the Established Church will know before long that if they are to keep their position, they must pay more attention to the will of the people. They must cease to come into their parishes as hierarchical autocrats. By the constitution of the Church of England, they are the servants of the people. The churches do not belong to them, nor even to the patrons of the livings. They are the property of the nation, and therefore the property of the inhabitants of the parish.

'In regard to this testimonial, I distinctly understand that it is presented to me without reference to any other person. Some, I know, have been deterred from subscribing, lest a wrong construction should be put upon it, or a wrong use made of it. This was a groundless fear, and one that would never have been entertained, had they known as much about it as I know. When I came to Ousebank, it was to take the duty for six Sundays. During that time your late Vicar frequently urged me to take the curacy [43] permanently. It was a great joy to him to find a man of some experience, on whom he could rely, while he felt his own infirmities increasing upon him. The salary he had to give, though larger than is generally given to Curates, was not so large as I could have had in London. He told me that it would be generally agreeable to the parishioners if I did stay, and intimated that it was the intention of some of them to do something equivalent to adding to the salary. I saw that there was work to be done, and that, salary or no salary, my staying among you was a duty. The testimonial was talked of at the end of the year, with a view to secure my remaining in the Parish, but when I found it was likely to cause differences, and knowing that it would not effect the object intended, I wished it to be deferred. The promoters were resolved that I should not leave the Parish without the presentation being made. It is made to-night. I will never regret having spent nearly two years in Ousebank, and I trust you will never regret the graceful and becoming act which you have now performed. I could have wished that I had been[54] able to do more for you, but the completion of a work of which you have all heard, and of which, judging from letters which I am daily receiving from eminent men, you are likely to hear more, has deprived me of much of the time which should have been spent in pastoral duties.

'Allusion has been made to what is now going on in your Parish Church. That subject is between you and your Vicar. It is not my business to enter into it. I must leave you to fight your own battles, or make the best truce you can. Several have come to me earnestly imploring advice, and the only advice which I have thought it my duty to give is, "*Whatever you do, do as Christians and as gentlemen.*" It is well known that the Vicar publicly condemned my doctrine, by silencing me in the pulpit as soon as he had taken possession of the living. I have defended myself firmly. He has followed a decided course, but there has been no approach to any misunderstanding or unchristian feeling between us. I trust the time is come when men can discuss theological subjects with calmness but with firmness, without reference to temporal interests, and without exciting angry passions. We have set you the example in Ousebank. I hope you will all follow it. Whatever differences you may have with your Vicar, you will always find him ready to reason with you. Do not be outdone by him in Christian feeling. Give him credit for right motives and whatever practical good he does. Jesus has taught us, in the beautiful parable of the man who fell among thieves, that it was the Samaritan with the erroneous creed who showed mercy, while the orthodox Jew passed by on the other side. Christian charity is better than orthodoxy. There are good men of all creeds; yet their goodness need not blind us to the falseness of their creeds. Their hearts are better than their heads—their lives better than their doctrines.

'It is due to you, and, I believe, many of you expect, that I will say something that may help you to understand the cause of the present

---

54   I had been] I been

excitement in the Church. I claim a special right to speak on this subject, for I have seen my way to clear Church of England principles, in which all that is really good in what is called the "Catholic Revival" may be retained, and all that is pernicious, which by the way is much the greater proportion, may be put away. There are many of the forms to which, considered in themselves, I do not object. Some of them are old Church of England forms, which may be restored or suffered to rest in oblivion, as people may fancy. There is no harm, for instance, in preaching in a surplice, though to my taste the academical gown is the more appropriate dress when the minister appears as the instructor of the people. It is, moreover, I believe, the vestment appointed by law to be worn in the pulpit. For some time after the Reformation, many of the priests in the country parishes retained, against the law, the old Roman Catholic vestments. The prejudice in the public mind against the surplice in the pulpit is connected with a dread of the restoration of these vestments—a prejudice which, I must say, as a Protestant, I very highly respect. There are some things on which I cannot pass a judgment. Not being a musician, I cannot speak of what relates to music. Intoning the prayers is distasteful to me, because it seems unnatural. But there are others to whom it may appear devotional. There is a point at which prayer passes into praise. I am not to be the judge for those who differ from me. But in all these matters regard should be had to the wishes and the tastes of the worshippers.

'Many things are real improvements, such as the restoration of Churches to their original architectural beauty—the abolition of the aristocratic square pews in which ladies and gentlemen used to show their position in the parish, and the substitution of seats that are alike for all classes, in that place where we should all appear as humble worshippers, and as equal in the sight of God. Beautiful Churches, like music and [44] painting, may be made conducive to sacred feelings. A German philosopher calls Architecture "a petrified psalmody." Every time I walk through the solemn aisles of a cathedral, I feel as if the very stones were singing psalms to God—they seem to speak of worship as the birds and the flowers speak of the spring time, or the dropping leaves of the sombre autumn. It is sad that the indulgence of this feeling is checked not only by the fact that in past times it was associated with superstition, but that in these days of light, as we are wont to call them, there is danger of this superstition returning.

'I do not object to turning to the east in some parts of the service, but I do not know that there is any authority for it, except that some of the Fathers speak of worshipping towards the east. It is a traditional custom of the Church.[55] The Jews prayed towards the Holy Temple. The western nations, after their conversion to Christianity, may have worshipped towards Palestine, but the origin of the custom was probably Pagan. It may be traced to Bactria and India—the birth places of the oldest Aryan religions. In ancient Persia the chief deity was the Sun. The people worshipped towards it. Temples were consecrated to it; and white robed priests singing holy songs knelt before the vestal flame. They had litanies to the Sun; and when the glorious king of day crowned with the diadem of light, glittering with the pearls of the morning, and bringing joy and gladness to the world, rose above the horizon, the priests began the daily service with the solemn invitation "Let us worship Mithras." Among the deities of Rome the Sun had still its worshippers. The profligate Heliogabalus, before he was made Emperor, was priest in the temple of the Sun, and Julian the Apostate tried to restore the worship of the Sun as a substitute for Christianity. His biographer says that he met it every morning with offerings of blood. Worshipping towards the east is a beautiful superstition. If we can give a reason for it, the beauty may be preserved when the superstition is gone.

'The "Catholic Revival" is to be distinguished from all forms of High-Churchism that have gone before it. It is the legitimate and logical tendency of them all, yet different from them all. There is the High-Churchism of the elevated ecclesiastic, who fills with dignity the chair of office. There is the High-Churchism of the mortified vicar, whose parish is so full of Dissenters that he cannot get everything his own way. There is the High-Churchism of the raw curate, who puts on the stiffened white neck-cloth and the long-tailed coat, whose lips are full of heresy, dissent,

---

55   This note is Hunt's, signalled by an asterisk in the original text.
     I am told that the greatest Church in the world, St. Peter's at Rome, has the chancel in the west. Socrates, the Ecclesiastical historian, says that the Church of Antioch, probably the first Christian Church ever erected, had its chancel in the west. St. Botolph's, Aldgate, in the City of London, has the chancel in the north. It is a very poetical idea to think of all the people of London, when they say their prayers, looking towards Whitechapel and Bethnal Green.

and schism, beginning and ending all things with "The Church, my Brethren." These are but incipient or transient forms of High-Churchism. The wearers of albs and copes and chasubles, who light candles and burn incense, accompanied by acolytes and thurifers, and their other manifold attendants, may also be excepted, but on other grounds. They are the indiscreet men who damage the cause by too much haste. The "Catholic Revival" is more inviting than any of these. When thinking men, who know with what dullness and want of life the Church service used to be performed, see the clergy doing their work as if they were in earnest about it, the first feeling is a thrill of joy. The old fabric lives once more. The holy fire burns in the sacred fane. A revival, we say, has come at last. But we examine it further, and the disappointment is bitter. One day last summer, I found a sparrow lying dead under the chesnut trees in the Vicarage garden. Wishing to preserve the skeleton, I placed it in the ivy for the ants to clean its bones. Three days after I went to examine it. Its breast heaved beautifully, like the heaving of a maiden's breast in sleep. It lived, but alas! it was a life worse than death. It was the life which follows death, the life of corruption. Such, I fear, is the boasted "Catholic Revival."

'We are better able, at the present time, to pronounce judgment upon the "Revival," than we have hitherto been. The leader of it has published a book called "Eirenicon," in which he proposes to make peace between the Church of England and the Church of Rome. The old divines of the Church of England, Bishop Hall for instance, delighted in such titles for their controversial pamphlets, as the motto of Hannibal and the Carthaginians when the Romans invaded their country *Nulla pax cum Roma*, no peace with Rome. There was something in this of the true Protestant spirit of the Church of England, but now her divines write *Eirenicons*, or how to make peace with Rome. I have just read the "Eirenicon," and the judgment which I passed upon it the other day [45] in a letter to a friend, was, that "there is as much nonsense in this book as would make even the Virgin Mary weep." The ridicule which it has called forth among the French Catholics has given an unusual interest to their current literature. Recent articles in the *Revue du Monde Catholique*, sparkle with the wit of the Jesuits, plentifully lavished at the expense of Dr. Pusey. Archbishop Manning is only restrained by his position from saying that Pusey is insane, or something worse, and it would be difficult for any member of the Church of England, in his right senses, to pronounce any other judgment.

'Dr. Pusey's reconciliation between the two Churches is to be accomplished by showing that the Church of England is not a Protestant Church, and that the Church of Rome is not infallible, in other words is not *the* Catholic Church. The word "Catholic" is one of those words, that from the variety of its meanings, requires definition every time it is used. The only lawful meanings which it has in the formularies of the Church of England are, where it refers to the Church visible, as in the "Prayer for all sorts and conditions of men," in which it is plainly defined to consist of *"all who profess and call themselves Christians;"* and, where, as in the Creed, it refers to the Church invisible—the mystical body of Christ, which is, to use the words of Archbishop Usher, 'the whole universal company of the elect, that ever were, are, or shall be gathered into one body'—that Church which, as Hooker says, "is Christ's mystical body, and consisteth of none but only true Israelites, true sons of Abraham, true servants and saints of God." In conventional language the word Catholic is applied to the Church of Rome; and all who are in communion with that Church are called Catholics. As the word Catholic properly means universal, that is obviously a wrong use of it, for not more than the half of the Christian world is in communion with the see of Rome. Dr. Pusey's Catholic Church consists of the Church of England, the Church of Rome, and the Greek Church. It is Catholic because of the universal acceptance of the three creeds of the ancient Church, and the continuance of the Episcopal succession from Apostolic times. All others who profess and call themselves Christians do not belong to the "Catholic Church," though the Prayer-book expressly says that they do. Dr. Pusey's "Catholic Church" is universal, but it is not "one." It consists of three Churches which anathematize each other—three Churches which hold no communion with each other—Churches of which the priests of the one cannot minister at the altars of the others. The word Protestant is not so various in its meanings, but it is sometimes misinterpreted. It does not mean that we protest against the Catholic Church in either of the senses in which it is used in the Prayer-book, but only that we protest against the errors of the Church of Rome. The word Protestant is in this sense a precious word. We should ever be proud of it. It is the watchword of free enquiry, free thought, and free speech. It comes to us laden with the history of the struggles of our forefathers, when they fought for the right, and shared in the glorious battle of freedom—that battle which

> "Once begun,[56]
> Bequeathed from bleeding sire to son,
> Though baffled oft, is ever won."

It is a word pregnant with great things for the future—a word we must never abandon. When you speak of the Church of England, you may call it, if you like, a branch of the Church Catholic, but never forget that it is our Protestant Church of England.

'Dr. Pusey wishes to explain away the Protestantism of the Church of England. He wishes to say that our Reformers protested not so much against the doctrines of the Church of Rome, as against the abuses of these doctrines, which abuses were, in a great measure, corrected by the Council of Trent. He lingers over the many points on which the two Churches agree, and speaks of those on which they differ as unimportant. Were Dr. Pusey to go to Professor Huxley, that gentleman would show him that the points on which a man and a chimpanzee are the same, are very numerous, and those on which they are unlike very unimportant. Professor Huxley would show that the chimpanzee is the complete analogue of the man—that it has the same skull, the same bones in the skull, the same brains beneath the skull, the same conformation throughout, even to the posterior lobe and hippo-campus minor—the same cervicals, dorsals, lumbars, sternum, clavicles; and all the other bones, which some of the doctors present know better than I do. He will even prove that a chimpanzee is not an animal with four hands as we used to suppose, but that it has two hands and two feet like any human being. And yet we all know that a chimpanzee is not a man, neither is the Church of Rome the same as the Church of England. [46]

'Dr. Pusey's method of showing the relationship, is to explain away nearly all distinctively Protestant doctrine. We say, for instance, that the sacraments are generally necessary to salvation. By this our best divines understand that it is the duty of Christians to use the sacraments when they may be had; but it is never said that men may not be saved without

---

56 'Once begun,] Once begun,

them. Yet Dr. Pusey interprets "generally" as meaning universally; so that we are to read "the sacraments are universally necessary to salvation." This may do for the Church of Rome, but we know better in the Church of England. Again in the article, which says that "transubstantiation, or the change of the substance of bread and wine into the body and blood of Christ overthroweth the nature of a sacrament, and hath given occasion to many superstitions," it is explained that this was directed against the doctrine of the schoolmen, which was not adopted by the Council of Trent. That Council declared that the "accidents" of bread and wine remained, and this is equivalent to our word "substance." It is very dexterous in Dr. Pusey to throw us back upon metaphysical terms, which sometimes have entirely opposite meanings in the lips of different men. But the Reformers who wrote our Articles were not metaphysicians. They were plain men, who used words carefully, and with the ordinary meanings. They said plainly that the change of the substance, which with them meant what it now does in common language, the essence of bread and wine overthroweth the nature of a sacrament, and hath given occasion to many superstitions. In the Article which denies that the Eucharist is a sacrifice, and where it is said very decidedly that the sacrifices of masses are blasphemous fables and dangerous deceits, Dr. Pusey finds that the Reformers did not mean the sacrifice of the mass, but only the buying of masses, which then prevailed in the Church, but which was afterwards corrected by the Council of Trent. I suppose it is due to Dr. Pusey to have been the first to discover the meaning of this article. I do not know that any divine of the Church of England ever so explained it before. The great Bishop Bull understood it of what he called "the monstrous sacrifice of the mass taught in the Church of Rome."

'I have given you some specimens of the mode in which Dr. Pusey wishes to eliminate the Protestantism of the Church of England. His ingenuity is very great. A life spent in the study of the fathers and the schoolmen makes a man very acute, and if not held accountable to reason it will make him, it appears, a noted divine, even in the Church of England. But after Dr. Pusey has ground our Articles to Catholic powder, and left us nothing to admire in the Reformation but the folly of the Reformers, there still remains an impassable gulf between the Church of England and the Church of Rome. And for proof of this we need not go further than to the "Eirenicon." Here it is that all men who have their eyes open, both Catholics and Protestants, see the weakness of Dr. Pusey's cause. The account which he gives of the character and extent of the worship of Mary in the Church of Rome seems to have astonished, not only the Protestants of this country, but even the Roman Catholics themselves. I always had a suspicion that the Church of Rome could give a reasonable explanation of the worship of Mary, and that the accounts we generally had were only the exaggerated statements of Protestant writers, but on any subject connected with the Church of Rome, Dr. Pusey is not likely to exaggerate. He has consulted the best sources, and thrown down a challenge to the whole Roman Catholic world. We have often heard English Catholics say that prayers addressed to the Virgin were simply prayers that she would intercede for them. Dr. Pusey shows that this is not correct—that Catholics pray to Mary to have remission of sins, to be led into the way of truth, to have grace, life, and glory. Catholicism, it is said, does not flourish in England, because English Catholics do not give sufficient worship to Mary. "Here in England," says a pious Roman Catholic writer, "Mary is not half enough preached, devotion to her is low and thin. It is frightened out of its wits by the sneers of heresy. It is always inviting human respect and carnal prudence, wishing to make Mary so little of a Mary that Protestants may feel at ease about her. Jesus is obscured, because Mary is kept in the background. *Thousands of souls perish because Mary is withheld from them.*" Catholic priests in Italy have lamented by the death beds of their English converts that they are but half converted, for when dying they put their trust in Jesus, and never pray to Mary. Dr. Pusey has often been told that before he can expect to be converted, he must learn to pray to Mary. In the Church of Rome, Mary is all in all. She is called "The Queen of Heaven and the Mistress of the world," "the Great One Herself," "the Holy Mother of God," "Companion of the Redeemer," "Co-Redemptress," "Authoress of eternal salvation." "The Destroyer of heresies throughout the world," "The Ring in the chain of creatures," "The Mediatress not of men only but of angels," "The Complement of the [47] Trinity. One Catholic writer says that in the Eucharist they eat and drink not only the flesh and blood of Christ, but the flesh and blood of the Virgin Mary, and that there is present in the sacrament, not only the blood of the Lord Jesus Christ, but also the Virgin milk! of his Virgin mother! Another writer says, that the regenerate are born not of flesh, nor of blood, nor of the will of man, but of God *and Mary*.

This is the Church with which Dr. Pusey wishes to unite the Church of England! Of course he wishes it to lay aside its mariolatry, and to renounce its last and most favourite dogma, the immaculate conception of the Blessed Virgin. He asks an "infallible Church" to say that it is fallible. He might as well ask the Pope to say that he is not the Pope. For the Church of Rome to retract any of its dogmas would be suicide. It must bear its own burdens with which it is self-burdened. It is committed irretrievably to idolatry, to the worship of the Virgin Mother. It stands condemned in the light of scripture and in the eyes of reason. Let it sink under the weight of its errors. Let the chain of infallibility drag it downwards. It is caught in its own craftiness. It has woven destruction for itself.

'Dr. Pusey's scheme is to bring back the Church of England, the Church of Rome, and the Greek Church to the position in which they stood before the separation of the Eastern and Western Churches. And here the futility of his plan is manifest to all men. He supposes the Church to have been infallible up to the time of the great schism between the east and the west, but after that, the decrees of the Church of Rome, not being the decrees of the whole Church, were fallible. If the three Churches could be again united, it is expected, I suppose, that infallibility would return. A man who has spent his life in study, as Dr. Pusey has done, ought surely to have learned that if infallibility had belonged to the "Catholic Church," it would never have been divided into Greek, Roman, and Anglican.

'"A[57] return to the Catholic Church—restoration of Catholic truth," is the cry of Dr. Pusey and his disciples. When we ask them what they mean they do not know. They are like unto men that dream. A vague something which they call "Catholic" has possessed their minds. They follow it as bewildered travellers follow the phosphoric light, that leads them to the bogs and the swamps and sinks them they know not where. I do not like to call ill names, I do not like to ascribe bad motives to those who differ from me. I believe Dr. Pusey and his disciples are sincere. They excite our compassion rather than our hatred. It is a pity to see so

---

57 '"A] "A

much earnestness lost, to see men erecting a scaffolding which is sure to fall. The Church of Rome is the inevitable goal of all their efforts. This is proved by the soundest arguments, and alas! ratified by experience. The best and most consistent men in the original Oxford movement are all in the Church of Rome. Their friends, as Dr. Newman testifies, saw where they were going, but they did not believe it themselves, till they had gone too far to be able to return.

'This vague "Catholic" Church is called the Church of the Fathers, especially of St. Augustine. Alas! how easily are men deceived with great names. No one can read the story of St. Augustine's life without being affected by it. He has told it himself with all the ingenuousness of a truly great man, how he wallowed in sin, how his mother followed him with her prayers, how at last he came with his friend Alypius, and his gifted boy Adeodatus, to the waters of Baptism; and there was plunged in the flood to signify that now he was dead to sin and that henceforth he would live to righteousness. The conversion of St. Augustine was a great event for the Church, his powerful mind impressed itself on its history, its dogmas, its destiny. Let us give to St. Augustine all that is due, but why should we go back to his theology? God has given us light which was withheld from him. In the knowledge revealed to us by the patient study of science—in the better understanding which we have of the spirit of Christianity—in our more worthy conceptions of the Divine Being, and His relations to the universe, we leave St. Augustine far behind. Indeed, it is with the two great errors of his theology that we have yet mainly to contend; the doctrine that God only wills some men to be saved, and the belief that unbaptized infants must everlastingly perish—two of the darkest heresies that ever found shelter in the Christian Church.

'The present movement in the Church of England is an anxious question to all thinking men, and especially to all sincere Protestants. Quiet church going people are driven away from their parish Churches by doctrines and practices to which they are unaccustomed. In past times when the Parish Church did not please the people they built a meeting house. The same course is open still. But does this serve the end? Are the people to go on building Dissenting chapels, and leave the Churches and Church property in possession of that party which is the most opposed to the judgment and [48] common sense of the people? If the national Church ceases to represent, at least, the majority of the nation, is it likely that the nation will suffer it to stand? What, then, are Dr. Pusey's disciples doing? Professing to build up the Church; in reality pulling it down. But, my friends, do not be alarmed. This is only a temporary madness. Dr. Pusey, by the publication of his "Eirenicon," has inflicted a blow on his cause which it cannot survive. Every one who is capable of putting two ideas along side of each other, will see that he and his disciples have not an inch of ground on which to stand. The cause why so favourable a reception is given by many of the clergy to what is called "Catholic" doctrine is doubtless to be found in the vantage ground which they seem to have through their connection with the episcopal succession over the Dissenters. It is not my business to take the side of the Dissenters. But no national Church can exist in England which does not acknowledge as branches of the Church Catholic the great bodies of nonconformists. The future of the Church of England depends on which of the two parties in the Church shall finally prevail—those who follow scripture, and reason, or those who follow scripture and tradition. If the latter, its existence as the national Church is doomed. If the former, it may work the well being of the nation, and be the great bulwark of sound religion and the enemy of superstition throughout the world. Let the clergy be properly educated in theology as a science. Let the temporalities of the Church be so distributed, that there may be some connection between merit and reward, so that men capable of guiding the intellect of the nation may be induced to come into her service. And then in a higher sense than the prophet intended shall be fulfilled the prophecy—The kings of Tarshish, and of the Isles shall bring presents unto Him, and the Queen of Sheba shall offer gifts. Then shall be found among the Church's worshippers, not merely emotional women and confiding children, but men whose minds have battled with all the problems of life. Then the merchant-man weary with the toils of business shall find religion a reasonable service. Then the man of science shall come with the fruits of his study as an offering to God, acknowledging that in Christianity he has found that which satisfies his reason, commends itself to his conscience, banishes fear, and gives peace to his anxious mind. 'It has been a great pleasure to me that I have been able to speak some plain words, among you. I have tried to make you think for yourselves. I have tried to persuade you to love righteousness for its own sake. I have lived at peace among you and have done my best to promote peace and good will between man and man. And now my last desire and prayer for you all is, that God may be with you now and evermore.'

The address was loudly applauded. I had spoken the sentiments of the Ousebankians, and of the intelligent laity of the Church throughout the land. I tried to check all ebullition of the feelings usual at such partings, but it could not be done entirely. The last exclamation I heard was from a poor woman—'Good bye, sir, good bye!' she cried, 'May you be as well respected, wherever you go, as you have been here.'

The Church is troubled. All its teachers are perplexed, from the Bishop who rides in his carriage, to the Curate who rideth on the top of an omnibus. We do not know whether or not we are sacrificing priests! One half of the clergy are surprised to hear that it is even supposed; the other astounded that everybody does not know it. Wisdom may be crying aloud in the streets, but it is in another sense that she is *crying* in the Church. Like Rachel, she laments there for her children, because *they are not*. Can we expect it otherwise, when no encouragement is given to men able and willing to do the Church's work; when, of the material that is available for the ministry, it is impossible to make anything better than innocent Evangelicals, or brainless Ritualists—preachers of platitudes, or performers of attitudes. Shall it ever be that in religion, as in other things, men will listen to the solemn voice of Reason?

FINIS.

Clergymen Made Scarce, Second Edition (London: Hall, 1867), With the Annotations of Mrs Eliza Hunt.

Appendix II

The Anatomist Curate

THE Rev. John Hunt, Curate of St. Botolph, Aldgate, is not, it may be fairly presumed, a man of much discretion, but that does not exactly justify a coroner's jury in laying down *ex cathedrâ* the limits of clerical education. That function, one would think, if it rests anywhere, is vested in the Episcopal Bench, and not with twelve worthy tradesmen assembled to judge whether a stillborn child had or had not come to a natural end. Mr. Hunt, it would seem, is a curate who, whether from taste, original destination in life, or a conscientious conviction, thinks it expedient that a clergyman should study something beyond Latin and Greek and a somewhat superficial system of theology. He even ventures to believe that an English incumbent, who is incessantly brought by his office into contact with the very poor, with the diseased, the sick, and the dying, with crowds who defy habitually all the laws of hygiene, and a few who from time to time are left to perish for want of the skill they cannot command, would be made more efficient by a practical knowledge of medicine. As in many another 'viewy' person, however, Mr. Hunt's wide ideas are not corrected by average common sense, and instead of pursuing his studies like a reasonable being in connection with some hospital or infirmary, he must pursue them in private, obtaining subjects secretly from his medical friends. Indeed, if the truth were known, we dare say that, though wise enough to perceive the value of surgical knowledge to a Christian pastor, he was priestly enough to be a little ashamed of pursuing a study so secular.' At all events he pursued it privately in his lodgings, greatly, we suspect, to his landlord's annoyance, and in one instance obtained from a medical friend a stillborn child for dissection. This body, with an infatuation of which one would think only a scientific curate could be guilty, he would not keep in his lodgings, but deposited in the vault of his church, without concealment, but without clearly informing the sexton of the mode in which he obtained it. That official of course, full of the idea that a clergyman's only business with bodies was to bury them, suspected unutterable things, there was an inquest, a protracted examination, a great deal of evidence nasty enough out of a dissecting room, though not damaging to Mr. Hunt's character except for ordinary discretion and sense, and finally this special verdict returned by the coroner's jury:— 'That the deceased child was stillborn, and the jury, while admitting the right of the Rev. Mr. Hunt to study medicine, are of opinion that it would be better if he confined his studies to matters of a clerical character, to the exclusion of the study of anatomy.'

We do not know that we ever read a more curious exhibition of that middle-class *quasi*-reverential feeling which is fast reducing the English clergy to a position between that of men and women. The first impulse of every educated man on reading the verdict is probably to utter an anathema on its deliberate and formal impertinence, the jury having exactly as much to do with Mr. Hunt's studies as with those of the Archbishop of Canterbury or Lord Palmerston, but the anathema would be unjust. The decent but ignorant people who usually sit on coroner's juries never know, and cannot fairly be expected to know, the limits of their authority, while the coroner is far too rejoiced at getting any intelligible verdict at all to quarrel greatly with its form. Ignorant people always like to publish their 'sentiments' on any matter of interest, and this particular jury, we doubt not, really felt the 'sentiment' which they expressed. They really considered medicine, or at least its foundation— anatomy, a very unclerical study, and being entirely unrestrained by taste, judgment, or knowledge, they said so, characteristically enough guarding in the words of their verdict against any invasion of Mr. Hunt's legal right. They did not know if they denied Mr. Hunt's right of study what dreadful consequences might not follow to the unhappy curate, and being sufficiently fair people, as well as more than sufficiently stupid, they carefully protected *that*. He had a 'right' to study anatomy, only being in orders he had better not use it. Why not? Because anatomy is a wicked pursuit, or useless, or frivolous, or injurious to the mind? Not a bit of it. Even a coroner's jury is not exempt from disease, and consequently is not inclined to deny that anatomy may be a valuable study, but it is in their judgment as men of the world not consistent with the 'clerical' character, that is, with the total incapacity to do anything except preach or keep a school which the English middle class choose to think a qualification for the pastorate. The verdict is really directed not against this special study, but any study whatever not obviously essential to sermons. Not only is a knowledge of anatomy *not* 'unclerical,' but the most successful missionaries ever employed either by the Established or Nonconformist churches have been at once pastors and surgeons, have preached to the heathen in the morning and cured their ailments in the afternoon, have gained a hearing by distributing pills and secured converts who trusted them first because they cured painful sores. The world would be much the worse for the absence of Medical Missionaries. Dr. Judson, one of the most successful preachers who ever lived, was a skilled anatomist, and missionaries have been heard to regret keenly that knowledge of medicine is not made an absolute condition of selection. The use of such knowledge is at least as great in an English parish, where in hundreds of cases the poor man must either go without aid or obtain it from the only man in the parish who will give him the assistance of science without expecting reward in cash. Be he ignorant or well trained, the people still come to the pastor, and the only difference is that while if he has studied the 'unclerical' science he can relieve them skilfully, if he has not he is compelled to fall back on old women's recipes, or the cram rules of some homœopathic manual, or his own intelligence, which, as intelligence does not even teach a man where his own stomach is, is not worth a great deal. His wife's practice is even more risky, for women have a brave faith in drugs, and the minister's wife is consulted in cases where palliatives are of little avail. We do not hesitate to say that the general study of medicine by English clergymen would do more to reduce the sum of English misery than any single change likely to occur in society, and that it would directly strengthen their strictly 'clerical' influence. There is no man to whom you listen so readily as the man who has assuaged your pain, no man who may pray by the bedside of the dying so heartily as he who has striven in vain to postpone the dread hour which he now strives to soothe. There are no two functions in life more directly *en rapport* than those of physician and pastor, but what need of long-drawn argument when an unanswerable illustration lies so close at hand? The verdict of this sapient jury amounts to an assertion that it is highly 'unclerical' for a minister of Christ to qualify himself to imitate as closely as possible his Master's walk on earth. The single secular office assumed by Jesus was that of physician—healer, and the fact that He had and could have no need of study cannot diminish in any degree the weight of His example. Mr. Hunt cannot heal without means, but that is a reason for studying how to use means, not a reason for neglecting them. He cannot forgive sins either, but a jury would hardly aver that he was therefore never to study theology, never lay bare the bones of the heart in order to heal its diseases.

We have assumed of course all through that the jury did not intend to imply, as their words might seem to do, that it is possible to study medicine to purpose without studying anatomy first, or that the practice of medicine may be praiseworthy while that of surgery is 'unclerical.' If they meant either of those absurdities their opinion is not entitled even to the respect of contempt, but we do not believe they did. They were simply expressing the feeling becoming engrained in the popular mind that a pastor should be ignorant of all but theology, that art and science are irreligious, that a minister should confine himself to preaching and visiting, with good books for his sole reading and gossip for his only recreation. There are parishes in England where the clergyman must study chemistry on the sly, and geology in silence, and there is scarcely one in which the sight of an easel in the vicar's sitting room would not give deep offence. By an odd but explicable whim the study of astronomy, of all sciences the most absorbing, is exempted from censure, but it is the only one which would provoke from a party in the parish no kind of hostile comment. Such narrowness is, we are bound to say, almost confined to laymen, but it is lay opinion which in England creates the external law of the Church, and the opinion expressed so clearly by the City jury has two permanent and most pernicious effects. It forces on the clergy a kind of hypocrisy, an appearance of ignorance they do not feel, and it lowers throughout the country the clerical ideal. The true pastor to our minds is the man who, learned in all human learning, familiar with all human practice, physician and teacher, *savan* and divine, farmer and orator, uses those rich stores of capacity to higher ends than gain, who, touching life at all points, comprehends it in all, and derives from his comprehension the power of healing the physician obtains from the study which the St. Botolph's jury have taken on themselves to condemn. There must be anomalies, it would seem, in every condition of English life, but the limit of reason is surely passed when we contrive to create an opinion under which St. Luke would have been pronounced 'unclerical,' and St. Paul have been condemned by a jury for knowing how to make tents for the Roman army.

Spectator, 19 November 1864, pp. 1324–1325.

An Inquest on an Inquest (*Punch*)

An inquest was held on Tuesday last week by *Mr. Punch*, upon an inquest which had been held the day before by Mr. W. Payne upon a body. The circumstances of the case were these:—

A Clergyman, the Rev. John Hunt, Curate of St. Botolph's, Aldgate, had systematically studied anatomy for the very best of reasons, among them because 'he held it to be his sacred duty as a theologian to inquire into every quarter of Nature's kingdom, to search out her mysteries, and see her glorious and miraculous works.' He obtained, from a physician, the necessary means for acquiring anatomical knowledge, and in so doing neither infringed the Anatomy Act nor violated the decencies of life or death. That which he had procured for his purpose was the most unobjectionable thing for it that could possibly be conceived. However, a churchwarden, Mr. DAVID KING, found the thing in his possession, had suspicions about it, thought it formed a matter for investigation, 'refused to allow the case to drop, and would not have hushed it up for £1000.' Accordingly, he sent to the Coroner; an inquest followed; everything was quite satisfactorily explained. The Coroner, in charging the jury, was pleased to remark that 'it was clear the rev. gentleman had pursued medical studies; but whether wisely, or not, it was not for him to say.' He added, however, the following considerably more pertinent observation: —

'Certainly in a country district a Clergyman might be called in to a woman to give her religious consolation, and it might so happen that she might become suddenly ill, and his medical assistance would be of great use.'

The jury then laid their heads together to consider their verdict, and the conclusion which they arrived at was as follows: —

'That the deceased was stillborn, and the jury, while admitting the right of the Rev. Mr. Hunt to study medicine, are of opinion that it would be better if he confined his studies to matters of a clerical nature to the exclusion of the study of anatomy.'

Mr. Punch, after having pointed out the logical difficulty of accepting the statement that the 'deceased' was stillborn,' said he would only remark that ignorance of natural knowledge, and especially of anatomy, was particularly objected in the present-day against the clergy, and greatly impaired their influence and usefulness. His jury would now consider the verdict of that other jury, and give their own thereon.

Without a moment's deliberation the jury empanelled by Mr. Punch returned a verdict of 'Snobbish Impertinence'. They added that, whilst admitting the lamentable fact that vulgar blockheads are eligible to serve on Coroners' juries, they are of opinion that it would be better that such persons should cease to be so, and should be obliged to mind their own business, and confine their attention to their awls, or their geese, or to dispensing candles, red herrings, penn'orths of cheese, balls of twine, small parcels of sugar, tea, coffee, tobacco, snuff, vinegar, and pepper, and other groceries, or the like commodities, over the counter, to the exclusion of any office whose performance affords them an opportunity of making uncalled-for, offensive, and ridiculous remarks on the meritorious conduct of gentlemen.

Punch, 26 November 1864, p. 215.

Clergymen Made Scarce (*Punch*)

It used to be a saying, 'Make the greatest fool in the family a parson.' That saying still holds good, with a condition. Make the greatest fool in the family a parson, if he will let you. For he will not let you unless he is such a fool as the greatest fool in a very foolish family. That is, if you have not got a good fat living for him to step into as soon as he is ordained.

It is a bore to be obliged to wear a white 'choker'[1] when you prefer a black tie[2] or bird's-eye 'fogle.'[3] So it is to be obliged to refrain from going about smoking a short pipe if you wish to do so.[4] It is a monstrous bore to have your personal habits controlled and your natural freedom limited in any degree by the opinion of old women, or the power of old womanly bishops. No consideration but a very high pecuniary one would induce a man who has the least respect for himself to submit to any such dictation.

Fancy yourself being in such a position as to be liable to the censure of a set of snobs constituting a coroner's jury, because you, a curate, choose to study anatomy!

Then fancy your Rector, who ought to stand by you, and back you against those vulgar and impertinent blockheads, truckling to them and to their kind, and giving you the sack, to starve, or get your living how you can—that is, by begging or stealing, unless you possess a patrimony; for once a parson always a parson; and having once entered the clerical profession, no other is open to you; neither can you keep a shop or a public-house. But no. This last case is not to be fancied. No clergyman can be capable of the conduct supposed in it. The rumour that the rector of St. Botolph's, Aldgate, has, under circumstances such as these above stated, discharged his curate, the REV. MR. HUNT, is evidently an invention of the Jesuits, designed to damage the Church of England.

Punch, 17 December 1864, p. 251.

---

1 An ironic reference to the clerical neck-cloth, which is likened to the close-fitting and frequently broad necklace favoured by Victorian women (cf. https://en.wikipedia.org/wiki/Choker).

2 This could refer to either evening or day wear. Charles Dickens in *Our Mutual Friend* (1864–1865) describes the daytime wearing of 'formal black tie': 'Bradley Headstone, in his decent black coat and waistcoat, and decent white shirt, and decent formal black tie, and decent pantaloons of pepper and salt pantaloons', Charles Dickens, *Our Mutual Friend* (New York: Bradburn, 1864), p. 8.

3 Bird's eye fogle was a modish slang expression (first attested c. 1828), meaning 'a silk handkerchief with a bird's-eye pattern' (*Green's Dictionary of Slang* 2011). A fogle could be worn as a cravat around the neck.

4 Smoking a short pipe was regarded as working-class. Cf. *The Nautical Magazine and Naval Chronicle for 1842*, p. 156.

Extraordinary Charge against a City Clergyman

A most protracted inquiry of a very extraordinary character was held on Monday by Mr. W. Payne, coroner for the City of London, at the Vestry-room, Fountain court.

The inquest was held on view of the body of a newly-born male child, and owing to the revolting rumours afloat, the proceedings created in the locality remarkable interest.

Mr. Clines, vestry clerk, attended to watch the case on behalf of the parish authorities; and the Rev. Mr. Roberton, incumbent of St. Botolph, Aldgate, and the Rev. Mr. John Hunt, curate; and Mr. Churchwarden King, C.C.,[5] were also present.

The first witness called was Walter Parkhole,[6] 2, Spital-street, Mile-end, who said that he was steeple-keeper and gaslighter of the parish of St. Botolph. On the previous Friday at twelve o'clock he saw the body of the deceased child in the vault of the church of St. Botolph, Aldgate. It was wrapped up in a newspaper. Miss Hammond, the sextoness, brought him a message from the curate, the Rev. Mr. Hunt, to come to him in the Vestry-room. Witness accordingly went there, and Mr. Hunt told him that there was a parcel down in the vaults, and that he wanted the skeleton of a child. He said, 'There is no other way of doing it but to boil it.' Mr. Hunt gave witness a shilling to buy a saucepan to boil it in. Witness had the shilling now. He was to bring the pot to Mr. Hunt on the Saturday evening. Witness went out and told Mr. William Bigg and the sextoness.

By the Coroner: It was after that conversation that witness went into the vault and saw the body in a parcel. Witness took it up and put it in a shell lest the cats should get at it. Witness did not buy the pot as he did not think it right.

Mary Hammond, sextoness to the church, said that on the previous Wednesday the curate came to the church and said to witness, 'Open the vault door, and let me down there.' He said no more, and witness opened the vault and turned on the gas. The curate had a parcel, and he took it down into the vault and left it there. Witness thought it was

---

5   The postnominals indicate that he was a Common Councillor. Cf. 'City of London Corporation', *Wikipedia*, 2021 https://en.wikipedia.org/w/index.php?title=City_of_London_Corporation&oldid=1003604034

6   The name is spelled in various ways in the different newspaper articles.

a bundle of clothes. Witness then locked the vault. The Rev. Mr. Hunt came on Friday to churchings and baptisms. He told witness not to let the steeple-keeper go away before he (Mr. Hunt) saw him. The steeple-keeper came out and told witness that Mr. Hunt had given him a shilling to buy a pot to boil the child in.

Mr. David King, C.C., said that he was churchwarden of the parish of St. Botolph. From information given to him on Friday last be locked up the vaults of the church. On Saturday he requested the Rev. Mr. Roberton, the Rev. Mr. Hunt, and Mr. Clines, the vestry clerk, to meet him in the vestry-room, and at three o'clock he met them there. He cautioned the Rev. Mr. Hunt as to any statement he might make, and asked him for an explanation of the charge. The rev. gentleman treated the matter with great levity. He said that the body was that of a fœtus and not of a child, and that he only wanted to boil it to get the skeleton. When asked 'How and from whom did you get it?' he declined to answer. A surgeon was then sent for, and from what transpired they sent to the coroner. Afterwards Mr. Hunt stated that he wanted the child for scientific and anatomical purposes.

Mr. Andrew Holman, M.R.C.S., said that he had examined the body of the deceased. It had been only very recently born. No marks of violence were visible, but there was a very peculiar appearance over the whole body. It was perfectly bloodless. The umbilical cord was not tied, as was usual when medical men were present at the birth. The general practice among medical men was to tie the cord before it was cut, in order to prevent haemorrhage. In the present case it was cut with a sharp, and not, as was usual, with a blunt instrument. Witness said to the churchwarden, 'It is very suspicious; the child has bled to death.' Upon making a post-mortem examination, he found that the child was a well formed seven months child. The lungs were gorged with blood. He believed the child must have been alive up to the moment of birth, but might have died during birth. It might perhaps have given one cry, but it had not fully breathed. The lungs sank in water. He believed that it was the first child of a woman, and that the poor creature had delivered herself.

The Rev. John Hunt, 4, George-street, Minories, was then sworn. He said that he was curate of the parish of St. Botolph. On the defence which he could make for himself depended the judgment of the public, for a case in which a clergyman was concerned was not terminated by the verdict of a jury. He was charged, be supposed, with having placed under the church of which he was curate a human fœtus, and with having signified his intention to dissect the same. The first question the multitude would ask was, 'What has a clergyman to do with dissection?' Most people would answer, 'Nothing at all; his doctrine is to be derived from the written Word of God.' But others would remember that there was also a book of nature, wherein he might see God too, and wherein, with purified hearts and minds, communion might be held with the Eternal. He might be in the minority perhaps of his own profession, but he held it to be his sacred duty as a theologian to inquire into every quarter of nature's, kingdom, to search out her mysteries, and see her glorious and miraculous works, for in studying nature he was studying God. The greatest both in theology and science had declared that the two studies should never be divorced, and that from their union the best results might be expected. It had been urged against him that, as a clergyman, he could have no acquaintance with practical science, and that his only object in dissecting a fœtus was the gratification of an idle and improper curiosity. That he denied. He always had in view the interests of theology. He had attended a complete course of lectures of Mr. Savory, the eminent lecturer on anatomy and physiology at St. Bartholomew's Hospital, and that gentleman entirely agreed with him as to the benefit a theologian would derive from those studies. He had also attended other lectures at other hospitals. Dr. Hadlow, the medical officer of the parish, knew that for weeks past he had been engaged in close study of the homologies of vertebrate animals, and that he had written an article since forwarded to a scientific journal. Dr. Thynne gave him the fœtus as a present. Having no convenience at his lodgings he took it to the vaults and told Parkhole to bring a pot of warm water for the purpose of dissection. He found afterwards that he could not attend to it on Saturday night, and he therefore went earlier, when the sextoness told him that Mr. Churchwarden King ordered the vault to be kept locked. As the words 'boil' and saucepan' are by no means[7] agreeable associated with the idea of fœtuses, he must[8] solemnly declare in the sight of God and in the face of that assembly that the

---

7   no means] nomeans
8   must] most

words were not used by him. He first heard them from the lips of Mr. Churchwarden King. It was too ridiculous to suppose that he was so ignorant of dissection as to think of doing what would only have defeated his object. He offered either to remove the fœtus or to dissect it in their presence. Both proposals were refused. In conclusion the rev. gentleman complained bitterly of the conduct of Mr. King in bringing about the present inquiry. The breath of public suspicion, and distrust of his brethren in the ministry, or the disapprobation of his diocesan, might produce irreparable injury to him. He then called, for the defence,

Dr. Thomas Thynne, 140, Minories, who said that he had known the Rev. Mr. Hunt intimately. He had asked witness for a fœtus some months back. On the Wednesday witness was called in to a woman nearly confined. The child was dead. Witness obtained the child, which was premature, and gave it to the Rev. Mr. Hunt. The mother had had a fall previous to her delivery.

Dr. Hadlow said that the Rev. Mr. Hunt lived in his house, and was always devoted to medical studies.

Dr. Barnes said that the Rev. Mr. Hunt had studied medicine with him.

The Coroner said that it was clear that the rev. gentleman had pursued medical studies, but whether wisely or not it was not for him to say, Certainly in a country district a clergyman might be called in to a woman to give her religious consolation, and it might so happen that she might become suddenly ill, and his medical assistance would be of great use. In the present case the church wardens had done their duty. The public mind would not have been satisfied without an inquiry.

The foreman then said that the verdict of the jury was as follows:—'That the deceased child was stillborn, and the jury, while admitting the right of the Rev. Mr. Hunt to study medicine, are of opinion that it would be better if he confined his studies to matters of a clerical character to the exclusion of the study of anatomy.'

The proceedings then terminated.

Reynolds's Newspaper, 20 November 1864, p. 3

Singular Freak of a Clergyman

SINGULAR FREAK OF A CLERGYMAN.—An inquest has been held in the Vestry-room, Fountain-court, City, on the body of an infant child which was found in the vaults of St Botolph's Church, having been placed there by the Rev. John Hunt, curate to the Rev. Mr Robertson [sic, read *Roberton*], incumbent. —From the evidence it appeared that the rev. gentleman gave Walter Porkhall, the steeple-keeper, a shilling to buy a saucepan, which Porkhall thought was intended to boil the corpse in. Horrified at the idea, he told the incumbent and the churchwardens, which ended in the inquest being held.—Mr Hunt tendered himself for examination, and treated the charge of boiling the child with scorn. He said he was fond of scientific inquiries, which he believed had a direct bearing on theological truth; and a medical friend of his, knowing his tastes, had presented him with this fœtus—for it was no more—for the purposes of dissection.—This was clearly proved to be true by the evidence of the accoucheur who had delivered the mother and made the present to Mr Hunt; and the jury being satisfied of the facts returned a verdict that the child was still born, but recommending Mr. Hunt to confine his attention for the future to studies bearing more directly on his sacred profession.

Bedfordshire Times and Independent, 22 November 1864, p.8.

Presentation of a Testimonial to the Rev. John Hunt

ST. IVES. —*Presentation of a Testimonial to the Rev. John Hunt*. The Rev. John Hunt, who has been curate of this parish during the last two years, being about to leave St. Ives, several his friends decided to present him with a testimonial as a token of their respect and esteem for the efficient manner in which he had performed the duties of his sacred office. On Friday evening week a public meeting was held in the Institution Hall, for the purpose of making the presentation to the rev. gentleman. Mr. Read Adams having been called to the chair, said he had both an agreeable and unpleasant task to perform; it was agreeable to have to present the testimonial to the rev. gentleman, but unpleasant to have to take leave of him. Mr. Hunt was a talented and able scholar of the Protestant Church of England, and a stern opponent of the Ritualistic and semi-Popery practices which were being introduced into the Church; and it was because of this, and his refusal to preach Catholic doctrines that he was about leaving St. Ives. Addressing the rev. gentleman, he said he had the honour of presenting him with a purse containing 30 guineas, subscribed by fifty-two of the inhabitants of St. Ives, and he hoped he would enjoy long life and every happiness (loud cheers).—The Rev Jno. Hunt, in acknowledging the testimonial, said he was proud to receive it, and in looking over the list of subscribers he found, with but few exceptions, the names of all the principal church-going people of the town, and also those of several Dissenters. It is true that some of the subscriptions were small, but when he knew that the testimonial was in contemplation, it was his wish that it should be made up of small sums rather than a few large ones. It was more gratifying to him to find that his services had been appreciated by the whole parish than only by a few persons in it. He expressed the wish that no one might be allowed to give more than 2s. 6d., but this was overruled by those who had the management of the testimonial. It was at his own request that it should be in money, rather than as something which would be merely an ornament; not that he was in want of money, but because money was one of the most useful things in the world. He should not tell them how it would be spent but should keep it till some great occasion required it that he might, with greater gratitude, remember the gift. He then referred to the propriety of such gifts to curates when they do their work satisfactorily in a parish, as those curates who have only their own merits to depend upon, have but few chances of promotion in the Church. This[9] was great evil, and deprived her of the services of many able men, and there were in consequence not a sufficient number of educated men to supply the ranks of the clergy. To devise remedies for this must be left with those who have the government of the Church. He thought it would be well that if in every parish where there is a curate the parishioners would unite to provide his salary, and claim in return a voice in his election. The clergy of the Established Church well know that before long, if they are to keep their position, they must pay more attention to the will of the people. They must cease to come into their parishes as hierarchical autocrats. By the constitution of the Church of England they are the servants of the people. The churches do not belong to them, nor even to the patrons of the

---

9   This] this

livings. They are the property of the nation, and therefore the property of the inhabitants of the parish. He regarded this testimonial as being presented to him without reference to any other person. He knew some had been deterred from subscribing lest a wrong construction should be upon it, or wrong use made of it. This was a groundless fear, and would never have been entertained had they known as much about the history of this testimonial as he did. He should never regret having spent nearly two years in St. Ives, and he trusted they would never regret the graceful and becoming act which you have now performed. He wished he had been able to have done more, but being engaged in the completion of a work, it had deprived him of much of the time which otherwise would have been devoted to his pastoral duties. Allusion has been to what is now going on in your parish church; that subject is between you and your Vicar. It was not his (Mr. Hunt's) business to enter into that. You must fight your own battles, or make the best truce you can. Several had come to him earnestly imploring his advice, and the only advice which he thought it his duty to give was, *whatever you do, do it as Christians and as gentlemen*. It is well known that the Vicar publicly condemned his (Mr. Hunt's) doctrines by silencing him in the pulpit, as soon as he had taken possession of the living. He (Mr. Hunt) had defended himself firmly. The Vicar has followed a decided course, but there has been no approach to any misunderstanding or unchristian feeling between us, and trusted the time had come when men could discuss theological subjects with calmness, but with firmness, without reference temporal to interests, and without exciting angry passions. We have set you this example in St. Ives, and he hoped they would all follow it. Whatever differences you may have with your Vicar, you will always find him ready to reason with you. Do not be outdone by him in Christian feeling. Give him credit for right motives, and whatever practical good he does. Jesus has taught us, in the beautiful parable of the man who fell among thieves, that it was the Samaritan with the erroneous creed who showed mercy, while the orthodox Jew passed by on the other side. Christian charity is better than orthodoxy. There are good men of all creeds, yet their goodness need not blind us to the falseness of their creeds. Their hearts are better than their heads—their lives better than their doctrines. The rev. gentleman then referred to the cause of the present excitement in the church, which was caused, he considered, by the semi-popish practices which many of the clergy were introducing into it, and warned his hearers to be on their guard not to be led away from the Protestant Church of England, and went on to say we should ever be proud of the word Protestant; it is the watchword of free arguing, free thought, and free speech. It comes to us laden with the history of the struggles our forefathers, when they fought for the right, and showed in the glorious battle of freedom, that battle which

> Once begun,
> Descends from bleeding sire to son.
> Which, baffled oft, is ever won.

It is a word pregnant with great things for the future, a word we must never abandon. He animadverted, in severe terms, on Dr. Pusey and his followers; and referring to Dr. Pusey's work *Eirenicon*, he said it had inflicted a blow on his cause which it cannot survive, for every one who is capable of putting two ideas alongside of each other will see that he and his disciples have not an inch of ground to stand upon. He then went on to say that no National Church can exist in England which does not recognise as branches of the Church catholic the great bodies of Nonconformists. The future of the Church of England depends on which of the two parties in the Church shall finally prevail—those who follow Scripture and reason or those who follow Scripture and tradition. If the latter, its existence as the National Church is doomed. If the former, it may work the wellbeing of the nation and be the great bulwark of sound religion and the enemy of superstition throughout the world. The rev. gentleman concluded by saying he should not bid them farewell, as he had promised to deliver a lecture during the winter for the Mutual Improvement Society. And, after again expressing his regret that he had been able to do so little amongst them, dismissed them with the prayer 'God be with you all.' During the delivery of his address, he was frequently and loudly applauded.

Cambridge Independent Press, 20 October 1866, p. 6.[10]

---

10 Cf. also *Cambridge Chronicle and University Journal, Isle of Ely Herald, and Huntingdonshire Gazette*, 20 October 1866, p. 6.

Lecture on St Augustine

ST. IVES.— Lecture. On Thursday evening last week, a lecture was delivered in the Institution Hall by the Rev. Jno. Hunt, formerly curate of this parish, on St. Augustin, Bishop of Hippo, Regius Confessor, and Doctor.' There was a very good attendance, and the Rev. J. K. Holland presided. We regret to state that the audience was much annoyed by the disgraceful conduct of certain persons—who, from their position in society, ought to have known better—interrupting the rev. gentleman nearly all the time he was speaking by hissing, scraping of feet, and other discordant noises, the cause of which was not that they disapproved of the subject of the lecture or what the speaker said, but because of a personal ill-feeling towards him arising from a pamphlet published by him shortly after he left this town, entitled, *'Clergymen Made Scarce,'* a portion of which seems to have given great offence to these persons. We certainly think it showed very bad taste on their part to assail the lecturer in the way they did, particularly as the subject and the opinions he expressed had not the remotest connection with the pamphlet in question. If they had any objection to the statements it contained, why did they not wait until the conclusion of the lecture, and then ascend the platform, and discuss the matter with the rev. gentleman, or invite him to attend another evening to argue the points in dispute; such a course would have been far more creditable to them than the one they adopted. Although the audience evinced its disapprobation of their conduct by loud and repeated cries of 'Shame, shame!' it had not any effect upon them. But the worst part of the affair remains to be told. Shortly before the audience began to assemble, one of the committee of the 'Mutual Improvement Society,' by whom the rev. gentleman was engaged, happening to go into the hall, found that a most filthy and sickening odour pervaded it, so bad indeed was it that it was almost impossible for anyone to remain long in the place; on searching about for the cause, it was discovered that some dastardly fellow had placed a quantity of asafoetida under the platform. This was speedily removed, and disinfectants being freely used, the effects of the cowardly act became partly neutralized. We hope that the perpetrator will be discovered and receive the punishment he so richly deserves.

Cambridge Independent Press, 30 March 1867, p. 6.

Review of *Religious Thought in England* I

If the labour of writing this volume was at all commensurate with the labour of reading it, no one can charge the author with lack of conscientiousness. It has seldom been our fate to come across so ponderous and dreary a digest of theology. It is really a most remarkable monument of laborious care, to supply a fresh controversial manual for a public which by this time is almost satiated with religious discussions. As a matter of course Mr. Hunt begins by claiming credit for fairness and impartiality, while the first sentence of his work shows that nothing can be further from his intention than to take the impartial view of his subject. He writes in fact as a virulent Protestant, equally opposed to the High Anglican as to the Roman systems. Before he has got over his first page he falls foul of Dr. Pusey, the main reasoning of whose 'Eirenicon' he is content to dismiss in a foot-note, with a mere passing sneer; and this promising opening sufficiently indicates what the reader has to expect who can summon courage to pursue his weary task. We give Mr. Hunt, however, the fullest credit for diligence. His work consists mainly of voluminous extracts from writers of the Church of England and almost every conceivable sect of Protestantism, with his own comments thereon. Among such names as those of Cranmer, Ussher, Hooker, Milton, and Baxter, he has unearthed many whose names are quite obscure, and others whose works have been long practically consigned to oblivion. He shows a singular lack of any power of arranging these copious materials, and there seems to be not even the attempt at a summary or analysis of the disconnected matter which he has brought together. Possibly he intends something of the kind in a later volume, for which those whose taste lies in that direction are obliged, as the rest of us may be very well contented, to wait yet awhile.

'Review of *Religious Thought in England. From the Reformation to the End of Last Century*. A Contribution to the time History of Theology. By the Rev. John Hunt, M.A. Vol. I.—London: Strahan and Co., 1870', in *John Bull*, 1 October 1870, p. 683.[11]

---

11   Numerous reviews of Hunt's work, especially his *Religious Thought in England*, were published. These show something of the impact of Hunt's scholarship and its mixed reception.

Review of *Religious Thought in England* II

THE volume before us is a further instalment of Mr. Hunts laborious task—the history of religious thought in England from the Reformation to the end of the eighteenth century. Mr. Hunt has now reached the end of the seventeenth, and given notices of the principal Deist writers in the beginning of the eighteenth century. So far as industry and impartiality can entitle a writer to praise, he is entitled to it in no common degree; and it may also be said with confidence that his book is calculated to be of great service to future students of English theological literature.

There is, however, a further question upon which we must dwell rather more fully. In his preface Mr. Hunt defends himself against certain criticisms—our own being apparently among the number—which had been directed against his first volume. Why, we asked on that occasion, had not a man who was so well qualified for the task gone a little further? why did he not trace the connection of doctrines prevalent at a given time with those prevalent at different times or in other countries? why, in short, did he not give us a philosophical account of the genesis of opinion, instead of a bare statement of facts? To this demand his answer is in one sense conclusive. He says that he intended only to collect and arrange materials, and not to give his own theories. He considered himself to be writing 'part of the history' of religion, and not 'the philosophy of the history of religion.' Of course there is nothing more to be said. Beggars must not be choosers. Mr. Hunt was under no moral or legal obligation to give us anything, and if, out of his mere grace and bounty, he throws us half-a-crown, it is perhaps ungrateful to murmur because it is not a sovereign. We will, however, add that the criticism implied a compliment. We should have liked a little more philosophy from Mr. Hunt, because we think him capable of being philosophical, and we regard it as a misfortune that a man who has collected so many valuable materials should not have chosen to construct an edifice with them. The misfortune is that somebody will very likely attempt to give us the philosophy without the material. Let us hope that Mr. Hunt will anticipate such a result by doing the work himself at some future period.

Meanwhile, however, Mr. Hunt, not content with claiming his indisputable liberty to abstain from writing a philosophical treatise, has put in some further pleas, of which we must venture to speak. He says in the first place: 'Merely to have given my own conclusions or my own theories would have been easier to me, and perhaps more agreeable to my readers.' We take leave to dispute this altogether. If Mr. Hunt means, indeed, that it would have been easier to run up some flashy theory without troubling himself about the facts, he is speaking within bounds. But nobody ever asked him, so far as we know, to do anything so foolish. What he was asked to do was to form some intelligent theories on the mass of crude fact, and then to make the theory and the narrative of fact mutually illustrate each other. He was asked to give us a philosophical history, not a philosophy without the history; and to do this as it ought to be done would involve much severe intellectual labour in addition to, and not in the place of, all that he has actually undergone. It would therefore have been harder for him, though, as we fancy, much more agreeable to his readers. Mr. Hunt, indeed, speaks almost as if he doubted the possibility of such a performance. 'It has been intimated,' he says, 'that there is a principle of progress or development to be traced in this history, but I have not been forward to trace it.' The whole value of the history seems to us to depend upon the fact that there are such principles of development, whether supplied by the writer or the reader. Without it, a history of ideas is as barren as the old-fashioned history of events. It is of no interest to a rational being to be told that at one time a man wrote a book about justification by faith, and at another time somebody else wrote a book about the law of nature, without any attempt to show why particular subjects[12] were interesting at given times and why particular methods of inquiry were in favour, any more than to be told that a battle was fought here and a treaty made there, without any attempt to trace out the political and social changes with which they were inseparably connected. The so-called history becomes a mere string of barren statements without any significance until they have been made a foundation for subsequent conclusions. Mr. Hunt's view of his duties explains another sentence in his preface. 'A history of ideas,' he says, 'could not be expected to have the same interest as a history of events.' That is a matter of taste. In our opinion, a well-managed history of ideas would be far more interesting to any one with a soul above sensation novels. It would be more interesting because the facts can be more satisfactorily ascertained, because they

---

12 subjects] subject

are generally more important, and because it is easier to trace the 'principle of development,' of which Mr. Hunt speaks, in a progress which is less dependent upon external accidents. As a matter of fact, few more interesting books have been written than some histories of this nature. The statement is apparently made under the impression that Mr. Hunt's critics made unfair demands upon him, and imputed to him a dulness which was inherent in the subject. We confess—though it may make against our claims of impartiality—that we have in fact found Mr. Hunt dull. Yet we venture to assert that our weariness was not owing to any want of interest in the subject; on the contrary, we know of few subjects on which we should receive with greater pleasure the views of so intelligent a writer if only he would condescend to give them. The dulness is due to the simple fact that Mr. Hunt has chosen to give us, not a philosophy of the history, nor a philosophical history, nor even, to speak correctly, a history of any kind, but simply a collection of annals. A history would imply grouping of facts; some attempt in this particular instance to present a coherent and systematic picture of the theological ideas current in England during a given period; some attempt to tell us what were the topics upon which the thinkers of the time employed their intellects and the methods by which they endeavoured to arrive at a solution of the problems presented to them. Such a picture may be formed by the reader himself if he has sufficient memory and patience; but he will not find it prepared for him. Mr. Hunt has simply given us a number of careful analyses of the principal books written during the period he is considering. An abstract is proverbially dull reading, and a whole series of abstracts is inconceivably depressing after a time, even if, as in this case, they are intelligently and carefully performed. So far from there being any effective grouping, it is difficult to discover the principle on which Mr. Hunt has arranged his book. In a general way he roughly follows a chronological order; occasionally he becomes biographical, and puts together all the works of any given author, however distant may be the periods of their publication, and sometimes he follows the order of ideas and puts together all the books bearing upon one particular issue. Thus, for example, the controversy about Toleration and the Trinitarian controversy are followed out as continuous subjects, and towards the end of the volume the Deist controversy naturally absorbs all other topics. Yet Toland is separated from Shaftesbury, Collins, and Tindal by many pages, including accounts of South, Bishop Bull, the theology of the Quakers, and various other subjects. Culverwell, whose 'Light of Nature' was published in 1652, precedes Wollaston, whose 'Religion of Nature Delineated' appeared in 1722, and next comes Shaftesbury, whose works had appeared from ten to fourteen years earlier than Wollaston's. This is an arrangement by subjects; but in another chapter we have an account of Archbishop Sharp's views on predestination, on the Sabbath, and on the Eucharist, Bishop Kidder's appeal to the Jews, Patrick's theory of the sacraments, Fowler's Platonism, and Stillingfleet's theories of Church unity, all following each other in succession, apparently on mere chronological grounds. We do not, of course, deny that it would be extremely difficult to arrange all these complex subjects in a perfectly clear and consecutive manner; and, equally of course, a writer who almost prides himself on being nothing but an annalist will care comparatively little for a confused effect produced upon the mind of the reader.

Our criticism comes, indeed, chiefly to this—that Mr. Hunt's book is rather useful for purposes of reference than as a narrative of the ordinary kind, though even here we have one more criticism to add. Mr. Hunt, in his preface, says that some of his critics—we believe that we were again among the number—complained of a want of dates. He has endeavoured, he says, to comply with the demand; but he does not admit that the first volume was deficient. 'Dates were not always given,' he says, 'but it was generally mentioned who was Archbishop of Canterbury at the time of any controversy or the public activity of any great writer.' We confess that we had not noticed that help. But even if the Archbishop was generally mentioned, that still leaves considerable latitude. Sheldon was Archbishop for fifteen and Tenison for twenty-one years. Now, though Mr. Hunt does not seem to observe it, dates may be of great importance even in matters of this kind. Great books are frequently in close connection with great events. The writings, for example, on Toleration were prompted by the contemporary legislation, and such a book as Samuel Johnson's on passive obedience can only be understood fairly by reference to a particular crisis. We may wish to know what writer had the priority in suggesting a particular argument, whether he was writing under circumstances, which made a full confession of faith dangerous, at what age he had arrived at certain conclusions, and so on. We wish in using a book of reference to have such facts staring us in the face, and not to be obliged to make a vague inference from the contemporary Archbishop, or to be sent to hunt in a biographical dictionary. Again, when a reference is given it is not pleasant to be told that the 'subject will indicate the chapter, which may be easily found from the table of contents;' and that where the page is not given, 'the substance of what is said will be found not far from the quotation.' The practical result is simply that if you wish to verify some interesting remark, you must take the trouble of hunting through a table of contents and a chapter. The process may only occupy ten minutes; but when by a little trouble on the part of the author the ten minutes might have been reduced to one, you are apt to lose temper. An excess of clearness, rather than a defect, is a high merit in a book of this class.

However, with all its shortcomings, Mr. Hunt's book will be a considerable assistance to students of theological literature. We have been forced to indulge chiefly in criticism of an adverse kind; but we should be doing the work great injustice if we did not fully admit its substantial merits.

'Review of *Religious Thought in England*. By the Rev. John Hunt. Vol. II. (London: Strahan and Co. 1871)', in *Pall Mall Gazette*, 29 November 1871, p. 12.

Review of *Religious Thought in England in the Nineteenth Century*

THIS is an annoying book, because in some respects it is so good that it ought to have been better in all, and might easily be made so. Mr. Hunt has done well to continue into the present century his history of religious thought in England since the Reformation. It would be more accurate, however, to describe the present work as a history of books on or bearing upon religious subjects, since for the most part the author is content to examine the theological literature of successive periods of the century, and summarize its contents and tendency. No doubt this is a useful study in itself, and the record is one of great value to the theological student. But we should not ourselves describe it as a history of religious thought. The course of a people's thought in religion must be traced outside the limits of its expression, not merely in theological books, but in books of any sort. Mr. Hunt's readers should understand the somewhat esoteric sense in which he employs his title.

Nor can we unreservedly commend the way in which the author has carried out his task. Mr. Hunt is painstaking and industrious indeed, but ponderous beyond belief or endurance. Compared with such a work as Dean Church's history of the Oxford movement, or even Messrs. Abbey and Overton's record of the English Church in the eighteenth century, Mr. Hunt's book is painfully hard reading. Moreover, the space allotted to some teachers — notably S. T. Coleridge and Frederick Maurice — is absurdly inadequate; although, so far as he goes, the author's summaries are very fairly accurate and impartial. Some of them — as the chapter on the Bampton and Hulsean lectures — are particularly well done, and furnish a most useful magazine of reference. Mr. Hunt need not have disclaimed partisanship with quite so much emphasis in his preface, for he allows his own sympathies to appear on almost every page, and even spends ink and paper in an attempt to show that the Thirty-nine Articles are Calvinistic! Surely they are not sufficiently definite for that: they are, of course, and were meant to be, a deliberately ambiguous compromise. In a future edition many exasperating little mistakes will call for correction — e.g. Disciplina *Arcana* (p. 126); Denison was Archdeacon of Taunton, not Frome (p. 172); where is Well Street? (p. 209); and what are archaicisms? (p. 214). Mr. Hunt's own errata seem to indicate a desire to improve the English language.

'Review of *Religious Thought in England in the Nineteenth Century. By the Rev. J. Hunt, D.D. (London: Gibbings & Co. 1896)*', in *Saturday Review of Politics, Literature, Science and Art*, 6 February 1897, p. 154.

Review of *Religious Thought in England in the Nineteenth Century*

Religious Thought in England during the Nineteenth Century. By the Rev. John Hunt, D.D. (Gibbings and Co.)—Dr. Hunt quotes a saying of Goethe (referring to a question of natural history that was being hotly debated), 'I do not judge; I only record,'[13] and adopts it as his own rule.

---

13 The original, of which this is a not very accurate translation, is 'Ich lehre nicht, ich erzähle', a translation by Goethe of Montaigne (Zur Morphologie: Principes de

It is easy to see, however, that if he is neutral, his neutrality is benevolent to parties and individual thinkers who have advocated liberal views. The first chapter is given to a brief account of various divines who really belong to the eighteenth century rather than to the nineteenth, Paley to Vicesimus Knox. It is impossible, however, to keep strictly to time limits, and these and other writers to whom Dr. Hunt devotes some of his pages have to be considered if we are to understand the religious history of the time. No account of the evidential controversy would be complete without a notice of Paley, however far we may have moved from his standpoint. Chap. 3 introduces us to Simeon and the Evangelicals; and in chaps. 4–5 we hear about the apologetic writers of the early half of the century; while in chap. 6 we have a reference to the Establishment Controversy, illustrated by the story of the Disruption in the Scottish Church. Further on we find a description of the Tractarian movement, and of the development of Coleridgean thought which went alongside with it. A separate chapter is devoted to 'Essays and Reviews,' and another to Unitarianism, Old and New. Chap. 19 is given to an account of various sceptical writers, among whom we are somewhat surprised to see the author of 'Ecce Homo.' Dr. Hunt should be aware that 'Ecce Homo' was an accommodation to circumstances. It was certainly intended to strengthen belief, not to weaken it. It is impossible that a volume so comprehensive should do equal justice to all the writers whom it seeks to represent. Of Dr. Hunt's industry, intelligence, and candour there can be no question. The press might have been more carefully corrected. 'Catagorise' disfigures the preface, and on p. 10 Bishop Porteus (born in 1731) is said to have promoted a petition in 1722.

'Review of *Religious Thought in England during the Nineteenth Century*', in *Spectator*, 2 October 1897, p. 25.

Dr. Hunt's Travels.

The Vicar of Otford, the Rev. Dr. Hunt, gave an interesting lecture on his travels at the National Schools on the 4th inst. In the course of his remarks, the Rev. gentleman said:—'There are certain reasons why men

---

Philosophie Zoologique. Discutés en Mars 1830 au sein de l'académie royale des sciences par Mr. Geoffroy de Saint-Hilaire, Paris 1830, II. Abtheilung: 7. Band, 1892), https://goethe.chadwyck.com

travel—one is to see the country, another is to learn the language, and a third is to see something different from what they see at home.

We English may be very great people, but we live in a small island. The world outside of us is very large. To see the manners and customs of many men, and many nations makes a man very learned. As to languages, I have been learning them for many years. I taught German, French and Italian when I was 20 years of age—but to know a language in a book is a very different thing from speaking it. When I had to speak German I had not the word at hand, which I wanted. I had to look in the dictionary for it, and when I found it I had to think a long time till I ventured the next word. When I was in France, I found they called their mothers mères,[14] and their daughters filles. They run all the words together. I should have known them if had word for word, but they so jumbled them together, they seemed like monkeys talking gibberish. When I tried Italian, which is an easy language, German came in my head, and I talked German to them better than I talked to the Germans. Now for my travels.

In the first place I went from here to Westgate, from thence I might have gone to Dover,[15] but the Archbishop had a garden party, and we must appear amongst the grand people. We went to the Archbishop's, where we were archiepiscopally treated. Then I learned that the man whom I had engaged for my duty was the same man whom ten years ago the last Archbishop would not allow to come. He was

in the black books

at Lambeth. After a day's toiling in the burning sun, we found another, of whom the Archbishop approved. We bought our tickets to Basle, at the Belgium State Railway Office, in Regent St., and proceeded by train to Dover. A very interesting journey, which, as you have all, I doubt not, enjoyed, I shall not say anything more about. We got on board the steamer bound for Ostend, and stayed on deck until a servant of the ship asked for 2s. from me, because I was a second class passenger, and the second class passengers were below. I remonstrated that a second class passenger had a right to be on the deck. Then he became facetious, and he said that at certain times I married people for a certain sum, but

---

14 mères] meres
15 Dover,] Dover.

at other times I charged much more. I promised I should marry him at any lawful time for 5s., provided he found a bride, so I did not pay the money. In four hours time we were in Belgium, and in half-an-hour more we were in Bruges. It is no great distance, but it is an altogether new country. Bruges was once a famous commercial town, when the population was four times what it is at present. Now it has little trade, the beautiful bells ring every quarter of an hour. The churches are many, and the people attend them with a regularity that would put us to shame. But by 12 o'clock religion is all over, and then they give themselves up to amusement. They are not accustomed to keep the whole day sacred. They begin their music and merriment, which goes on sometimes till past midnight. How the people can be so serious in the morning, and then throw it off by mid-day, is beyond our comprehension. We attended several churches, especially one of the Capuchins. The prostrations of the priests, their

bowings and crossings

were strange to us. But doubtless their belief is different. They believe that the Host is the actual body of Jesus Christ. At the end of the sermon an image of the Virgin Mary was carried around the church. The sermon was extempore, and the congregation very devout. We left Bruges for Ghent. There was a fete on. I suppose it was some Saints Day, but the people hallooed and howled the whole night. We had no rest, and hastened away by the earliest train the next morning, leaving them to continue the fete. We came to Brussels and took the precaution not to have a hotel near the station. It is a beautiful city. We visited the famous Wiertz gallery. After a long day's journey we came to Strasburg. We had some altercation with the porters about the money. Strasburg belonged to Germany, and our money was Belgian. Next day we arrived at Spiez. On our way there a gentleman asked in the train 'If I were Dr. Hunt?' I said I knew him, but I did not know his name. He answered that his name was Mulzenberg. He said I was not altered since he saw me 12 years before; I did not look a bit older than I did then. He asked where I was going, and I said to his house. This gentleman stayed with me 14 years ago to learn English. He was then a very young man, just engaged to be married, and the first thing he wanted to know was the English for the young woman he was engaged to. And I told him he must say

'The girl I walk with'! or another form 'The girl I keep company with.'! His hotel was larger than it was years ago. When I was there last it was a very modest building, but the railway has come since that time, and he has added an immense building, that now he can accommodate 150 people. Mr. Mulzenberg, who was a slender young man when he was at Otford, has now grown a jolly hotel keeper. We crossed the lake in the steamer, and were taken up Beatenberg in a *funicular* railway. I called it a vernacular, being more familiar with that word. This is a railway that goes up a mountain. When got up, we had a glorious view of the Swiss Mountains, clad in everlasting snows, the Jungfrau, the Monk, and the Eiger, and many others. It was a glorious panorama of snow mountains, and we saw it in the middle of summer.

After this we set out for Gruyères.[16] We could have gone by Berne, but we preferred

a romantic route.

We went by diligence two-thirds of the journey, and the rest by rail. We arrived late in the evening. You can imagine us toiling up a steep hill, twice as high as Otford Mount. At a late hour in the evening we arrived at our destination, had supper and went to bed. We awoke next morning, in what is said to be the oldest town in Switzerland. It consists of one street. An old Castle at one end is inhabited by a Geneva goldsmith. At the other end was the dwelling of some pigs and cows. We went one morning to see the pigs, when a young woman said to us that they were very 'dégoutant,'[17] but made good 'jambon.'[18] That is, they were very disgusting, but they made good ham. There were two fountains, and every day the women were busy washing. There was also a school for teaching the deaf and dumb to speak; the Roman Catholic Sisters bestow much labour on these unfortunates. We heard them speak, but we could not speak to them. They were deaf, so that their education was of doubtful benefit.

But the grand sight at Gruyères was the church. It was Roman Catholic, but there was no other place to go so we went there; we thought it better to go to the Roman Catholic Church than not to go anywhere. It

---

16 Gruyères] Gruyeres (passim)
17 dégoutant] degoutant
18 jambon] jambor

is doubtless an open question. There are many things done in the Roman Catholic Church which we regard as a perversion of Christianity. But it was a delight to see the crowds that attended the services on Sundays. The bell begins at 6 a.m. in the morning and the church was thronged until mid-day. Down the steep hills and up the valleys of Gruyères came the cowherds, with a prayer book in their hands, and their sleeves washed white, to offer their early oblation. The church, which was large, was not only full to the door, but there were some praying outside. On a tombstone erected to the memory of a former Curé, it was written 'He loved the sheep and the sheep loved him.' It happened while were there that the new Pope was elected. The priest told the young men to light bonfires on the tops of the mountains. When they were lighted it was a grand sight, but in the evening came such a storm of thunder, lightning and rain, that the fires were soon extinguished, and the very rocks seemed to rend and the trees to burn with fire. Before I leave Gruyères[19] I want to tell you something about my hat. You all know my hat. It is broader in the brim than most men's hats. I mean my old hat, but they are all alike. It was coveted by a woman in Gruyères. Mrs. Hunt thought it was for her son, but to her amazement found she intended wearing it herself, with the addition of a feather, as her Sunday hat. From Gruyères we made a journey to Lausanne and Geneva. Lausanne we found a clean industrious Protestant town. Thence to Geneva. The rail runs along the edge of the lake through fields of vines, with the vast mountains of the Jura to the right. Geneva is the chief town in Switzerland. It is the town of

anarchists and revolutionists.

The population is equally divided between Protestants and Roman Catholics. Here was one of the chief centres of Reformation. It was in Geneva that the great Calvin lived and laboured. We heard a sermon in the Cathedral, but it was a poor echo of Calvin. On the bridge, where Mont Blanc is visible, the mountain is seen like a great giant towering above its fellows. From Geneva we returned to Spiez. We arrived at Lucerne in the evening, and after staying a night we took the steamboat to Flüelen;[20] here are mountains all round, and here is Pilatus, from which Pontius Pilate is said to have thrown himself down in remorse for

---

19   Gruyères] Gruyerès (passim)
20   Flüelen] Fluelen (passim)

having condemned the Just One; here was the Rigi, to which the ascent is by a funicular railway; here we have the legend of William Tell; the shooting of an apple from his son's head. All the country is celebrated by Schiller, who has devoted a play to the subject. At Flüelen we prepared to go through the St. Gothard Tunnel, the largest in the world. We are now on the other side of the Alps, and settled at Giubiasco,[21] a forlorn village near Bellinzona.

This is a new country and a different people. This is Italian Switzerland. The people are Italians. They are evidently poorer than those on the other side of the Alps; they are certainly not so clean; they work as hard and fare worse; the children are dirty, bare-footed wretches; the mothers are not much better, but though not able to buy shoes they wear clogs. The people called me the 'learned man' or the 'English Priest.' They all knew I was a clergyman and showed me great reverence. I was told they did not know the difference between Roman Catholic and Protestant, but they had great respect for all clergy. I was disposed to laugh at some of the pictures in the Churches and the holy houses. They were the work of country artists and often comic in their simplicity, but a young man warned me that they, the people, would be much offended if they saw me laughing either at their pictures or their images. 'The people,' he said, 'are ignorant and stupid, but they are sincere.' In a back street in Milan the people called after me 'A Pope. A Pope,' and I had the same salutation from some women in Rome. Even a troop of soldiers, on horseback, who passed me one day when walking outside the walls of Rome, all put their hands to their chin and shouted 'Barba. Barba.' At another place some girls were dancing to a hurdy-gurdy, who, as soon as they saw me, took to their heels and vanished.

Of Giubiasco I had pleasant remembrances. Ten years ago I spent a happy Christmas Day there, and I had pleasant recollections of the pheasants which we had for dinner. I went to the door of the hotel expecting to see my old friends, but they were not there. The servant had not understood what I said, so she ran to her mistress. She was equally confounded, but she sent for a German woman, who lived opposite, and she came when we conversed freely. The landlady began to talk, and in time we understood her. We learned the former landlord was dead, and the present occupiers were from Milan. The landlady

---

21   Giubiasco] Guiliasco (passim)

was tall, handsome and young; she had been at Shanghai where she had learned some English, but had almost forgotten it. The landlord was a young man, with the Roman blood in his veins. We explored the old town; the houses had been good, but decay seemed written on everyone. The burden of life falls heaviest on the women of all ages. We saw them groaning under loads of wood which they carried home for fire. We had daily walks in the green lanes, gathering bramble berries, or what you call blackberries, which there are ripe in the month of July. One Sunday night was very riotous. The people drank in a large public room below our bedroom, played and sang all night, so we had no sleep. We had stayed a week and learned that the anniversary of the Canton was to be held on the week following, so we thought it best to move on and leave the merry making to the people themselves. In the early morning we went to Lugano to take the steamer on the lake. The lake Lugano is very beautiful; on either side there are choice villas on the slopes; the sail was enchanting. In leaving the lake we left Switzerland, and after a railway ride through the mountains we arrived at Menaggio, on Lake Como. This is a choice resort of visitors and tourists. On one side is Bellaggio, which is called Paradise, for its beauty; on the other side Cadenabbia, with its magnificent hotels; a little further on is Tremezzo, where we intended to take up our abode for a time. On my arrival I asked for a glass of beer, but it was not to be had. I then asked for a bottle, for which I paid about 1s. 6d. There was no draught ale to be had; wine is the chief drink and it is cheaper than beer. In the evening I sat in the front of the hotel, in the gardens on the edge of the lake and watched the moon, with its accompanying star-rise above the mountains. It was interesting to see it gradually rising later and later till it disappeared. On Sunday we went to Cadenabbia to church. Here we had an English Church, but in everything it imitated the Roman Catholic. The clergyman held up his hands at the celebration of the Eucharist, and the bell tolled at the moment when the bread and wine were supposed to be transubstantiated into something else. When the administration took place the clergyman gave me a wafer, which I did not eat. It was so like that given by Roman Catholics that I kept it as a curiosity. I would much rather have the real Roman Catholic thing than this poor imitation. After 10 days at Tremezzo we again sailed on Lake Como. The steamer we sailed by was called 'Plinio,' from Pliny, who was born at Como. This is an elegant little town which

I had visited before, but this time we made for Milan. The interest of Milan centres around the Cathedral. It is a magnificent building of pure marble, and seems as if every block had some design upon it. There we bought the tickets for a tour round Italy. We arrived first at Verona. You will have heard of the 'Two Gentlemen of Verona,' if you have not read the play. Here we saw the house of the family of Juliet, the supposed tomb of Juliet of the famous play. From Verona we went to Venice. We reached Venice in a great storm of rain. We asked for a gondola to take us to the hotel 'Vapore,' but the porter put our luggage in the gondola belonging to the hotel 'Vittoria.' It contained some other passengers whom I found to be Americans. The gondoliers followed with a few more strokes of the oars, and we reached the watery entrance of a very large hotel. We visited St. Mark's, one of the wonders of architecture, where the campanile, or tower, fell two years ago. We were amused with the myriads of pigeons in the square where they came on our arms and shoulders to be fed. We visited the Bridge of Sighs, which crosses a canal and connects the Doge's Palace with the prison house. Lord Byron wrote: 'I stood in Venice on the Bridge of Sighs.' At the hotel we had large nets over our beds. These were to keep the mosquitoes from biting us. Our next town was Bologna. A fine old town full of porticoed streets, and from thence to Florence. This is the most beautiful city in Italy, and the most beautiful in its surroundings. We went four or five miles out by rail to the ruins of an old Etruscan town, Fiesoli. Here was lately unearthed the ruin of a theatre and a temple of Jupiter. It was a beautiful evening in September and the scene was

like a fairyland.

About here was the Vallombrosa[22] of the poets, a shady vale, where all was harmony and beauty. One Sunday morning we set out for the English Church, but when we got there it was closed for September. There are several bridges over the Arno, but one of them is a picture gallery, a mile in length. In the centre of the town we stood on the place where Savonarola, the Rreformer of Florence, was burned. We left Florence for Rome, but as it would be too late before we arrived there we spent a night on the way. We stopped at a place called Orte, but we

---

22   Vallombrosa] Vallambrosa

found that there was only one Inn if it might be called by that name, where we could obtain accommodation and the place was so awfully filthy that we regretted having come out of the train. The bed we had was clean, and the food was plentiful, but everything besides was filthy in the extreme. Mrs. Hunt called for two candles; I told her the one we had was sufficient, but she would have another as she wanted a light to let her see to sleep. We were glad when the morning came, and we left for Rome. When I first entered Rome, a boy said if I would give him a penny he would take me to a barber where I could get shaved. The Italians cannot grow beards, so a man with a beard is a strange phenomenon. Rome is a place which no one can see but with feelings of awe for the mighty past. The woman, who sitteth upon the hills and was drunk with the blood of the saints and martyrs of Jesus, is come to desolation. The prophecy of St. John in the Revelation is fulfilled. 'The woman was arrayed in purple and scarlet colour and decked with gold, and precious stones and pearls, having a golden cup in her hand and full of abominations, and filthiness of her fornication, and upon her forehead was written a name "Mystery of Babylon the Great, the Mother of Harlots, and abominations of the earth."' When I went the first time to Rome I went direct to the Coliseum[23] and sat down in deep meditation till the moon and the stars appeared overhead, and then I thought it was time to look out for a lodging. The Coliseum is a memorial of Ancient Rome in the days of its cruelty and persecution. Here the gladiators fought with each other and wild beasts, and here Christians were thrown to the lions to make a 'Roman holiday.'

It is seated for 80,000 spectators who delighted in this scene of blood. When Charles Dickens saw the Coliseum, he said, 'Thank God, it is a ruin. Beside the Coliseum stands the Roman Forum. I have said stands, but it would be more correct to say lies, for it *lies* in the dust. Here the Roman Orators harangued the people; here stood the statues and the temples of the gods, and by the side of the Forum the Palace of the Caesars. The Arch of Titus, on which is engraved the seven-branched candlesticks copied from the Temple at Jerusalem. At no great distance stands the Capitol, where Julius Caesar was stabbed, and the Mamertine prison in which St. Paul was said to have been imprisoned.

---

23 Coliseum] Colisseum (passim)

Time would fail me to tell of the Campus Martius, the Circus Maximus, the Ghetto, and other things both in Ancient and Modern Rome. I will just ask you to think of a power which conquered Gaul and Britain in the Far West and Mesopotamia in the Far East, and planted Colonies of Romans throughout the world. One day we went to St. Paul's Gate. Tradition says that the great Apostle was led out by this gate to martyrdom. About five or six miles out of Rome he was beheaded. Where the head first fell there sprang up a well of hot water, where it rolled a well of tepid water, and where it lay finally a well of cold water. About three miles from Rome is the magnificent church of St. Paul without the Gate. At St. Paul's Gate stands the pyramid of Caius Cestius, who lived in the time of Augustus. Behind the tomb is the Protestant Cemetery. Here was buried Keats, the poet; here were placed the ashes of Shelley after cremation, who was drowned in the Bay of Spezzia. We saw St. Peter's, the greatest Church in the world, and we visited the sacred steps at San Giovanni Laterano. They are the stairs on which Jesus came down from the judgement Hall of Pontius Pilate, and were brought to Rome by Helena, the mother of Constantine. You ascend them on bended knees, kissing them all the way, and you are rewarded by a plenary indulgence. It was ascending these steps that this verse occurred to Luther: 'The Just shall live by faith,' and he turned and walked down.

We visited the Catacombs of St. Callixtus[24] in the Appian Way.[25] Underground we went with candles and read the inscriptions on the tomb stones. A Capuchin Friar, in his brown cloak, led the way, and we followed with lighted tapers. We were glad to see the end of it and return it to the light of day. The Appian Way is the road by which the brethren came as far as Appii[26] Forum to meet St. Paul. Along this way the Romans had their sepulchral monuments, many of which still exist, the chief being that of Cecilia Metella.

After 10 days spent in Rome, we went to Naples. We took our hotel at the North of Naples, in Posillipo, looking out on Mount Vesuvius. It was smoking very gently; when I saw it before it reminded me of a tall smoking chimney in one of the manufacturing towns. While at Naples we resolved on a visit to the ruins of Pompeii. This town was buried in

---

24 Callixtus] Calistus
25 Appian Way] Appian way passim
26 Appii] Apii (passim)

ashes, at an eruption of Vesuvius in the year A.D. 79. It lies on the south side of the Mount, about 16 miles from Naples. The museum contains many articles of furniture, kitchen utensils, lamps, phials, and such like. There are also loaves of bread round like cakes, with a hole in the centre, so as to be carried on a pole. The same shape of bread, as is still, to be seen in Naples, and in the Museum are eight human bodies turned into stone recalling the story of Lot's wife turned into a Pillar of Salt; one is a woman lying on her face with her right hand under her forehead; one is a little boy about six years old, lying on his side, and all have fear and terror depicted on their faces. In one place we saw the bones of a prisoner who had been chained, and could not escape. The houses are for the most part roofless, and some of those on which the roofs remained had bathrooms and other conveniences, evidently done up for a rich luxurious people. We took a cab and drove through the streets outside of Naples. As an instance of the poverty of the country, there were great holes on the road, into which we occasionally went down to the great danger of our lives. The cabman was a merry fellow. He proposed to come to England to be our servant, and we asked if he had a wife. He said he had, and such a beauty, so fat, as fat as the *monsieur*. And what would you do with her? Oh, I should shed a few tears and leave her. He asked Mrs. Hunt how old she was, and I know no woman cares to tell the truth concerning her age, but I believe she said 60 years. How many children have you he asked; I suppose she said six boys and six girls. And why did she marry such a young man. When we were drawing near to Pompeii, the cabman advised us where to lunch, and with an engaging smile said 'Macaroni for me.' We answered 'Yes,' and his face brightened at the prospect. You should see an Italian eating Macaroni; He twists it round and round on his fork, and then it is like a great many serpents hanging out of his mouth. The Neapolitans are the happiest people under the sun. They never care to work after they have earned four pennies in the morning, one for bread, one for fruit, one for Macaroni, and one for wine. The children are all playing in the street, boys and girls, with scarcely a rag upon them; They have their milk brought to them by cows and goats, which are milked at the doors, and those who live in high houses when they want a pennyworth of grapes or other commodities they let down a basket by a string and put it up again.

We saw a sight one Sunday at the hotel which

reminded us of Otford.

The landlord of the houses was to give a dinner to 20 old men only. They came to the table unwashed and unshaved. All women were forbidden, which they felt very much, and two or three times one or two made an effort to sit down with the men. One woman took up a bottle of wine and drank it off without ceremony to the great amusement of all present. The landlord saw her and chased her away.

One day we went to 'Pozzuoli'[27] called in the Bible 'Puteoli.' Here St. Paul landed, after he had been almost shipwrecked and here began his journey to Rome. When the Christians at Rome where [sic] out as far as the Appii Forum and three Taverns to meet him and accompany him along the Appian Way to the great city. At Pozzuoli are the ruins of a temple of Serapis an Egyptian god, whose worship was forbidden at Rome. There is also the Solfatara, a crater extinct, beyond the memory of man. About five months ago it showed signs of life, and began to burn. Behind this is the Bay of Baiæ, the winter resort of the old Romans. There is 'no Bay' says the poet Horace more delightful than Baiæ, near to it is the lake Avernus–the Lake of Hell. It was here that Nero caused his mother to be put in a ship, and when they that were with her had gone far enough out in the sea they were to save themselves and leave her to sink. She managed, however, to swim ashore. When Nero heard of this he sent a soldier to stab her. We returned to Rome, went to Pisa, Genoa, Turin, Aix-les-Bains, Dijon, and Paris; Then with great joy to Otford.

Sevenoaks Chronicle and Kentish Advertiser, 5 February 1904, p. 8.

---

27   Pozzuoli] Pazzaoli (passim)

John Hunt, the Poor Man's Friend[28]

On Friday, 12 April 1907, shortly before midnight, the Reverend John Hunt, D.D., Vicar of Otford, died at the Vicarage (The Grange)[29] in his eighty-first[30] year.

This was the passing of no ordinary man, for, although he was a man[31] of simple tastes, a lover of nature and all mankind, and happy in his parish ministrations, his name was known and honoured far outside the confines of Otford, outside the Rochester Diocese, outside the County of Kent, outside England.

John hunt was born at Perth, Scotland, on 21 January 1827. He took Holy Orders in 1855, having become a student at the University of St. Andrews eight years before, and after serving the Church of England in curacies in Deptford, Bishopwearmouth,[32] Fulham, Hoxton, St. Ives (Huntingdon), Aldgate, and Lambeth.[33] He was installed as Vicar of Otford in 1878, immediately following two years at St. Nicholas's Church, Sutton, Surrey. In the same year, the University of St. Andrews conferred upon him the degree of Doctor of Divinity.

It has been said that Hunt was a thinker and writer who loved a simple country life. We read that 'His mind soared in high spaces of thought and that this saved him from undue concern with many things that unprofitably disturb or absorb the minds of multitudes.'[34] We also know that he was a deeply religious man, who, until the end, had a great zest for the style of life which he led. We are told that he was humble, straight and honourable in all his dealings, and transparently truthful.

---

28 This paper, entitled *John Hunt, the Poor Man's Friend*, was written by Harold W. Hart and dated in his own hand '6/10/58'. A copy of the essay was given to the Otford and District Historical Society for comments by the Committee. Duplicated, typewritten copies were sold in 1959 by the Rev. Francis Bunch, Vicar of Otford (1956–1984), priced 3d. Two copies are in the Otford and District Historical Society archive. I am most grateful to Mr Edwin Thompson for supplying me with these. Contrary to my practice elsewhere in this study, since the original is unpublished, I have edited and annotated the text, correcting or improving spelling, punctuation, phraseology, etc. Only significant changes are noted in the footnotes.
29 Vicarage] vicarage (The Grange has been added by hand.)
30 eighty-first] eightieth. Born on 21 January 1827, he died on 12 April 1907, aged eighty.
31 although he was a man of simple tastes] although of simple tastes
32 Bishopwearmouth] Bishop Wearmouth
33 Aldgate, and Lambeth. He] also in Aldgate and Lambeth, he
34 Quotation not referenced by Hart.

What else can be said of him, of his desires, his difficulties, his successes, and his disappointments?[35]

His Services to Literature

Firstly, it can be said that Hunt was a writer of great intellectual force.

His first literary works, *Poems from the German*, were published as early as 1852, to be followed, in 1853, by *Luther's Spiritual Songs translated from the German*. Some five years later, came *Lectures on Wesley and Wesleyanism*.

What might well be termed his great works began with *An Essay on Pantheism*, which was published in 1865. This is still considered to be one of the best treatments of the subject and was extremely well received by the Protestant churches, although it quickly formed an entry in the Papal Index. His next works, *Contemporary Essays in Theology*, appeared in 1873.

These were followed by his *History of Religious Thought in England*, which covered the period from the Reformation until the end of the Eighteenth Century. Some years later, a further volume appeared, which treated the same subject so far as the Nineteenth Century was concerned. These were received even more enthusiastically[36] by philosophers, clergy, and teachers than was the *Essay on Pantheism*. In addition, he wrote a number of articles on matters of a religious nature for various reviews and other periodical publications.

During the last decade of the Nineteenth century, he penned a number of poems. Most of these were of a simple and direct style, against a background of natural history, and appeared from time to time in issues of the parish magazine. One poem, 'The Galilean King', which he wrote after reading Renan's *Life of Jesus* is, however, in a style on a level with the best hymns in the English language.

Hunt's work in the field of Literature was duly recognised by the Government, and in 1901, he was awarded the sum of £100 per annum in recognition of his services to theological literature. [2]

---

35 disappointments?] disappointments.
36 enthusiastically] enthuastically

His Views on Sunday Observance

To anyone reading his pastoral letters, it becomes obvious that Hunt was a strict Sabbatarian. Perth, or rather his Scottish upbringing in the fifties of the last century,[37] no doubt increased this feeling of veneration for Sunday in a man already of firm Christian principles, and it was his dearest wish to see church attendance representing all families in the parish who were members of the church which he served.

In 1891, he inaugurated the parish magazine, and in an introductory pastoral letter, he charged the parish with lack of church attendance. 'After thirteen years', he wrote, 'your indifference to the services of religion has been to me a continual sorrow. The Sunday is spent in idleness, with no higher aspirations than belong to the cattle of the fields.' Speaking of those[38] who did not attend church, simply because others did not, he quoted 'Thou shalt not follow a multitude to do evil.'[39]

This strong feeling in respect of Sunday observance was with him throughout his life, and, writing some years later in the magazine, he quoted 'I have laboured in vain, I have spent my strength for naught and in vain, yet surely my judgment is with the Lord and my work with God.'[40]

He felt that a working man should be ashamed to be seen in his working clothes on a Sunday, unless it were a necessity, whilst as late as 1907, in a New Year letter, he wrote 'years and time pass quickly', and again, appealing to those who never sat under him, made mention of those 'persons in the parish who never go to the house of God, who never pray, who never wish to be instructed in the ways of wisdom, and who put off these things until it is too late, when the Archangel shall have sounded his trumpet that time shall be no longer.'

On one occasion, he said that there was no Commandment more neglected than the Fourth, but it is not clear whether he was referring to the country generally or to Otford in particular.

His views on this question might well be rounded off by quoting a stanza from his poem 'The Rector of Effingtree':

---

37 Hunt went to St Andrews, aged twenty, in 1847. His Scottish upbringing occurred mainly in the 1840s.
38 Speaking of those] whilst speaking of those
39 Exodus 23:2.
40 Isaiah 49:4.

'The Church was old and in part decayed
The people that came were few,
The lab'ring folk lay all in bed
And the Squire was an idler too.'

His Views on the Church

In this, it is convenient to touch only upon his few criticisms, which were, however, always strongly voiced, without fear of consequences.

A Scotsman, and an Episcopalian,[41] he was a staunch supporter of the Church of England and also incidentally of the Church Schools. He was strongly opposed to ritualism, and it must be remembered that he lived through the somewhat troublous times of the Oxford Movement. In actual fact, Hunt was brought face to face with the effects of this movement within the Church, as the Vicar of one of the churches where he had been curate was involved in some difficulties in connection with what might be termed 'Luxuries of worship'.[42]

He was, however, of the opinion that the times through which he was living saw a more sincere and spiritual Church[43] than that which had existed during the first decades of the Nineteenth Century, or, for that matter, for many years, and he once said that the clergy had at one time held two or three livings and lived in none of them and that the minister of the period was usually more familiar with the faces of the dogs in the squire's pack than with the faces of his parishioners. [3]

The question of benefices was another matter which engaged his attention, and he was a strong opponent of their sale, some of his articles in the reviews of the period leaving no doubt as to the stand which he took. Neither did he hesitate to bring Bishops to task where he considered that they were abusing the system. On the subject of High-Church dignitaries,[44] he wrote that 'for the most part, canonries and deaneries, to say nothing of bishoprics,[45] have been held by men whose names sound like the very essence of emptiness'.

---

41 Hunt was not a member of the Scottish Episcopal Church, but, having joined the Church of England, he accepted episcopal ministry.
42 This refers to Goldie at St Ives.
43 Church] church
44 High-Church dignitaries] high church dignatories
45 canonries and deaneries, to say nothing of bishoprics] Canonries and Deaneries, to say nothing of Bishoprics

His View on Temperance

Hunt was a believer in temperance, as was only natural, but he interpreted the word in its broad meaning.

So far as the parish was concerned, the first record of the Vicar's views on the question appear to be recorded in some lectures which he made on the work of General Booth, and it is obvious that he was deeply affected by the General's efforts on behalf of the submerged thousands'.

It does, however, seem that he was no particular admirer of total abstainers, and he certainly viewed with a tolerant eye the twin deities Beer and Tobacco, providing the words 'in reason' were coupled with them. It is recorded that, on the occasion of the Queen's Jubilee celebrations in Otford, Hunt drank to the health of the Westerham brewers, who had supplied six gallons of beer to encourage the festivities. These Jubilee gambols must have appeared strange to the villagers, as we read that, on this occasion, Scottish dances were danced by some Scottish visitors, and that Scottish and, for some unexplained reason, but possibly in honour of the late Prince Consort, late even at that time, German songs were sung.

There is, however, no doubt that he viewed with marked disfavour anything in the nature of excessive drinking, and in one issue of the parish magazine, he printed, without comment, the following extract from a Brewing Trade circular, which certainly speaks very well for itself:

> 'The market has been very dull during the last month and we have nothing but complaints from all sides. With regard to the Budget we think the Trade may congratulate itself that for once it has been left alone, and it is just possible, with the amount devoted to free education, that the working men, relieved of the expense of educating their children, may spend more on drink.'

His Views on Politics

In the political field, Hunt held Liberal views and was a Free Trader, although it is certain that he was not a member of the Party, holding the view that 'a man should come to a political meeting with an open mind as a free man and not as a slave.' His liberal views did, however, allow him to go to the lengths of taking the chair at local Liberal meetings, if he thought that, by so doing, he would assist the proceedings; and from the records still in existence, it can be readily seen that his work in this direction met with marked general approval.

An ardent admirer of Gladstone, he took the opportunity of preaching a funeral sermon upon hearing of that great man's death, taking as the text 'Know ye not that there is a prince and a great man fallen this day in Israel.'[46]

Speaking in 1898, on the reign of Queen Victoria, he expressed his opinion that the reign had been a prosperous one as well as a long one, and after mentioning railways, the telegraph, and other benefits to the public, remarked that the people of Britain were republicans in all but name. [4]

His Journeys Abroad

Turning to the European or foreign field, it can be said that John Hunt was a traveller who observed as he travelled. His visits to the Continent of Europe and to North Africa can be divided into two groups, the first being those undertaken in his earlier life and which were mainly in pursuit of theological study, and the second, those made in his latter years, when he combined education with a certain amount of relaxation. This first group received attention in his *Contemporary Essays in Theology*, whilst the remainder were on the lines of journals and appeared from time to time in the parish magazine. The first were for serious study, the second for general informative reading.

His earliest Continental travels concerning which information is available were made with the idea of studying at first hand the Old Catholic movement in Germany,[47] and if anything is clear from his writings, it is that he held strong pro-German views. No doubt this was partly due to the fact that he was a staunch Protestant and as such associated Germany with Martin Luther, the Confession of Augsburg, and other Reformation highlights. In his *Contemporary Essays* he went so far as to write 'Germany was the cradle of the Reformation. The Germans are Protestants. So are we. The name of Luther is a household

---

46 2 Samuel 3:38.
47 See Hunt, *Contemporary Essays in Theology*, Chapters XV and XVI, pp. 413–460, dealing with the period 1870–1872.

word in England. We pronounce it with feelings of reverence akin to worship.'[48] This statement was, however, qualified to some extent by the next paragraph where he wrote 'In number, not more than half the people are Protestants. That half is ... the more influential. It is among the Protestants that the German spirit has had its best and highest incarnations. Our interest in Protestant Germany makes us almost forget that there is a Catholic Germany. This forgetfulness, however, will be remedied as we become familiar with the ... recent vigorous protests of German Bishops, Archbishops and Cardinals against what is properly and strictly Romanism.'[49]

Hunt was, of course, referring to those dignitaries[50] of the Old Catholic Church who were endeavouring to make far-reaching changes in Roman Catholic doctrine, the Infallibility of the Pope being one point against which they were making a strong stand. His views on German Catholics are interesting, and it would have been entertaining, had he been[51] alive at the time, to have heard his views on the fact that, during Christianity's struggle against National Socialism, the German Catholics made a far stouter opposition than did the combined churches of Protestant Germany.

In 1871 or 1872, probably the former year, Hunt travelled to Germany, in order to become acquainted with the excommunicated professors of Munich and the leading personages of the Old Catholic Church. His interest in the movement was aroused chiefly by the fact that these 'reasoning German Catholics', as they were sometimes called, had made a breech with the Church of Rome and had tabled a number of modifications in Church government and also in the Church's services. So far as the latter are concerned, they were completely in favour of suppressing the Roman confessional.

Hunt travelled out via Holland and made a point of stopping at Rotterdam, the birthplace of Erasmus, after which he proceeded to Germany by way of Dordrecht. Anyone reading his story of this journey, which appeared in his *Essays*, will be instantly struck by his veneration

---

48 Hunt, *Contemporary Essays in Theology*, p. 81. This first appeared in the *Contemporary Review* 14 (1870), p. 313.
49 The quotation has been corrected in accordance with the original.
50 dignitaries] dignatories
51 had he been] were he

of Germany and of things Germanic. 'This year', he wrote, 'the English traveller embarks on the Rhine with a feeling of thankfulness that it is still German.'[52] — it must be remembered that the Franco-Prussian War was just over — 'The Rhine'. he went on to say, 'is the Highway of Europe, and Frenchmen cannot be entrusted with highways. I saw Germania ever present, with her sleepless eye and her powerful arm, keeping religious watch over the noble river.' The word 'religious' can hardly have been meant literally, as the inhabitants of the German Rhineland are of the same faith as the majority of Frenchmen, Roman Catholics. [5]

Continuing his journey southwards, Hunt visited Friedrichsdorf, a village in the vicinity of Homburg, where a colony of Huguenots made a settlement after the Revocation of the Edict of Nantes. On arrival at Munich, however, he found that Dr. Frohschammer, with whom he was already acquainted, had left for Bad Kreuth. Therefore, to Bad Kreuth travelled the Doctor, remarking after arrival that it was a place 'fortunately unknown to the English, frequented entirely by Germans, and where German life and manners reign in their uncorrupted simplicity'.[53] In this Teutonic Eden, he found ministers of state, university professors, Protestant clergy and Catholic priests discussing differences of faith with, as he puts it, mutual understanding. Here he also met Dr Frohschammer, who had been excommunicated by the Roman Church seven years before, when a University Professor, for maintaining the independence of science and the right of free enquiry.

After staying in Bad Kreuth, Hunt returned home but travelled by a circuitous route, which included places as scattered at Munich, Augsburg, Constance, and Strasbourg. This somewhat curious route was no doubt dictated by points of religious interest.

In Constance, his hotel proprietor was a Frenchmen, and, wrote the Doctor shortly afterwards, 'A Frenchman can cheat a guest with the dash of his pen, irrespective of consequences or conscience.'[54] The Landlord of 'The Pike' was likened to that voracious fish, and Hunt expressed the hope that he was collecting the milliards of Bismarck. The Frenchman's reply is not recorded.

---

52 Hunt, *Contemporary Essays in Theology*, p. 376.
53 Hunt, *Contemporary Essays in Theology*, p. 380.
54 Hunt, *Contemporary Essays in Theology*, pp. 393f.

Hunt also wrote that the only other trouble which he experienced on this particular journey was at the hands of another Frenchman, this time a railway employee in the ticket office at Strasbourg station.[55] This official wanted from Hunt an English Sovereign in exchange for twenty francs, which was probably not a very bad exchange for the times. Writing of his journey, Hunt said that this was the first time that he had seen the image and superscription of Queen Victoria dishonoured. He told the official before a company of assembled Strasbourgers that it was a good thing that they would soon be under German rule, and he hoped that, under Bismarck, they would make such progress that English travellers would no longer be annoyed by French folly and French perversity.

What tactlessness, but after all, what courage!

The Old Catholics held a second Congress in the following year, this time in Cologne.[56]

Dr. Hunt was cordially received by Professor Knoodt and the other German delegates, also by the Abbé Michaud, late Vicar of the Madeleine in Paris, and by some Russian representatives. On this occasion, the Bishop of Lincoln, the Bishop of Ely, and the Dean of Westminster took part in the proceedings.

It is not possible in a paper of this size to deal with the matters on the agenda of the Congress; in any event, they would not be in line with the scheme of this paper, but there were a number of incidents which are worth recording, especially as Hunt was closely connected with them.

The proceedings of the first day, a Sunday, were followed by a somewhat secular evening, and we read that Hunt the Sabbatarian 'almost trembled to recall'[57] how the time was spent, for, at the close of the meeting, two hundred or so of the delegates adjourned to the Casino for a banquet. Hunt was the only representative from this country present on the occasion, but he certainly found it impossible to conceive anything more incompatible with the English ideas of Sunday, as toasts were drunk and glasses rattled against glasses as the company toasted each other and the leading personages of the Congress. Even Bismarck was not forgotten. [6]

On returning to his hotel, Hunt found about fifty persons making what he described as the usual obstreperous commotion which the

---

55 Hunt, *Contemporary Essays in Theology*, pp. 394.
56 1872.
57 The quotation is inaccurate. See fn. 31, p. 98.

Germans think a necessary accompaniment to a comfortable dinner. Were his pro-German feelings beginning to become a trifle less sure of themselves? These persons were also Congress Delegates, and some of them suggested that a visit to the theatre might be a pleasant way of rounding off the day. Hunt, who had attended the banquet, as he considered it part of the Congress, considered an invitation to attend a theatre on a Sunday evening, however pleasantly put, to be something definitely in the nature of a last straw, and he declined making one of the party in such a marked manner that the proposal was dropped.[58]

Further shock was registered by the Doctor's nervous system, when in a café one Sunday, a gentleman took a pack of cards from his pocket and approached the Herr Pastor with the idea of his joining in a pleasant game. So put out was the Doctor on this occasion, that he hinted the probable presence of an individual who was so troublesome to Luther that the Reformer once aimed an inkstand at his head.[59] The Devil's counters were repocketed.

At one of the meetings of this same Congress, held in Bonn, a servant came into the hall with a tray of rattling glasses, whilst the Bishop of Lincoln was reading prayers. The Bishop, in turn, made himself troublesome later in the day, by refusing cigars, with the result that, as none of the delegates wished to smoke before he, the Bishop, did, one and all were deprived of the consolation of tobacco.

On the following day, at the Wiener Hof in Cologne, the Germans counter-attacked by way of an early start and lit up, before the British contingent arrived, with the result that the Bishops had to make their speeches amid the rattling of plates and glasses and dark surging clouds of tobacco smoke. In addition to these distractions, whilst the Bishop of Lincoln was discoursing in French on the necessity for, among other things, Bishops, a hotel waiter was jostling aside the Dean of Westminster, in order to convey beefsteaks and Brauenberger to a German professor.[60] The following day, however, saw a German defeat. Large 'no smoking' notices appeared all over the building.[61] Lincoln had been at work. One

---

58   Hunt, *Contemporary Essays in Theology*, pp. 427f.
59   This refers to the legend that Luther, in his study in the Wartburg, threw an inkwell at the Devil. Cf. Scott H. Hendrix, *Martin Luther: A Very Short Introduction* (Oxford: Oxford University Press, 2010), p. 4.
60   Hunt, *Contemporary Essays in Theology*, p. 429.
61   Hunt, *Contemporary Essays in Theology*, pp. 429f.

does wonder as to the extent of the popularity of the British on this occasion.

Turning from Germany to France, there is no doubt that Hunt showed a lively interest in the French Protestant Churches, and his essay on the subject shows that he followed the proceedings of their assemblies and synods with close attention. It is also evident that he entertained the highest regard for most, is not all, of their leaders.

As has been mentioned earlier, Hunt did feel a dislike for things French, and this attitude of mind unfortunately showed itself in the essay from which the following is a quotation: –

> 'When we look[62] at the frivolous and volatile creature who is the typical Frenchman of the present day, we can scarcely believe that Calvin and Beza were Frenchmen, and that their countrymen formed the Church of the Huguenots.'[63]

This same essay does, fortunately, end on a happier note, for he says: 'The Church of England has not forgotten its old helper and ally, the Church of the Huguenots. With their Evangelicals, our Evangelicals[64] have the deepest sympathy.'[65]

As regards Hunt's later travels, these consisted for the most part of visits to Switzerland, Italy, Egypt, and the Holy Land, and his journals throw a deal of light upon the man himself, particularly on his love of children and the fact that he could play jokes, at the same time taking those against him in good part. [7]

There was one matter concerning foreign hotel registrations, which did, however, annoy him in the extreme. This was the police regulation under which it was necessary for hotel guests to state their age, but he managed to turn this against the authorities by making a point of entering his own age as 165. This information taken in conjunction with his long white beard and his venerable appearance caused, as can be expected, considerable curiosity and astonishment, and although there can have been very few who were taken in by this little deceit, there was never any unpleasantness.

---

62 we look] one looks
63 Hunt, *Contemporary Essays in Theology*, p. 344.
64 Evangelicals, our Evangelicals] Evangelists, our Evangelists
65 Hunt, *Contemporary Essays in Theology*, p. 375.

The beard caused considerable mirth when, one day on his travels, he encountered a party of Italian cavalry. His appearance was the immediate signal for the men to stroke their chins and call our Barba! The same beard was also blamed by Hunt himself for putting to flight some little Italian girls, who were dancing to a hurdy gurdy and among whom he made a sudden appearance.

There is one particularly interesting link between Switzerland and Otford brought about by his travels. One day, in a Swiss church, Hunt came across this version of the following words on a memorial to a Curé:

'He loved the sheep and the sheep loved him.'[66]

Hunt turned to his wife and asked her what more a minister could wish for by way of an epitaph. His words were obviously remembered, for they are inscribed on his own stone at Otford.

Finis

Towards the end of his life, he was a staunch opponent of the Education Bill wherein was the proposal to take over the Church schools whilst, although a minister of the Established Church, he looked upon the member of any congregation as one of his own flock, if he were approached for help of a material or of a spiritual nature. He gave freely to charities but was strongly against the publication of the names of the recipients and the amounts received. He provided a very large number of books for the church library. He contributed towards the cost of church repairs and renovations. His name was known far around for his treats to the aged. Perhaps one of the first improvements which he carried out after his induction at Otford, was the planting of the churchyard with varieties of trees, and a number of those existing at the present time, especially some of the yews, were planted by his hands.

Dr Hunt married twice. His first wife, Eliza, who died in 1890, was buried in Otford, where her name can be seen on one side of his memorial cross and his on the other. He married a second time Margaret Foote of Kelvinside, Glasgow, the ceremony taking place in 1899. This lady survived him.

On the last night of his life, he quoted Pope: 'He can't be wrong whose life is in the right'; but he could indeed have quoted instead some lines from his own poem 'Age':

---

66   Inscription on a tombstone in Gruyères (Clarke and Stoyel, *Otford in Kent*, p. 234).

'There is a calm at the close of life
When man's race is nearly won
And he rests like a warrior after the strife
With a sense of victory won.'

In conclusion, the inscription on one of his funeral wreaths might well be the last words of this paper. It read:

'To the poor man's friend.'[67]

John Hunt's Obituary

Death of the Vicar of Otford[68]

Dr. Hunt's Sudden Demise.

In the early hours of Saturday last, the inhabitants of this ancient and delightful Kentish village were startled by the sad news that their esteemed Vicar, the Rev. John Hunt, D D., had died suddenly in the night. The rev. gentleman, who was in his 81st year, had gone to bed at his usual hour, and was then in the best of Spirits and, with the exception of a slight bronchial attack, was in good health. He was, however, seized with a sudden illness shortly after retiring to bed and despite the unremitting care of his wife he expired about the middle of the night, just prior to the arrival of his medical attendant (Dr. Desprez, of Shoreham). The deceased gentleman had been Vicar of Otford for nearly 30 years and was held in the highest esteem by all who came in contact with him; more especially by his poorer parishioners, for whose comforts he had been a most assiduous worker sparing neither time nor trouble in looking after the various charities &c. It was also a well-known trait in his character (though he was occasionally imposed

---

67 'From the churchwardens and sidesmen of Otford, in loving memory of the poor man's friend' (recorded in his Obituary, p. 231, below).

68 *Sevenoaks Chronicle and Kentish Advertiser*, Friday 19 April 1907. I am grateful to Mr John Hunt for supplying me with the newspaper cutting and to Mr Edwin Thompson for identifying the source. A photograph of Hunt as an old man precedes the main text. The sometimes faulty spelling and punctuation have been retained.

upon) that he always helped the truly needy without regard to creed or character. It was sufficient if he thought they were in want, in fact, in all matters appertaining to the Parish and its welfare he was always prepared to do his best for the general good and was to those who knew him well, a level-headed, rugged kind-hearted Scotsman. Born at Perth, N.B., in 1827, he was educated at St. Andrew's University, and ordained 50 years ago. He served the Church in various Curacies (the last being at Sutton, Surrey,) till the year 1878, when he was appointed to the living at Otford by the Dean (Dr. Stanley) and Chapter of Westminster. The living at that time included Dunton Green, and so remained until 1890 when, with funds raised by Dr. Hunt, a new Church was built at Dunton Green and handed over to the charge of the Incumbent at Riverhead. During the early years of his residence at Otford he was a well-known figure of the Religious Literary World. For 15 years he was on the staff of the *Contemporary Review* — the whole period of its existence. He was also principle [sic] contributor to Strachans [sic] 'Day of Rest'. His first effort at literary work was a translation of Luther's hymns. He published his essay on 'Pantheism' in 1866 (placed by the Pope of Rome in the Index Expurgatorious [sic]). Contemporary essays in theology in 1873; Religious Thought in England 1870–1873; religious thought in the nineteenth century 1896. An essay on the rise of Dissent, in a volume entitled 'The Church: Past and Present' edited by Professor Gwatkin, 1900. He received from his Alma Mater (St. Andrew's University) the degree of Doctor of Divinity in 1878 and a few years ago he was awarded an annual pension of £100 from the Civil List for Historical Research. The rev. gentleman's life was essentially a busy one and only a few hours before his death he had prepared his sermon for the following Sunday, thus he may be said to have died in harness. The text he had chosen for his sermon was taken from I John iv., 8, 'God is love.' This was preached at the morning service on Sunday last by the Curate, the Rev. John Martin, and the following is culled from the Sermon after reading the text. It continued: 'It is easy to credit tradition concerning this Apostle (John) that when advanced in life and unable to say much in his master's name, he used to meet in the Christian assemblies and address them with nothing more than his favourite words "Little children love one another", and it is difficult to restrain the imagination from dwelling with him on the Isle of Patmos, banished indeed from the society of loving Christians, but only to be more favoured by the love of God, this is a lovely sentiment "God is Love". It is worth all the wisdom of all the books in the world. If it is not wrong to say it, it is better than all the rest of the Bible put together. It is not said "God is holiness," "God is truth," "God is justice," but it is said "God is Love."' Further on in the discourse the following passage occurs: 'Some wells are dry in summer time, but the well of God's mercy, the well of God's love in Christ, is like those springs that rise in the mountain's bosom.' At the conclusion of the service the organist (Mr. R. Hoff) played 'The Dead March' in Saul, with great expression, the congregation standing in mournful silence, and with an expression of deep sorrow at the loss of a dear friend and guide.

The Funeral.

Yesterday, the remains of the dearly esteemed old vicar of Otford, were laid to rest in a brick grave at the south side or the churchyard, where his first wife was buried. The entire village was in mourning, shops being closed and blinds drawn in almost every house. Outside the ancient Church, the school children lined the path, the sad procession passing between the scholars to the tolling of the bell, in the old fashioned belfrey. The sacred building which was draped in black was crowded, many of the mourners being very old parishioners. Beautiful wreaths were placed in front of each of the reading desks and the choir stalls, and there were also many other floral tributes on the coffin. The impressive service was conducted by the Rev. Mr. Thorpe [sic, read Thorp], vicar of Kennington, (brother of the late Mrs. Hunt), the Rev Canon A. Hall Hall (Rector of Chevening), and the Rev. J Martin (Curate of Otford). Amongst the other clergy present were: The Rev. H. Somers-Cocks (who represented the Bishop of Rochester, who could not attend owing to indisposition); the Revs. H. Percy Thompson, J. P. David. E. S. Buchanan, H. T. Knight, G. F. Bell, C. A. Stubbs (Crockham Hill), H. D. Madge, B. P. Thompson (St. Lawrence, Seal), W. Jones (Knockholt), and Rev. Hancock (Woodlands). There were also present Major Wreford, Dr. Desprez, Mr. W. W. Knocker, Mr. R. Edwards, Mr. B. Lightfoot, Mr. H. T. Willins, Mr. J. J. Beale, Mr. H. Wellband, Mr. Booker, Mr. Greenlees, Mr, Turk, Mr. Isaacs, and others. Mr. T. H. Knight, churchwarden, had made ample arrangements for the large crowd of mourners. The choir preceded the coffin as it was carried up the centre aisle, followed by the clergy. The chief mourners were Mrs. Hunt (Widow), Dr. Tom Hunt (nephew), Mr. Harry Hunt (nephew), Mrs. Franks, and Mrs. Swan. Mr. Hoff, who officiated at the organ, played Mendelssohn's Funeral March, and the hymns were 'Days and moments quickly flying,' and 'Now the labourer's task is o'er'. The breastplate on the coffin was 'John Hunt, D D., born 21st January, 1827, died 12th April, 1907.'

There were many beautiful wreaths, crosses, and other floral tributes sent, including one from the widow 'In ever loving remembrance—from one who revered and adored her husband as a man apart—"The pure in heart see God"'; 'In never dying remembrance of a Christian scholar and sage, who was in heart as a little child—J. Martin, curate'; 'To uncle John, in loving remembrance from his neice [sic], Jane'; 'To dear uncle John, in loving memory from Dorothy, and Greta'; 'From the churchwardens and sidesmen of Otford, in loving memory of the poor man's friend'; 'In loving memory from Otford choir'; 'In grateful memory of our vicar—from the teachers and children of Otford school'; 'With kindest sympathy from Dr. H. S. and Miss Desprez'; 'In deepest sympathy from Mr. Francis Mildmay, Shoreham Place'; 'With deepest sympathy from Mr. and Mrs. R. Edwards'; 'Miss Leveaux, with kind remembrance'; ' With sincere sympathy from Mr. and Mrs. R. B. Polhill-Drabble'; ' With deep sympathy from Major, Mrs. and the Misses Wreford'; 'Mr. and Mrs. J. L. Leveaux, with kind remembrance'; 'The Rev. H. A. and Mrs. Soames '; 'With sincere regard from Countess Stanhope'; ' In affectionate remembrance from M. and B. Alexander'; 'In remembrance from Mr. and Mrs. Arthur Cornwallis'; 'From the trade of Otford, in kind remembrance and deepest sympathy'; ' With sincere sympathy and kind respect from Mr. and Mrs. H. Wellband and family'; 'With deepest sympathy and respect to our dear vicar from members of our Mother's Meeting 'O Lamb of God I come!'; ' With Mr. and Mrs. Percy Arden Simmon's deepest sympathy'; ' With deepest sympathy from the servants at Otford House; ' 'With deepest sympathy, to Dr. Hunt, from his maids.'

Bibliography

Select Works by John Hunt

[Hunt, John], *Clergymen Made Scarce. Five Years' Experience as a Curate in the Diocese of London: A Letter to the Right Hon. and Right Rev. the Lord Bishop of the Diocese by a Presbyter. Second Edition, with a Postscript, Containing Two Years' Further Experience in the Country* (London: Hall & Company, 1867), https://books.google.co.uk/books?id=2v9fAAAAcAAJ

Hunt, John, *An Essay on Pantheism* (London: Longmans, Green, Reader and Dyer, 1866), https://catalog.hathitrust.org/Record/001921935

Hunt, John, *Contemporary Essays in Theology* (London: Strahan, 1873), http://archive.org/details/a588115100huntuoft

Hunt, John, *Pantheism and Christianity* (London: W Isbister, 1884), https://archive.org/details/pantheismandchr00huntgoog/page/n5

Hunt, John, ed., *Poems by Robert Wilde D.D., One of the Ejected Ministers of 1662, with a Historical and Biographical Preface and Notes by the Rev. John Hunt* (London: Strahan, 1870), https://books.google.co.uk/books?id=J78wAQAAMAAJ

Hunt, John, *Religious Thought in England, from the Reformation to the End of Last Century: A Contribution To …*, 3 vols (London: Strahan & Co., 1870), I, http://archive.org/details/religiousthough02huntgoog

Hunt, John, *Religious Thought in England, from the Reformation to the End of Last Century*, 3 vols (London, Strahan, 1871), II, http://archive.org/details/religiousthough200huntuoft

Hunt, John, *Religious Thought in England from the Reformation to the End of Last Century*, 3 vols (Strahan & Co., 1873), III, http://archive.org/details/religiousthough03huntgoog

Hunt, John, *Religious Thought in England in the Nineteenth Century* (London, Gibbings & Co., limited, 1896), http://archive.org/details/religiousthough00hunt

Hunt, John, 'Review of Horatius Bonar, The Life of the Rev. John Milne of Perth', *Contemporary Review* 10 (1869), 456–460, https://babel.hathitrust.org/cgi/pt?id=uc1.b2972914&view=1up&seq=466

Hunt, John, *Select Poems: From the German*, translated by John Hunt (Preston: H. C. Barton, 1852), https://books.google.co.uk/books?id=52cCAAAAQAAJ

Hunt, John, *The Two Sacraments. Two Sermons Preached in the Parish Church of S. Ives, August 5th, 1866, by the Rev. John Hunt, Curate, Second Edition, With an Appendix* (St. Ives, Hunts: W. Lang, 1866), https://books.google.com/books?id=7MVQhNACKJwC&num=100

Hunt, John, *Wesley and Wesleyanism: Three Lectures* (London; Sunderland: Hamilton, Adams, and Company; Vint and Carr, 1858).

Other Works Cited

'1851 England Census | Ancestry®', https://www.ancestry.co.uk/

'1861 England Census | Ancestry®', https://www.ancestry.co.uk/

'1871 England Census | Ancestry®', https://www.ancestry.co.uk/

Altholz, Josef L., 'Alexander Haldane, the "Record", and Religious Journalism', *Victorian Periodicals Review* 20 (1987), 23–31.

'The Anatomist Curate', *Spectator*, 19 November 1864, pp. 1324–1325, https://hdl.handle.net/2027/mdp.39015023494894

Anon., 'Review of *An Essay on Pantheism by the Rev. John Hunt*', *Spectator*, 24 November 1866, p. 20, http://archive.spectator.co.uk/article/24th-november-1866/20/an-essay-on-pantheism-by-rev-john-hunt-curate-of

Anon., *The Whole Case of the Unbeneficed Clergy; Or, a Full, Candid, and Impartial Enquiry Into the Position of Those Clergy Commonly Called the Curates of the Established Church. By a Presbyter of the Church, Etc.*, 2nd edition (London: Hatchard & Son, 1843), https://books.google.co.uk/books?id=YeFhAAAAcAAJ

'Archdeacons: Huntingdon | British History Online', https://www.british-history.ac.uk/fasti-ecclesiae/1541-1847/vol7/pp14-15

Austin, B. F., *The Gospel to the Poor versus Pew Rents*, CIHM/ICMH Microfiche Series = CIHM/ICMH Collection de Microfiches; No. 06703 (Toronto: Montreal: W. Briggs; C. W. Coates, 1884), https://catalog.hathitrust.org/Record/100250786

Bank of England Inflation Calculator, https://www.bankofengland.co.uk/monetary-policy/inflation/inflation-calculator

Bennett, John Charles, Abstract of *The English Anglican Practice of Pew Renting, 1800–1960* (unpublished doctoral dissertation, University of Birmingham, 2011), https://etheses.bham.ac.uk/id/eprint/2864/

'Biographical Register 1747–1897', https://arts.st-andrews.ac.uk/biographical-register/data/documents/1387291364

Bonar, Horatius, *Life of the Rev. John Milne of Perth*, 5th edition (New York: Carter & Brothers, 1870), https://www.electricscotland.com/webclans/m/lifeofrevjohnmil00bona.pdf

Bradley, James E., *Religion, Revolution and English Radicalism: Non-Conformity in Eighteenth-Century Politics and Society* (Cambridge: Cambridge University Press, 2002).

'Brewster, Sir David (1781–1868), Natural Philosopher and Academic Administrator', *Oxford Dictionary of National Biography*, https://doi.org/10.1093/ref:odnb/3371

'Browne, Edward Harold (1811–1891), Bishop of Winchester', *Oxford Dictionary of National Biography*, https://doi.org/10.1093/ref:odnb/3672

Burke's Genealogical and Heraldic History of the Landed Gentry (London: Harrison, 1875), https://books.google.co.uk/books?id=ZNEKAAAAYAAJ

The Cambridge University Magazine (W.P. Grant, 1840), https://books.google.co.uk/books?id=efUHAAAAQAAJ

Carter, Mary, *19th Century St Ives* (St Ives: Friends of the Norris Museum, 2010).

Chadwick, Owen, *The Victorian Church*, Part I, *An Ecclesiastical History of England* (London: Adam & Charles Black, 1966).

Chadwick, Owen, *The Victorian Church*, Part II, 1860–1901, *An Ecclesiastical History of England*, 2nd edition (London: SCM Press, 1987).

Charles Dashwood Goldie, Vicar of St. Ives with the Chapelries of Old Hurst & Woodhurst Annexed [Mandate for Induction Record], 1866, in *Huntingdonshire Archives*, AH26/239/7, https://discovery.nationalarchives.gov.uk/details/r/be10958d-2c8b-460e-bb5a-f2f94f813f29

'Church Missionary Society College, Islington', Wikipedia, https://en.wikipedia.org/w/index.php?title=Church_Missionary_Society_College,_Islington&oldid=995991744

Civic Society of St Ives, Annual Report 2013 (St Ives, 2013), http://www.stivescivic.org.uk/images/report-archive/CS-Annual-Report-2013.pdf

'Civil List Pensions' (London, 23 June 1902), in *House of Commons Parliamentary Papers Online* (ProQuest Information and Learning Company, 2005), no. 235.

Clarke, Reginald Dennis and Anthony Stoyel, *Otford in Kent: A History* (Otford: Otford and District Historical Society, 1975).

The Clergy List ... Containing Complete Lists of the Clergy in England, Wales Scotland, Ireland & the Colonies ... (London: Kelly's Directories, limited; [etc., etc.], 1917), https://catalog.hathitrust.org/Record/005782706

'Clergymen Made Scarce', in *Punch, Or, The London Charivari* (Published for the Proprietors, at the Office, 13, 1864), 17 December 1864, p. 251, https://books.google.co.uk/books?id=fxtcAAAAQAAJ

Crockford's Clerical Directory for 1860: Being a Biographical and Statistical Book of Reference for Facts Relating to the Clergy and the Church (London: Crockford's, 1860), https://babel.hathitrust.org/cgi/pt?id=hvd.hn4jj2&view=2up&seq=43

Crockford's Clerical Directory for 1865: Being a Biographical and Statistical Book of Reference for Facts Relating to the Clergy and the Church (London: Horace Cox, 1865), https://babel.hathitrust.org/cgi/pt?id=hvd.hn4jj1&view=2up&seq=5

Crockford's Clerical Directory for 1885: Being a Biographical and Statistical Book of Reference for Facts Relating to the Clergy and the Church (London: Horace Cox, 1885), in 'UK, Crockford's Clerical Directories | Ancestry®', https://www.ancestry.co.uk/search/collections/1548/

Crouch, William, 'St. George's-in-the-East and St. George's Mission', in William Crouch, *Bryan King and the Riots at St. George's-in-the-East*, Chapter IV (London: Methuen, 1904), pp. 31–44, http://anglicanhistory.org/ritualism/crouch_king1904/04.html

Deceased Wife's Sister's Marriage Act 1907, https://en.wikipedia.org/wiki/Deceased_Wife%27s_Sister%27s_Marriage_Act_1907

Descendants of Quintin Riddell, Probably Born Late 1300s, http://www.airgale.com.au/riddell/d15.htm#i33543

Dickens, Charles, *Our Mutual Friend* (New York: Bradburn, 1864)

Dickson, Neil T. R.: 'A Scottish Fundamentalist? Thomas Whitelaw of Kilmarnock (1840–1917)', in *Evangelicalism and Fundamentalism in the United Kingdom during the Twentieth Century*, eds. David W. Bebbington and David Ceri Jones (Oxford: Oxford University Press, 2013), pp. 35–52.

Directory of Bedfordshire & Huntingdonshire, 1862 (London: Thomas Danks, 1862), http://specialcollections.le.ac.uk/digital/collection/p16445coll4/id/257748/rec/3

Dugmore, Ruth: 'Review of The Curate's Lot: The Story of the Unbeneficed English Clergy by A. Tindal Hart', *Journal of Ecclesiastical History* 23 (1972), 206–207.

Dunn, William McKee, *Is Marriage with a Deceased Wife's Sister Lawful?* (London: Rivingtons, 1883), https://en.wikisource.org/wiki/Is_Marriage_with_a_Deceased_Wife%27s_Sister_Lawful%3F

'Dunton, (Walter) Theodore Watts- (1832–1914), Writer and Poet', *Oxford Dictionary of National Biography*, https://doi.org/10.1093/ref:odnb/36785

'Edmonton: Churches | British History Online', https://www.british-history.ac.uk/vch/middx/vol5/pp181-187

Eliot, George, *Scenes of Clerical Life* (Edinburgh and London: William Blackwood, 1858), https://books.google.co.uk/books?id=6zcJAAAAQAAJ

'Enderby's Printing Mill, of London Road, St Ives', St Ives in Cambridgeshire, https://stives.cambs.info/locations/detail.asp?GetLocID=683

'Ferrier, James Frederick (1808–1864), Philosopher', *Oxford Dictionary of National Biography*, https://doi.org/10.1093/ref:odnb/9369

Flanagan, Bridget: *A Commanding View: The Houses and Gardens of Houghton Hill* (Godmanchester: Great Ouse Valley Trust, 2019).

'The Fortunes of the Clergy', St. George-In-The-East Church, http://www.stgitehistory.org.uk/media/stipends.html

'Fosbroke [Fosbrooke], Thomas Dudley (1770–1842), Antiquary', *Oxford Dictionary of National Biography*, https://doi.org/10.1093/ref:odnb/9954

Fowler, H. W. and F. G. Fowler, *The King's English* (Oxford: Clarendon Press; London; New York: H. Frowde, 1908).

Fowler, H. W. and R. W. Burchfield, *The New Fowler's Modern English Language* (Oxford: Clarendon Press, 1996).

Fowler, Henry Watson, *A Dictionary of Modern English* Usage (Oxford: Clarendon Press, 1926).

The Gentleman's Magazine and Historical Review (J. H. and J. Parker, 1866), https://books.google.co.uk/books?id=ZlNFAAAAYAAJ

The Gentleman's Magazine, Early English Newspapers (F. Jefferies, 1859), p. 540, https://books.google.co.uk/books?id=02Q3AQAAMAAJ

GENUKI, 'Genuki: Anglican Churches in Islington, Middlesex in 1890, Middlesex' (GENUKI), https://www.genuki.org.uk/big/eng/MDX/Islington/churches

GENUKI, 'Genuki: Christ Church, Hoxton, Church of England, Middlesex' (GENUKI), https://www.genuki.org.uk/big/eng/MDX/Shoreditch/Christ Church

GENUKI, 'Genuki: Edmonton, Middlesex' (GENUKI), https://www.genuki.org.uk/big/eng/MDX/Edmonton

GENUKI, 'Genuki: Holborn Deanery Anglican Churches in 1890/1903, Middlesex' (GENUKI), https://www.genuki.org.uk/big/eng/MDX/HolbornStAndrew/churches

GENUKI, 'Genuki: St John, Walham Green, Church of England, Middlesex' (GENUKI), https://www.genuki.org.uk/big/eng/MDX/Fulham/StJohn

GENUKI, 'Genuki: St Jude, Southwark, Church of England, Surrey' (GENUKI), https://www.genuki.org.uk/big/eng/SRY/Southwark/StJude

'Charles Goldie (Cricketer)', Wikipedia, https://en.wikipedia.org/w/index.php?title=Charles_Goldie_(cricketer)&oldid=938240178

The Guardian (Anglican Newspaper)', Wikipedia, https://en.wikipedia.org/w/index.php?title=The_Guardian_(Anglican_newspaper)&oldid=959850312

Gwatkin, Henry Melvill, *The Church, Past and Present: A Review of Its History by the Bishop of London, Bishop Barry, and Other Writers* (New York: Thomas Whittaker, 1899), http://archive.org/details/churchpastpresen00gwat

Haig, Alan Graham Leigh, 'The Church of England as a Profession in Victorian England' (unpublished doctoral dissertation, Australian National University, 1980), https://doi.org/10.25911/5d778863e864a

Haig, Alan, *The Victorian Clergy* (London; Sydney: Croom Helm, 1984).

Harrison, Stephen J., 'Apuleius Writer and Orator, b. c. 125 CE', *Oxford Research Encyclopedia of Classics*, 2015, https://doi.org/10.1093/acrefore/9780199381135.013.628

Hart, A. Tindal, *The Curate's Lot: The Story of the Unbeneficed English Clergy* (London: J. Baker, 1970).

Hart, Harold W., 'John Hunt, the Poor Man's Friend' (unpublished typescript, Otford and District Historical Society Archive, 1958).

Hatts, L., and P. Middleton, *London City Churches* (Bankside Press, 2003), https://books.google.co.uk/books?id=JezJorTtQnUC

Henderson, Jeffrey, *Horace, Odes and Epodes*, Loeb Classical Library, https://www.loebclassics.com/view/LCL033/2004/pb_LCL033.iii.xml

'Here's One I Made Earlier', in *Inspire: The Newsletter of the Free Church* (*United Reformed*) *Saint Ives*, December 2017, pp. 6–7, https://d3hgrlq6yacptf.cloudfront.net/5f41930a02cae/content/pages/documents/1511978737.pdf

Hesketh, Ian, *Of Apes and Ancestors: Evolution, Christianity, and the Oxford Debate* (Toronto: University of Toronto Press, 2009).

History, Gazetteer & Directory of Huntingdonshire, 1854 (Huntingdon: James Hatfield, 1854), https://specialcollections.le.ac.uk/digital/collection/p16445coll4/id/278541

Hodgson, H. J., and J. Steer, *Steer's Parish Law: Being a Digest of the Law Relating to the Civil and Ecclesiastical Government of Parishes, Friendly Societies, Etc., Etc.: And the Relief, Settlement, and Removal of the Poor, nineteenth century Legal Treatises* (London: Stevens and Norton, 1857), https://books.google.co.uk/books?id=iLEDAAAAQAAJ

'Holloway v. Webber; Holloway v. Holloway', in *The Law Times*, xix (1869), pp. 514–516.

'Houses of Benedictine Monks: The Priory of St Ives | British History Online', https://www.british-history.ac.uk/vch/hunts/vol1/pp388-389

Howlett, Sue, 'Burley on the Hill' in Robert Ovens and Sheila Sleath, eds., *The Heritage of Rutland Water* (Oakham, Rutland: Rutland Local History & Record Society, 2008), pp. 55–92, http://www.rutlandhistory.org/HRW/chapter-004

Hunt Family Tree, Ancestry®, https://www.ancestry.co.uk/family-tree/tree/90393463/family?cfpid=77012743749

Hunt, Eliza [Mrs John Hunt], *The Wards of Plotinus*, 3 vols (London: Strahan, 1881), http://archive.org/details/wardsofplotinus01ward

'An Inquest on an Inquest', in *Punch*, 26 November 1864, p. 215, https://books.google.co.uk/books?id=7oZEAAAAcAAJ

Jackson, Samuel Macauley, Philip Schaff, and J. J. Herzog, *Encyclopedia of Living Divines and Christian Workers of All Denominations in Europe and America; Being a Supplement to Schaff-Herzog Encyclopedia of Religious Knowledge* (New York: Funk & Wagnalls, 1887), https://catalog.hathitrust.org/Record/005768313

Jervis, William George, *Startling Facts Respecting the Poverty and Distress of Four Hundred Clergymen of the Church of England* (London: Edward Thompson, 1860), https://books.google.co.uk/books?id=IXxIqRs_ycAC

Jones, Philip, 'Ecclesiastical Sequestration', *Ecclesiasticallaw*, 2012, https://ecclesiasticallaw.wordpress.com/2012/11/17/ecclesiastical-sequestration/

Jordan, J., *A Curate's Views of Church Reform, Temporal, Spiritual and Educational* (London: Longman, 1837), https://books.google.co.uk/books?id=KeXd8fpWE24C

Juvenal, *The Satires*, ed. William Barr, trans. Niall Rudd (Oxford; New York: Oxford University Press, 2008).

Kelly, E. R., *Hampshire, Including the Isle of Wight, Ed. by E.R. Kelly. (County Topogr.)*, 1875, https://books.google.co.uk/books?id=6wsHAAAAQAAJ

Kelly's Directory of Beds, Hunts & Northants, 1898, https://specialcollections.le.ac.uk/digital/collection/p16445coll4/id/167113

Kennett, Debbie, 'Cruwys News: Rev. Francis Cruse of Worthing, Sussex', *Cruwys News*, 2007, https://cruwys.blogspot.com/2007/02/rev-francis-cruse-of-worthing-sussex.html

Kirtlan, Norman, *Places of Worship in Old Sunderland* (Washington: Stone Boy Studio, n.d.), http://www.sunderland-antiquarians.org/assets/Uploads/OPGM/WAP/PlacesofWorshipinOldSunderland.pdf

Knight, Frances, *The Nineteenth-Century Church and English Society* (Cambridge: Cambridge University Press, 1998).

Landow, George P., 'Charles Haddon Spurgeon at Exeter Hall, London', Victorian Web, http://www.victorianweb.org/religion/sermons/exeter.html

The Legal Guide, vol. IV (London: John Richards, 1840), https://books.google.co.uk/books?id=wp9GAQAAIAAJ

Livingstone, E. A., ed., *The Concise Oxford Dictionary of the Christian Church* (Oxford: Oxford University Press, 2014), https://www.oxfordreference.com/view/10.1093/acref/9780199659623.001.0001/acref-9780199659623

'Maltby, Edward (1770–1859), Bishop of Durham', *Oxford Dictionary of National Biography*, https://doi.org/10.1093/ref:odnb/17900

'Mansel, Henry Longueville (1820–1871), Dean of St Paul's and Theologian', *Oxford Dictionary of National Biography*, https://doi.org/10.1093/ref:odnb/17988

'Maurice, (John) Frederick Denison (1805–1872), Church of England Clergyman and Theologian', *Oxford Dictionary of National Biography*, https://doi.org/10.1093/ref:odnb/18384

Memories of St Ives, Cambridgeshire, http://saintives.org.uk/memories.html

Milton, John, *Paradise Lost: A Poem in Twelve Books* (New York: Hurd and Houghton, 1868).

The Monthly Chronicle of North-Country Lore and Legend (Newcastle-upon-Tyne: W. Scott, 1890), https://books.google.co.uk/books?id=m9EGAAAAYAAJ

Mottram, Phil, 'John Macduff Derick (c.1805/6–59): A Biographical Sketch', Ecclesiology Today 32 (2004), 40–52.

Nicoll, W. Robertson, *'Ian Maclaren': The Life of the Rev. John Watson, D. D.* (New York: Dodd, Mead & Company, 1909), http://hdl.handle.net/2027/wu.89099242844

Nicholls, Paul, 'The Social Expectations of Anglican Clergy in England and Australia, 1850-1910' (unpublished doctoral dissertation, University of Oxford, 1988), https://ora.ox.ac.uk/objects/uuid:52828db5-d273-41db-8516-c873e1e7a91a

Nichols, J., *The Gentleman's Magazine* (London: E. Cave, 1840), https://books.google.co.uk/books?id=TCVIAQAAMAAJ

Nicoll, William Robertson, *'Ian Maclaren': The Life of the Rev. John Watson, D. D.* (London: Hodder and Stoughton, 1908), http://hdl.handle.net/2027/wu.89099242844

Norris, Herbert E., *History of Saint Ives. From 'The Hunts County Guardian'* (St. Ives: Hunts County Guardian Offices, 1889).

'Oddities of St Ives', St Ives, Cambridgeshire, http://saintives.org.uk/oddities1.html

'Paddington: Churches | British History Online', https://www.british-history.ac.uk/vch/middx/vol9/pp252-259

Parish Register: St Mary, Lambeth, England, 2 September 1870 [retrieved from Ancestry.com].

'Parishes: Buckden | British History Online', https://www.british-history.ac.uk/vch/hunts/vol2/pp260-269

'Parishes: Burley | British History Online', https://www.british-history.ac.uk/vch/rutland/vol2/pp112-119

'Parishes: St Ives | British History Online', https://www.british-history.ac.uk/vch/hunts/vol2/pp210-223

Post Office Perth Directory for 1845–6 (Perth: Fisher, 1845), https://digital.nls.uk/directories/browse/archive/85660224

Post Office Perth Directory for 1850–51 (Perth: Sidey, 1850), https://digital.nls.uk/directories/browse/archive/85662586

Post Office Perth Directory for 1854–55 (Perth: Sidey, 1854), https://digital.nls.uk/directories/browse/archive/85744588

Post Office Perth Directory for 1858–59 (Perth: Sidey, 1858), https://digital.nls.uk/directories/browse/archive/86532093

'Potto Brown', Wikipedia, https://en.wikipedia.org/w/index.php?title=Potto_Brown&oldid=994016050

de Rivoire de La Bâtie, G., *Armorial Du Dauphiné* (Lyon : Perrin, 1867), https://books.google.co.uk/books?id=f_dCtzspcusC

'Robertson, Frederick William (1816–1853), Church of England Clergyman', *Oxford Dictionary of National Biography*, https://doi.org/10.1093/ref:odnb/23792

Rogers, Charles, *History of St. Andrews* (Edinburgh: Adam & Charles Black, 1849), pp. 123–128, https://books.google.co.uk/books?id=f7MHAAAAQAAJ

Rosman, Doreen M., *Evangelicals and Culture* (Cambridge: James Clarke, 2012).

Sanderson, Michael, *Education, Economic Change and Society in England 1780–1870*, 2nd edition (Cambridge: Cambridge University Press, 1995).

'Scott, Thomas (1808–1878), Freethinker', *Oxford Dictionary of National Biography*, https://doi.org/10.1093/ref:odnb/24922

Shea, V., and W. Whitla, eds., *Essays and Reviews: The 1860 Text and Its Reading*, Victorian Literature and Culture Series (Charlottesville and London: University of Virginia Press, 2000), https://books.google.co.uk/books?id=sJcf9rWn8nAC

Short History of the Watergate, Made in Perth—Official Website, 2014, http://madeinperth.org/a-short-history-of-the-watergate/

Smith, David Crawford, *The Historians of Perth, and Other Local and Topographical Writers, up to the End of the Nineteenth Century* (Perth: J. Christie, 1906), http://archive.org/details/historiansperth01smitgoog

'St Botolph's Aldgate', Wikipedia, https://en.wikipedia.org/w/index.php?title=St_Botolph%27s_Aldgate&oldid=1003379028

'St Ives 100 Years Ago: Read Adams', St Ives 100 Years Ago, https://stives100yearsago.blogspot.com/2020/06/read-adams.html

'Strahan, Alexander Stuart (1833–1918), Publisher', *Oxford Dictionary of National Biography*, https://doi.org/10.1093/ref:odnb/40987

Tait, A. C., *The Dangers and Safeguards of Modern Theology. Containing "Suggestions Offered to the Theological Student Under Present Difficulties" (a Revised Edition), and Other Discourses, 1861* (London: Murray, 1861), https://books.google.co.uk/books?id=T2BoAAAAcAAJ

'Tait, Archibald Campbell (1811–1882), Archbishop of Canterbury', *Oxford Dictionary of National Biography*, https://doi.org/10.1093/ref:odnb/26917

Temple, Philip, ed., *Survey of London. Vol. 47, Northern Clerkenwell and Pentonville* (New Haven; London: Published for English Heritage by Yale University Press on behalf of the Paul Mellon Centre for Studies in British Art, 2008), also in survey of London | British History Online', https://www.british-history.ac.uk/survey-london/vol47

'Thomas, Mesac (1816–1892)', *Australian Dictionary of Biography*, https://adb.anu.edu.au/biography/thomas-mesac-4708/text7805

Thomson, James and Otto Zippel, *Thomson's Seasons. Critical Edition, Being a Reproduction of the Original Texts, with All the Various Readings of the Later Editions Historically Arranged* (Berlin: Mayer & Müller, 1908), http://archive.org/details/thomsonsseasonsc00thomrich

The Topographical, Statistical, and Historical Gazetteer of Scotland: A-H (Edinburgh, London and Dublin: A. Fullarton and Company, 1853), https://books.google.co.uk/books?id=gXE_AQAAMAAJ

Trollope, Anthony, *Barchester Towers* (London: Oxford University Press, 1953), http://archive.org/details/AnthonyTrollopeBarchesterTowers

Venn, John and John Archibald Venn, eds., *Alumni Cantabrigienses: A Biographical List of All Known Students, Graduates and Holders of Office at the University of Cambridge, from the Earliest Times to 1900* (Cambridge: Cambridge University Press, 2011), https://doi.org/10.1017/CBO9781139093897

Waites, Bryan, *Who Was Who in Rutland, Rutland Record, Special Issue, no. 8* (Oakham: Rutland Record Soc., 1987), http://www.rutlandhistory.org/rutlandrecord/rr08.pdf

Walford, Edward, *The County Families of the United Kingdom; or, Royal Manual of the Titled and Untitled Aristocracy of England, Wales, Scotland, and Ireland ...*, 59th edn (London: Spottiswoode, Ballantyne and Co. Ltd., 1919), http://archive.org/details/countyfamiliesof591919walf

Walter, James Conway, *A History of Horncastle from the Earliest Period to the Present Time* (Horncastle: W. K. Morton, 1908).

'Wilberforce, Samuel (1805–1873), Bishop of Oxford and of Winchester', *Oxford Dictionary of National Biography*, https://doi.org/10.1093/ref:odnb/29385

'Wild, Robert (1615/16–1679), Nonconformist Minister and Satirical Poet', *Oxford Dictionary of National Biography*, https://doi.org/10.1093/ref:odnb/29395

Wilson, John Marius, *The Imperial Gazetteer of Scotland or Dictionary of Scottish Topography* (Edinburgh & London: A. Fullarton & Co., 1854), Vol. I Aan-Gordon, http://archive.org/details/imperialgazettee01wils

Wilson, John Marius, *The Imperial Gazetteer of Scotland or Dictionary of Scottish Topography* (London & Edinburgh: A. Fullarton & Co., 1866), Vol. II Gordon-Zetland, https://digital.nls.uk/gazetteers-of-scotland-1803-1901/archive/97473786

Yeandle, David, 'Music in Worship and Recreation at Little Gidding in the Time of the Ferrars', *The Seventeenth Century* 34 (2019), 1–21.

Yeandle, David, T*he Clash of Churchmanship in Nineteenth-Century St Ives: The Coming of Anglo-Catholicism* (London: Anglo-Catholic History Society, 2021), https://www.achs.org.uk

About the Team

Alessandra Tosi was the managing editor for this book.

Lucy Barnes performed the copy-editing and proofreading.

Anna Gatti designed the cover. The cover was produced in InDesign using the Fontin font.

Luca Baffa typeset the book in InDesign and produced the paperback and hardback editions. The text font is Tex Gyre Pagella; the heading font is Californian FB. Luca produced the EPUB, MOBI, PDF, HTML, and XML editions — the conversion is performed with open source software freely available on our GitHub page (https://github.com/OpenBookPublishers).

Index

Adams, Read 83, 84
advowson 69, 91
Allen, Hugh 41
All Saints', St Ives xi, 2, 36, 64, 66, 73, 79
anatomy 5, 51, 54, 57, 58, 85, 90
Anglo-Catholicism 74, 75
Ansley, Benjamin Frederick 70, 76
Ansley, Gilbert John 69, 70
Ansley, Mary Anne 70, 74, 75, 76

Baines, Cuthbert Johnson 69
Batty, William Edmund 27
Bishop of London 15, 17, 20, 33, 55, 57, 87
Bishop of Oxford 75, 78
Bishopwearmouth 20, 103, 216
Bridgend 1, 7, 8, 9, 101, 103
Broad Church 5, 73
Brown, Bateman 74
Brown, Potto 63
Burley 65, 90

Calvinism 17
Calvinist 19
Cambridge 19, 22, 36, 48, 77, 78, 81, 90
Catholic 48, 75, 79, 80, 85, 94, 98
Catholic Revival 85
catholic truth 79, 80, 85
Christ Church, Hoxton 48, 49
churchmanship 17, 57, 72, 81, 88, 89, 97
Church of England 5, 6, 16, 17, 18, 19, 32, 33, 39, 54, 55, 67, 76, 80, 85, 91
Church of Rome 76, 85, 100
Church of Scotland 9
class, social 6, 9, 67
Clergymen Made Scarce 15–18, 52, 59, 61, 76, 84, 87, 105, 108–180, 186, 196
Coldstream 65, 67, 69, 73

Colenso, John 55
Colnbrook 76, 78
Contemporary Review, The 11, 229
country parson 32
Cromwell, Oliver 13, 64
curacy 15, 16, 20, 21, 23, 25, 27, 28, 30, 35, 38, 41, 45, 47, 48, 54, 59, 61, 91
curate 12, 13, 15, 18, 21, 22, 23, 25, 26, 27, 28, 29, 32, 35, 36, 37, 39, 40, 41, 45, 46, 47, 48, 49, 51, 52, 54, 55, 56, 58, 59, 61, 65, 67, 72, 74, 78, 79, 80, 81, 84, 86, 87, 88, 89, 90, 91, 93, 96, 101
Curates' Registry 43

Deptford 20, 23, 24
desk, reading 78, 79
Dissenters 10, 51, 67, 71, 84
Dissenting 33, 63, 64, 69, 83
Durham University 90

Essay on Pantheism 12, 44, 67
Essays and Reviews 35, 36, 37, 38, 39, 89
Established Church 85
evangelical 5, 12, 24, 25, 28, 31, 32, 40, 41, 42, 43, 55, 59, 71, 73, 89
evangelicalism 9

Finch, George 32
Foote, Margaret Allen 14
Fosbroke, Yate 67, 68, 69, 71, 72, 73
French 99
Fulham 26, 33

Garratt, Samuel 39
Garratt, William 27, 28, 29, 30, 35, 39, 49, 50
gentleman 47, 63, 65, 67, 71, 73, 90, 91, 94, 100
gentleman parson 65, 94

German 30, 90, 99
Germany 94, 99
Goldie, Charles Dashwood 74, 75, 76, 77, 78, 79, 80, 81, 82, 83, 84, 85, 86
gown, preaching 73, 79
Guardian (church newspaper) 43, 44, 45, 61

High Church 44, 45, 46, 50, 61, 73, 76, 78, 80
Horncastle 78
Houghton 69
Hunt, Colin 9
Hunt, Eliza 15, 20, 27, 31, 33, 35, 36, 42, 49, 84
Hunt, John
  character 5
  degrees 11, 44
  education 9
  epitaph 5, 99, 101
  family 7
  humour and wit 6, 16
  marriages 13
  matriculation 11
  ordination 19
  politics 97
  poor man's friend 94, 101
  scholarship 11
Hunt, Thomas and Agnes 7
Huxley, Thomas Henry 76

income 23, 24, 72, 94
incumbent 20, 21, 24, 25, 26, 27, 28, 30, 36, 38, 40, 44, 45, 49, 50, 52, 54, 55, 59, 61, 64, 65, 69, 74, 76, 85, 88, 89, 90, 91
Islington 14, 21, 23, 24

King's College London 90
Kingsley, Charles 68

liberal 5, 6, 12, 17, 26, 36, 68, 86, 97, 99
literates 45, 90
living, ecclesiastical 15, 16, 68, 69, 70, 71, 72, 73, 74, 75, 76, 77, 85, 91, 93, 100
livings 17, 70
living, sale of 17, 68, 69, 70

Maltby, Edward 19
Mansel, Henry Longueville 42
Marchwood 75
Martelli, Horatio Francis Kingsford 75
Martelli, Thomas Chessher 75
Maurice, Frederick Denison 5, 12, 13, 26, 68, 94
Milne, John 9, 10

Neander, August 23, 68

Old Catholic Congress 94, 98
Otford 5, 15, 23, 86, 93, 94, 96, 97, 98, 99, 100, 101
Ousebank 61, 63, 67, 69, 70, 72, 73, 78, 82, 83
Oxbridge 19, 45
Oxford 19, 38, 42, 76, 78, 90, 91

Pastoral Aid Society 21, 25, 27, 28, 41, 43, 44, 89
patron of a living 69, 70
perpetual curate 21, 27, 78
Perth 7, 8, 9, 10, 20
pew rents 24, 94
Poems by Robert Wilde 61
Popery 73, 82
preferment 6, 16, 17, 20, 49, 81, 85, 86, 91, 94
Presbyterian 9, 17
Presbyterianism 10
presentation to a living 68, 69, 72, 73, 76, 83, 84, 85
Preston 11
Protestant 41, 80, 85, 99
pulpit 64, 73, 79, 80, 96
Punch 16, 52, 54, 58, 67
Pusey, Edward Bouverie 75, 85

rationalist 5, 71, 73, 89
Record (church newspaper) 25, 31, 38, 39, 43, 47, 58
Religious Thought in England 11, 12, 44
ritualism 74
ritualist 76, 78, 83, 85
Roberton, James Matthew 54

Robertson, Frederick 26, 55
Roman Catholic 30, 68, 75
Roman Catholic Church 30, 68
Rutland 31

Scotch 10, 16, 25, 30, 91
Scotland 5, 7, 10, 77, 80, 91
Scotsman 6, 17, 91, 95, 101
Scottish universities 90
Select Poems: from the German 11
sequestrator 82
sermons 24, 26, 28, 36, 39, 79, 80, 81, 88, 96, 98
shoemaker 7, 14
Snape, Alfred William 38, 39
Soapy Sam 76
Spectator 52
Spiritual Songs of Martin Luther 11
squirearchy 31, 90
St Andrews 9, 10, 44
Stanley, Arthur Penrhyn 13, 15, 68, 86, 93
St Bees 36, 37, 45, 90
St Botolph's, Aldgate 15, 49, 51, 54, 57
Steventon, Edwin Henry 38
St Ives 13, 15, 61, 64, 65, 67, 73, 74, 76, 77, 78, 82, 83, 84, 86
    Free Church 63, 64

St John's, Melmoth Place 26, 33
St Mary Magdalen's, Old Kent Road, Bermondsey 38
St Mary's, Lambeth 13, 86
St Nicholas's, Sutton 86
St Paul's, Lisson Grove 26
St Philip's, Arlington Square, Islington 21, 22, 23, 48
Strahan, publisher 12, 98
Sumner, John Bird 5
surplice 73, 82
Sutherland, James Rose 21, 22, 23, 25, 27, 28
Swallow, Lincs. 15, 58, 59

Tait, Archibald Campbell 17, 18, 23, 25, 87, 91
Tate, Thomas 36
testimonial 28, 39, 49, 84, 89
theological colleges 45, 90
Thorp, Eliza Meadows Shepard 13
Toynton 78
Trinity College Dublin 41, 90

Walham Green 26, 33, 35, 37
Wilberforce, Samuel 75, 76, 78

This book need not end here...

Share

All our books — including the one you have just read — are free to access online so that students, researchers and members of the public who can't afford a printed edition will have access to the same ideas. This title will be accessed online by hundreds of readers each month across the globe: why not share the link so that someone you know is one of them?

This book and additional content is available at:

https://doi.org/10.11647/OBP.0248

Customise

Personalise your copy of this book or design new books using OBP and third-party material. Take chapters or whole books from our published list and make a special edition, a new anthology or an illuminating coursepack. Each customised edition will be produced as a paperback and a downloadable PDF.

Find out more at:

https://www.openbookpublishers.com/section/59/1

Like Open Book Publishers

Follow @OpenBookPublish

Read more at the Open Book Publishers BLOG

You may also be interested in:

The Waning Sword
Conversion Imagery and Celestial Myth in 'Beowulf'
Edward Pettit

https://doi.org/10.11647/OBP.0190

God's Babies
Natalism and Bible Interpretation in Modern America
John McKeown

https://doi.org/10.11647/OBP.0048

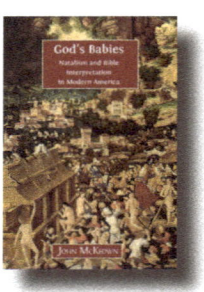

The Sword of Judith
Judith Studies Across the Disciplines
Kevin R. Brine, Elena Ciletti and Henrike Lähnemann (eds)

https://doi.org/10.11647/OBP.0009

www.ingramcontent.com/pod-product-compliance
Lightning Source LLC
Chambersburg PA
CBHW040903250426
43673CB00064B/1948